# EMERSON

## A COLLECTION OF CRITICAL ESSAYS

Edited by

*Milton R. Konvitz*

and

*Stephen E. Whicher*

GREENWOOD PRESS, PUBLISHERS
WESTPORT, CONNECTICUT

**Library of Congress Cataloging in Publication Data**

Konvitz, Milton Ridvas, 1908- ed.
Emerson : a collection of critical essays.

Reprint of the ed. published by Prentice-Hall, Englewood Cliffs, N. J., which was issued in series: Twentieth century views.
Bibliography: p.
1. Emerson, Ralph Waldo, 1803-1882--Criticism and interpretation--Addresses, essays, lectures.
I. Whicher, Stephen E. II. Title.
[PS1638.K58 1978] 814'.3 78-5739
ISBN 0-313-20469-1

# *Stephen Emerson Whicher*

## 1915-1961

At the time of his death on November 13, 1961, Stephen Whicher was variously at work on Emerson. On the day before he died, he wrote the Preface to this book, and was in the midst of work on Volume II of *The Early Lectures of Ralph Waldo Emerson,* of which he was co-editor. In the transition from life to death, he was, I like to think, guided by Montaigne's wise saying that "The premeditation of death is the premeditation of liberty . . . to know how to die delivers us from all subjection and constraint."

Except for the writings that bear our individual names, everything in this book was planned and prepared by us jointly. I dedicate everything in it that is mine to the memory of Stephen Emerson Whicher.

M.R.K.



Reprinted with the permission of Prentice-Hall, Inc.

Reprinted in 1978 by Greenwood Press, Inc.,
51 Riverside Avenue, Westport, CT. 06880

Printed in the United States of America

10 9 8 7 6 5 4 3 2 1

# Table of Contents

## IV



## V

# Preface

## *by Stephen E. Whicher*

Since this is the first selection of Emerson criticism ever made, a brief review of the state of the subject seems to be in order. The most influential single essay on Emerson is still by far Matthew Arnold's lecture of seventy-five years ago.[1] Because Arnold's influence, once perhaps for the good, has become unfortunate, a collection of more recent views of Emerson is necessary. His judgment that "we have not in Emerson a great poet, a great writer, a great philosophy-maker" has been widely accepted, often without his austere qualification, as "tried by the highest standards." Arnold meant this same judgment to apply to the *best* of American writers, and would certainly have said it of any other if the occasion had arisen. His compensatory pronouncement that Emerson is of even "superior importance" as "the friend and aider of those who would live in the spirit," on the other hand, has dwindled into a pious formula; even when we remember that Arnold meant to praise him as a friend and aider of those who, like Arnold, would achieve a stoic self-mastery, Emerson still seems to be relegated by such a verdict to the large shelf of moral tonics, from Plutarch to Tupper, whom past ages highly valued but for whom ours has lost the taste.

That Arnold's Concord Stoic has reality, few would deny, but if this were all that there were to Emerson the present volume would not exist. Twentieth century views of Emerson have gone beyond this judgment in a number of different ways. John Jay Chapman's essay of 1898,[2] the last and best of nineteenth century views and the proper starting point for a review of twentieth-century ones, showed one way of looking at Emerson by presenting essentially the same view as Arnold's, but with so vivid and personal a response, as a man and an American, that, to use Kierkegaard's language, he conveyed the full "inwardness" of Arnold's mere "results." Our first group of selections (Frost, James,

[1] Matthew Arnold, *Discourses in America* (1896).

[2] "Emerson." From *Selected Writings of John Jay Chapman*. (Garden City, N.Y.: Doubleday & Co., Inc., 1959).

Dewey) are of this kind, testimony by distinguished witnesses to the primary fact about Emerson, his peculiar awakening power. From Chapman and Dewey, too, has stemmed an emphasis on Emerson's role as an awakener of American democracy, the theme of the chapter on Emerson in Parrington's *Main Currents of American Thought* (1927). Since Parrington, the emphasis has shifted from Emerson's libertarian protest to his conservative, Whiggish side, or, more interestingly, to a careful dissection of the unresolved problems in his social thought and a dispassionate assessment of his strengths and limitations as a social critic. Our second group of essays are selections from this work (Santayana, Whicher, Arvin).

In 1888, Henry James, Jr.[3] opened another line of approach by his novelist's sensitivity to the human ambiguities and overtones in Emerson's character and writing. The tradition of appreciating Emerson as a man of complex intelligence and sensibility has become a major emphasis in the twentieth century. Smith's article, Matthiessen's *American Renaissance* (1941), and, I like to think, my *Freedom and Fate* (1953) have been influential contributions to it.

At the opposite pole a pejorative tradition has grown up that concentrates on his expressed opinions and condemns them and him. Santayana, in his bland way, did much to further it, with help from Woodberry; and the *coup de grâce,* as some supposed, was delivered when Yvor Winters, in *Maule's Curse* (1938), called him "a fraud and a sentimentalist." The most cogent member of this group has been Parkes, who elaborates upon a hint from Santayana and "exposes" Emerson as a product of the disintegration of Puritanism, as Perry Miller also did in a different way in his article "From Edwards to Emerson."[4] These negative views, intentionally extreme and polemical, have had their answers. Our third group (Smith, Miller, Aaron) centers on a major issue that they have raised, the charge made by Yeats, Eliot, and many others before and after them that Emerson "lacks the vision of Evil."

Henry James's concern, as a literary critic, to define Emerson's quality as an artist has also come in for much twentieth century attention. On the one hand there is James's remark that "with Emerson we never lose the sense that he is still seeking [his form]" and Emerson's own alleged admission that his work lacked structure; on the other hand there are repeated defenses of his coherence and an increasing interest in him as a pioneer of modern literature, especially in poetry, as well as of critical theory. Some influential discussions of Emerson as critic and as poet appear in our fourth group (Matthiessen, Foerster).

Finally, in the last decade, the question of Emerson's philosophical

[3] "Emerson." From *Henry James,* edited by Lyon N. Richardson (New York: American Book Co., 1941).

[4] Perry Miller, *Errand Into the Wilderness* (Cambridge, Mass.: Harvard University Press, 1956).

importance has been reopened by the most promising of recent views. Sherman Paul's *Emerson's Angle of Vision* (1952) revived the matter in a compelling defense of Emerson as a "reconciler," one of those who would heal the widening breach between man's rational self and his total self, the breach between knowledge and action, subject and object, thought and feeling, truth and poetry, man and nature. So viewed, Emerson becomes not the end of a "curve of history," but a harbinger, like William Blake, of the sustained effort in modern thought to free man from the "fallacy of misplaced concreteness" and to help him respond as a whole man to the full range of experience. Those who stress Emerson's anticipation of Pragmatism have been driving at a similar point, as have recent studies of Emerson and Christian Existentialism.

The most influential confirming statement has been Charles Feidelson's chapter in *Symbolism and American Literature* (1953), which juxtaposes Emerson and modern philosophers of symbolism such as Cassirer and Whitehead. Narrower, if more sophisticated than Paul, Feidelson shows an exclusive concentration on Emerson as a symbolist that ignores his stress on action as the completion of thought; yet the special "raking light" he throws on a supposedly familiar figure forces a reassessment by its very distortion. This fruitful direction of inquiry recently culminated in an essay by Pollock,[5] who unites Feidelson's knowledge of modern philosophy with his own broad grasp of Roman Catholic thought to reverse the argument of Parkes and treat Emerson as a renewer rather than a disintegrator of Western tradition. Our last group (Parkes, Feidelson, Paul), accordingly, juxtaposes contrasting views that sum up much twentieth century criticism of Emerson.

Thus, if sixty years have dimmed the vivid impression of Emerson as a personal force that controlled the generations of Arnold, Chapman, James, Dewey, and Woodberry—and that Frost still felt in his youth—and have called up in some quarters a wholesale rejection of all he is supposed to have stood for, they have also brought us at least to a new appreciation of his continuing importance as a pioneer in the reintegration of vision which is and must be a major endeavor of modern thought. And that he still lives as a personal influence is the point of the Introduction.

Another kind of cross section of opinion could have shown the geographical distribution of his modern critics. Interesting work has been done on him abroad, especially in France and Germany. However, unlike such authors as Whitman, Poe, or Melville, foreign interest in Emerson in recent times has been sporadic, tangential, and without influence. For example, the chief concern of the Germans is with his influence on Nietzsche. The best French piece on Emerson appeared during the

[5] Robert C. Pollock, "Ralph Waldo Emerson." From *American Classics Reconsidered*, edited by Harold C. Gardiner, Jr. (New York: Charles Scribner's Sons, 1958).

German invasion and has had no successors.[6] There is little or no interest in Emerson in England. In effect, Emerson's twentieth century reputation has been made in America, and a collection of recent views of him must reflect this fact. The purpose of these selections is to demonstrate the high level that criticism of Emerson has reached in our century and in our country, and the degree and range of interest that he has excited.

[6] Charles Cestre, "Emerson Poète," *Etudes Anglaises,* IV (1940), 1.

# Introduction

## *by Milton R. Konvitz*

In his lecture on Emerson, Matthew Arnold told his Boston audience that when he had been an undergraduate student at Oxford, voices were in the air that still haunted his memory, one of them that of Emerson: "a clear and pure voice, which for my ear, at any rate, brought a strain as new, and moving, and unforgettable as the strain of Newman, or Carlyle, or Goethe." [1] Other English critics confessed to the same lasting influence of Emerson. "What place Emerson is to occupy in American literature is for America to determine," said Augustine Birrell in 1887, ". . . but here at home, where we are sorely pressed for room, it is certain that he must be content with a small allotment, where, however, he may forever sit beneath his own vine and figtree, none daring to make him afraid. Emerson will always be the favorite author of somebody; and to be always read by somebody is better than to be read first by everybody and then by nobody." [2] Sixteen years later, in 1903, when the Emerson centenary was celebrated in England and the United States, Birrell told his audience that after thirty-five years he still remembered lines and passages from Emerson which he had first read "with a shiver of excitement." Thousands of readers on both continents will never forget to their dying day, he said, "the very place and year when first their souls vibrated to the strange charm, the infinite courage, the inbred composure, the spiritual independence of this New Englander." [3] Testimony abounds to the lasting impact that Emerson had on the minds and character of men in his own generation and later, in his own country and elsewhere. "The only firebrand of my youth that burns to me as brightly as ever," wrote Mr. Justice Holmes at the age of 89, "is Emerson." [4] And Robert Frost in 1959 expressed his belief that—with Jeffer-

[1] Matthew Arnold, *Discourses in America* (1896), 145. The lectures were delivered in 1883-1884.

[2] Augustine Birrell, *Collected Essays and Addresses* (London: Charles Scribner's Sons, 1922), II, 56.

[3] *Ibid.*, 68.

[4] Mark de Wolf Howe, ed., *Holmes-Pollock Letters* (Cambridge, Mass.: Harvard University Press, 1941), II, 264.

son and Lincoln—Emerson was one of the three greatest Americans.[5]

The judgment expressed by Emerson, however, as he reviewed the changes in the critical reception of John Milton in the one hundred and sixty years from the time of his death, also applies to the critical estimate of his own work in the span of more than a century and a quarter since the publication of his *Nature* in 1836. "The fame of a great man is not rigid and stony like his bust. It changes with time. It needs time to give it due perspective. . . . The aspect of Milton, to this generation, will be part of the history of the nineteenth century. . . . And as a man's fame, of course, characterizes those who gave it, as much as him who receives it, the new criticism indicated a change in the public taste. . . ." One may also adapt to Emerson his praise of Milton: "There is no name in [American] literature between his age and ours that rises into any approach to his own." [6]

What lies at the heart of this enduring fame and continuing influence? Again, Emerson's estimate of Milton helps us. "Better than any other man," he wrote of Milton, "he has discharged the office of every great man, namely, *to raise the idea of Man in the minds of his contemporaries and of posterity,*—to draw after nature a life of man, exhibiting such a composition of grace, of strength, and of virtue, as poet had not described nor hero lived. *Human Nature in these ages is indebted to him for its best portrait.*" [7] This task has been performed by Emerson preeminently among American writers.

This is not to say that Emerson had illusions about man, society, and human history; he did not close his eyes to past or present evils, sins, and crimes. He saw, for instance, that the business and commercial life of his fellow Americans was full of selfishness, distrust, concealment, and even theft and fraud; that men and women had forgotten the prayers and dreams of their childhood and had taken on themselves "the harness of routine and obsequiousness"; that men, so that they might live with themselves at night, atoned for the manner of acquiring wealth by the manner of expending it.[8] While his friend Bronson Alcott refused to eat rice (though he was a vegetarian) and to wear cotton clothes because slave labor had gone into their production, Emerson saw that if men were to refuse to benefit from commodities or services that were

[5] *Daedalus,* Fall 1959, p. 712. See also J. Donald Adams, "Speaking of Books," *New York Times Book Review,* July 30, 1961, p. 2.

[6] Emerson, "John Milton." From *The Early Lectures of Ralph Waldo Emerson,* edited by Stephen E. Whicher and Robert E. Spiller (Cambridge, Mass.: Harvard University Press, 1959), I, 145-146. Hereinafter this volume will be referred to as *Early Lectures.*

[7] *Ibid.,* 149. Italics supplied.

[8] Emerson, *"Man the Reformer."* From *Nature, Addresses, and Lectures,* Riverside Edition of *Emerson's Complete Works* (Boston, 1883), I, 221-222. Hereinafter refer ences to this work will be to the *Complete Works.*

tainted with cruelty and injustice, they would go naked, sick, and hungry. His castigation of the system of education of his day was no less sharp than that made today in support of bills to provide federal aid to our public schools, colleges, and universities: "Our modes of education aim to expedite, to save labor; to do for masses what cannot be done for masses, what must be done reverently, one by one. . . ." We do not want, he said, teachers to keep schools, but machines, automatons, for these facilitate "labor and thought so much that there is always the temptation in large schools to omit the endless task of meeting the wants of each single mind, and to govern by steam." [9] Teachers open the day with the "morning hope" of love and progress, but the day "is often closed at evening by despair." [10]

Emerson saw the evils that men do, and he knew the easy excuses that they find: how they offer in self-defense the plea made all too familiar by Nazi arch-criminals at Nuremberg. "Everybody partakes, everybody confesses," says Emerson, "—with cap and knee volunteers his confession, yet none feels himself accountable. He did not create the abuse; he cannot alter it. *What is he?* An obscure private person who must get his bread. That is the vice—that no one feels himself called to act for man. . . ." [11]

The inescapable central question for Emerson always was: *"What is he?"—What is man?* And he always, despite gnawing inner doubts and telling negative evidence, gave the biblical and classical answer:

> Thou hast made him little less than God and dost crown him with glory and honor.[12]

Emerson, unlike others, took with deep seriousness the biblical conceit that man is made in the image of God, that he is only a little less than God. It was this gospel, this news, that he wanted to teach and preach, and it was for this purpose that he left the pulpit and the obligation to engage in church rites that, he thought, obscured the truth and the way. The biblical view of man—man seen in all his greatness, grandeur, and sublimity, seen in all his divinity, although an earthly creature,—did not mean a failure to see his degradation, sinfulness, and criminality. On the contrary, the waywardness of man and the pathos of man's life stood out all the more sharply and grotesquely *because* the prophets judged man, and his acts and life, against the standard of what man is by divine intent. Man was a failure *precisely* when the human record

[9] *Complete Works,* X, 150.

[10] *Complete Works,* X, 149.

[11] *Complete Works,* I, 222.

[12] Psalm 8. Translation is that of the Revised Standard Version. The King James version is: "little less than the angels." But the Hebrew original is much more daring; it uses the word *Elohim,* correctly translated by the RSV scholars.

was put against the divine expectation, desire, and plan. In the Bible there is as much stress on man's failure as there is on the ideal vision; and it is this tension between ideal and fact that makes the Bible so compellingly true: it reveals man to himself as a being who is at one and the same time an ideal self and a phenomenal self. If man follows the worse, it is true, too, that he sees the better; and "the worse" has meaning as such only because there is a "better."

When Emerson is considered from the aspect of his interpretation of man, it is, I submit, clear that he is in the tradition of the Hebrew prophets and of Sophocles and Socrates. However, one difference should be noted: more than on the tradition out of which he speaks, Emerson's eye was on man as he could be or become rather than on man as he was or is. In a sense, Emerson's stance was an eschatological one: he kept his eye on the promise, on the blessing to come, on the hope. Just as Isaiah lost himself in the vision of the "latter end of days," when the lion in man will have learned to lie down peacefully with the lamb in man, just as the early Christians awaited the Second Coming, so Emerson was harried by love of the best.[13] The "mighty Ideal" always journeyed before his eyes, and this Ideal, he believed, was never known to fall into the rear. "No man," he said, "ever came to an experience which was satisfying, but his good tidings is of a better." [14] What was the nature of this madness of his if it were not like that of Socrates or Plato, who knew the Myth of the Cave, who saw that "man is not man as yet"? [15]

A significant aspect of Emerson's ideal view of man was his consuming interest in man's record, in becoming aware of how much of the ideal has already been achieved. For man is fulfillment as well as promise. He *has* exercised the dominion over the works of God which has been vested in him. If God has put all things under the feet of man, man has not been altogether indifferent to his power and trust. If man has the lordship over "whatever passes along the paths of the sea," [16] then the true ship is the builder of the ship[17]—it is he who must be the object of our wonder. If the "true poem is the poet's mind," [18] it is that mind that then must be the object of our wonder. Most of what Emerson wrote was, one might say, an elaboration of the paean to man in the chorus of the *Antigone:*

> man who crosses the sea in winter's storm, who tears away the earth with the plow that he has invented and can make the mules draw after them, who snares birds of the air and wild beasts of the woods and fish out of the salty sea, who has tamed the horse and the strong bull of the mountain, who

[13] *Complete Works,* IX, 11.
[14] *Complete Works,* III, 76.
[15] Browning, *Paracelsus,* Part 5.
[16] Psalm 8.
[17] *Complete Works,* II, 22.
[18] *Ibid.*

> uses language and thinks as fast as the wind, who builds cities and homes, and who has invented cures for his illnesses.[19]

But for Emerson there could be no complete catalogue of what man had wrought; even less, of what man might yet accomplish. For everything, he believed, teaches the infinitude of man, of every man.[20]

Emerson elucidated what was latent in the biblical and classical view of man. "A new Adam in the garden," he said, "is to name all the beasts in the field, all the gods in the sky." [21] The beasts in the field and the gods in the sky—Berkeley's choir of heaven and furniture of earth, Kant's starry heavens above and the moral law within—comprise nature, every part of which must pass through the alembic of man's mind in order that it may have a name, a significance. "Nature copies Art," said Oscar Wilde; "Nature copies Man," Emerson would say. Nature, he said,

> hastens to render account of herself to the mind. Classification begins. . . . But what is classification but the perceiving that these objects are not chaotic, and are not foreign, but have a law which is also a law of the human mind? The astronomer discovers that geometry, a pure abstraction of the human mind, is the measure of planetary motion. . . . Nature is the opposite of the soul, answering to it part for part. One is seal and one is print. Its beauty is the beauty of his own mind. Its laws are the laws of his own mind. Nature then becomes to him [this schoolboy under the bending dome of day] the measure of his own attainments. So much of nature as he is ignorant of, so much of his own mind does he not yet possess.[22]

Thus the world is the *"other me."* [23] Just as to John Locke property was a sub-person, an externalization of his labor, his sweat, and his imagination, so to Emerson nature and events were "sub-persons." [24] "Each creature puts forth from its own condition and sphere, as the . . . fish its shell." [25] Events exude from a man and accompany him;[26] history is the action and reaction of nature and mind—"two boys pushing each other on the curbstone of the pavement. Everything is pusher or pushed; and matter and mind are in perpetual tilt and balance, so. . . . Every solid in the universe is ready to become fluid in the approach of the mind. If the wall remains adamant, it accuses the want of thought." [27]

It is not that man is *master* of nature or *maker* of history. The rela-

[19] Cf. paean to man in Sophocles, *The Antigone,* verses 327 ff.
[20] *Complete Works,* X, 135.
[21] *Complete Works,* X, 136.
[22] *Complete Works,* I, 87.
[23] *Ibid.,* I, 96.
[24] *Complete Works,* VI, 42-43.
[25] *Ibid.*
[26] *Complete Works,* VI, 44.
[27] *Ibid.*

tion is not that of master and servant. Man masters *himself* as he masters nature by discovering its order, which is the order of the mind; for "always the mind contains in its transparent chambers the means of classifying the most refractory phenomena, of depriving them of all casual and chaotic aspect, and subordinating them to a bright reason of its own, and so giving to man a sort of property—yea, the very highest property in every district and particle of the globe." [28] Man owns all that he surveys even as he is owned by all that he has surveyed.

The prayer of Socrates at the end of the *Phaedrus,* Emerson would say, is always answered—"what we pray to ourselves for is always granted." [29] Socrates asked of Pan the grace that the outer and inner man be at one. "But they *are* at one," Emerson would say. There is always "this undersong, this perfect harmony." [30] Person and event make one another and reflect one another; events are "only the actualization" of what a man thinks. "The event is the print of your form. It fits you like your skin. What each does is proper for him. Events are the children of his body and mind." A man's fortunes are the fruits of his character. They are the children of his body and mind.[31] "Our first mistake," Emerson would gently remind Socrates, "is the belief that the circumstance gives the joy which we give to the circumstance. . . .[32] The pleasure of life is according to the man that lives it, and not according to the work or place. . . .[33] What if you shall come to discern that the play and playground of all this pompous history are radiations from yourself, and that the sun borrows his beams?" [34] Man determines his own existence. *He makes himself by making his world. He makes the world by making himself.* He lives in an open universe; he himself is man in the process of becoming man. God did not make the world in six days, and He did not make Adam on the sixth day; for the days of creation, are still proceeding one after the other, and Adam is born anew each day, with every man. When Kepler had discovered the three harmonic laws that regulate the motion of the heavenly bodies, Emerson recalled that the astronomer noted that God had waited six thousand years for an observer like himself.[35] God is always waiting. He is waiting not only for man the observer, but also, and even more, for man the maker, the doer—yes, the creator. There is always "more day to dawn." "Know then that the world exists for you.

[28] *Complete Works,* X, 130.
[29] *Complete Works,* VI, 43.
[30] *Early Lectures,* 25.
[31] *Complete Works,* VI, 43.
[32] *Complete Works,* VI, 295.
[33] *Complete Works,* VI, 44.
[34] *Complete Works,* VI, 302.
[35] *Early Lectures,* 22.

. . . What we are, that only can we see. All that Adam had, all that Caesar could, you have and can do. . . . Build therefore your own world." [36]

For Emerson, then, there is no antithesis between the practical and theoretical, between the humanistic and the scientific, between religion and science, between value and fact—as there is none between inner and outer, between man and nature, between character and event. There can be no such conflicts if man is central and if it is he who generates the world—a world subject to laws, that has an order that the mind discovers as it discovers its own order and powers. Man is one, mind is one, nature is one, the world is one. This, perhaps, is what the Bible means by its great affirmation of the oneness of God; for there is a single order, one set of laws that operates for man as well as for beast and star, in the marketplace as well as in the laboratory, in the mind as well as in the body. "There is one mind common to all individual men. Every man is an inlet to the same and to all of the same. He that is once admitted to the right of reason is made a freeman of the whole estate. What Plato has thought, he may think; what a saint has felt, he may feel. . . . I can find Greece, Asia, Italy, Spain, and the Island—the genius and creative principle of each and of all eras, in my own mind." [37] There is no escape from this Lord our God, as Job discovered—not in riches or poverty, not in sickness or in health:

> For we transcend the circumstance continually and taste the real quality of existence; as in our employments, which only differ in the manipulations but express the same laws; or in our thoughts, which wear no silks and taste no ice creams. We see God face to face every hour, and know the savor of Nature.[38]

Man is face to face with God every hour because man is made in the image of God, which means that ideals are as natural to man as feathers are to birds. Man is born for a high estate, as sparks fly upward. At the beginning of his lecture before the Mechanics' Apprentices' Library Association in Boston, Emerson told his hearers that he would assume that "the aim of each young man in this association is the very highest that belongs to a rational mind." Though the lives we lead are common and mean, says Emerson, every man feels the call to become "a free and helpful man, a reformer, a benefactor, . . . a brave and upright man, who must find or cut a straight road to everything excellent. . . ." [39]

[36] *Complete Works,* I, 79.
[37] *Complete Works,* II, 9.
[38] *Complete Works,* VI, 306.
[39] *Complete Works,* I, 218.

Each mind lives in the Grand Mind, and everything teaches the infinitude of every man.[40] "All that Shakespeare says of the king, yonder slip of a boy that reads in the corner feels to be true of himself." [41]

Keeping his eye on the centrality of man and his power to *become* a creature made in the image of God, Emerson was naturally led to devalue the past and tradition, and to emphasize instead the duty and the right of each man to trust himself. The Socratic "Know thyself!" became, in Emerson's thought, "Study nature!"—which also meant "Make nature!"—which in turn also meant "Trust thyself!"—which became "Make thyself!" As man makes the world and himself, he also *makes* the past, his past. Out of the abyss of

> The past! the dark, unfathom'd retrospect!
> The teeming gulf! the sleepers and the shadows!
> The past! the infinite greatness of the past! [42]

he must select those events and values that carry significance for him; these must be infused with his living breath and come to life in him, through him, and for him. Any other past is dead and, if carried, is a dead weight.

For the greatness of any part of the past is an attribute given it by a thinking, struggling, hoping, living man. All the rest of that infinitude is dead, utterly dead.

> Whence this worship of the past? The centuries are conspirators against the sanity and authority of the soul. Time and space are but physiological colors which the eye makes, but the soul is light: where it is, is day; where it was, is night. . . .[43]

Like a follower of Zen, Emerson complained that

> man is timid and apologetic; he is no longer upright; he dares not say "I think," "I am," but quotes some saint or sage. He is ashamed before the blade of grass or the blowing rose. These roses under my window make no reference to former roses or to better ones; they are for what they are; they exist with God today. There is no time to them. There is simply the rose; it is perfect in every moment of its existence. . . . But man postpones or remembers; he does not live in the present. . . . We shall not always set so great a price on a few texts, on a few lives. . . .[44]

It is not, of course, that Emerson meant that we should burn our libraries and refuse to learn about "Representative Men" who are no

[40] *Complete Works,* X, 134.
[41] *Complete Works,* II, 12.
[42] Walt Whitman, *Passage to India,* lines 10-13.
[43] *Complete Works,* II, 66.
[44] *Ibid.,* p. 67.

longer alive. He meant that the Bible is dependent on us, *who are alive this day,* for a meaning, a significance. It is not a "sacred text" for the man who cannot read, or for the man who reads it only for its chronicles of sinful, evil men and acts. Unless *I* stand at the foot of Sinai *today,* the Bible is a book like thousands of others and nothing more. "This should be plain enough. Yet see what strong intellects dare not yet hear God himself. . . ." [45] If Socrates has meaning today, it is only because I choose him to have life in me—me, a live dog living on a dead lion, who comes to life in me. "Whenever a mind is simple and receives a divine wisdom, old things pass away,—means, teachers, texts, temples fall; it lives now, and absorbs past and future into the present hour." [46]

The past, T. S. Eliot has said, in words that echo Emerson, is altered by the present as well as directed by it. The dead writers "are that which we know." [47] That part of them which we do not know is buried with their bones. Their existence, then, is dependent upon us. Tradition, Eliot has said in words that are a paraphrase of Goethe, "cannot be inherited, and if you want it you must obtain it by great labor." [48] Tradition is not like a piece of property that can be handed down from father to son by a legal document. If tradition, if the past, is to have any meaning, a living person must select from its limitless stores those elements that he wants to become *present.* The *pastness* of the past is without significance; it is only the *presentness* of the past that has meaning for the living man, and for that presentness it depends wholly on him. Once more, we see Emerson's application of the principle of the centrality of man, who is not only the measure but the very substance of all things.

The idea of the presentness of the selected, significant past leads naturally to Emerson's belief in a perpetual reformation. When early friends of the new Reformation doctrines called themselves Lutherans, Luther wrote to them: "Be not called after my name. Who am I? a lump of worms." [49] Every man, Emerson would add, is a lump of worms, whether his name is Luther or Calvin, Moses or Mohammed, Jesus or Paul. "If I have renounced the search of truth, if I have come into the haven of some pretending dogmatism, some new church or old church, some Schelling or Cousin, I have died to all use of these new events that are born out of prolific time into multitude of life every hour." [50] Every child, new-born, gives promise of a new reformation: "Give him time and opportunity. Talk of Columbus and Newton! I tell you the child just born in yonder hovel is the beginning of a revolution as great as

[45] *Ibid.*

[46] *Ibid.,* p. 66.

[47] T. S. Eliot, "Tradition and the Individual Talent" (1919). From *Selected Prose,* edited by John Hayward (London: Gerald Duckworth & Co., Ltd., 1953), 25.

[48] *Ibid.,* p. 23.

[49] *Early Lectures,* 127.

[50] *Complete Works,* X, 132.

theirs." [51] The trouble is that Luther, perhaps involuntarily, tried to make his neighbor another man like himself, just as a father tries to make his son conform, not to God but to the image of himself. On all such endeavors, to a degree unavoidable, Emerson made his judgment: "You are trying to make that man another *you*. One's enough." [52]

What T. S. Eliot has said of literature, Emerson would say of all culture, especially of philosophy, religion, and criticism: "It is part of the business of the critic to preserve tradition—where a good tradition exists. It is part of his business to see literature steadily and to see it as a whole; but this is eminently to see it *not* as consecrated by time but to see it beyond time. . . ." [53] To emancipate culture, as well as the human being, from a past that is inherited as a dead weight, Emerson would cry out with Schleiermacher: "The Reformation must continue." For every reformation needs to be reformed itself; every protest needs, in time, to be protested against. Every society, every man, every culture must submit to the process of self-transcendence, must listen to the voice of prophecy, to God as He speaks at the present time. For,

> it must be that when God speaketh he should communicate, not one thing, but all things; should fill the world with his voice; should scatter forth light, nature, time, souls, *from the centre of the present thought;* and new date and new create the whole. . . . If therefore a man claims to know and speak of God and carries you backward to the phraseology of some old mouldered nation in another country, in another world, believe him not.[54]

If a man takes his present thought as his center, he may find that today's thought contradicts yesterday's. If a man will fill his mind today with only yesterday's thoughts, he will be consistent, but will he be fully alive, will he be true to his genius? "Speak what you think now in hard words and tomorrow speak what tomorrow thinks in hard words again, though it contradict everything you said to-day." [55] It follows that a "foolish consistency is the hobgoblin of little minds" and that "with consistency a great soul has simply nothing to do." [56] For a man must shed his timidity and indolence, not only when he is faced with the past of "Socrates, and Jesus, and Luther, and Copernicus, and Galileo, and Newton," but even when he is faced with his own past. For only "the soul is light: where it is, is day; where it was, is night. . . .[57] A man

[51] *Ibid.*, p. 153.
[52] *Ibid.*, p. 136.
[53] T. S. Eliot, *The Sacred Wood* (London: Methuen & Co., Ltd. 1920), "Introduction," pp. xv-xvi.
[54] *Complete Works,* II, 66.
[55] *Complete Works,* II, 58.
[56] *Ibid.*
[57] *Ibid.*, p. 67.

must appeal from customs, traditions, neighbors, even from his own past. He must obey the first commandment: "I must be myself." [58]

Emerson's thought has an inner consistency. His justification of inconsistency and self-contradiction was not relevant to his own work. Perhaps this is so because even the most profound and productive thinkers have in the end only a few thoughts with which mind and imagination play their metaphysical games. Emerson's thought starts and ends with the centrality of man, and from this center he developed his ontological, epistemological, religious, and moral insights. The world, he said, "becomes at last only a realized will—the double of the man." [59] This world contains all of man's industry, poetry, religion—all of man's work, hopes, and frustrations. Man, once born, has no way to avoid his opportunity of making himself and his world, no way of avoiding his responsibility for what he thinks, does, makes, suffers and enjoys. The visible world is only the end product of his spirit, the metaphor, as Emerson liked to say, of the human mind.

There are thinkers who speak to us, and there are thinkers who answer us. The latter are masters who have disciples, they are founders of schools; they win domination over their followers, and their texts become the standard of what is orthodox and what is heretical. But they who speak to us are teachers who seek to liberate the mind from dominant traditions and schools. They have pupils but not followers. Their purpose is to set each man on his own quest, guided by his own candle. If their teaching has any content, it is that each man's world is his own creation, that each man's work is his own confession. They seek to broaden and deepen life by helping each man to discover and disencumber his own powers. They engage the soul in a dialogue and not in a catechism. It is to this small company of thinkers who speak to us that Emerson preeminently belongs.

[58] *Ibid.*, p. 72.
[59] *Complete Works,* I, 46.

# On Emerson

*by Robert Frost*

All that admiration for me I am glad of. I am here out of admiration for Emerson and Thoreau. Naturally on this proud occasion* I should like to make myself as much of an Emersonian as I can. Let me see if I can't go a long way. You may be interested to know that I have right here in my pocket a little first edition of Emerson's poetry. His very first was published in England, just as was mine. His book was given me on account of that connection by Fred Melcher, who takes so much pleasure in bringing books and things together like that.

I suppose I have always thought I'd like to name in verse some day my four greatest Americans: George Washington, the general and statesman; Thomas Jefferson, the political thinker; Abraham Lincoln, the martyr and savior; and fourth, Ralph Waldo Emerson, the poet. I take these names because they are going around the world. They are not just local. Emerson's name has gone as a poetic philosopher or as a philosophical poet, my favorite kind of both.

I have friends it bothers when I am accused of being Emersonian, that is, a cheerful Monist, for whom evil does not exist, or if it does exist, needn't last forever. Emerson quotes Burns as speaking to the Devil as if he could mend his ways. A melancholy dualism is the only soundness. The question is: is soundness of the essence.

My own unsoundness has a strange history. My mother was a Presbyterian. We were here on my father's side for three hundred years but my mother was fresh a Presbyterian from Scotland. The smart thing when she was young was to be reading Emerson and Poe as it is today to be reading St. John Perse or T. S. Eliot. Reading Emerson turned her into a Unitarian. That was about the time I came into the world; so I suppose I started a sort of Presbyterian-Unitarian. I was transitional. Reading on into Emerson, that is into "Representative Men" until she got to Swedenborg, the mystic, made her a Swedenborgian. I was brought up in all

"On Emerson." From *Daedalus* (Fall, 1959), 712-18.  The occasion of his receiving the Emerson-Thoreau Medal before the American Academy of Arts and Sciences.

three of these religions, I suppose. I don't know whether I was baptized in them all. But as you see it was pretty much under the auspices of Emerson. It was all very Emersonian. Phrases of his began to come to me early. In that essay on the mystic he makes Swedenborg say that in the highest heaven nothing is arrived at by dispute. Everybody votes in heaven but everybody votes the same way, as in Russia today. It is only in the second-highest heaven that things get parliamentary; we get the two-party system or the hydra-headed, as in France.

Some of my first thinking about my own language was certainly Emersonian. "Cut these sentences and they bleed," he says. I am not submissive enough to want to be a follower, but he had me there. I never got over that. He came pretty near making me an anti-vocabularian with the passage in "Monadnock" about our ancient speech. He blended praise and dispraise of the country people of New Hampshire. As an abolitionist he was against their politics. Forty per cent of them were states-rights Democrats in sympathy with the South. They were really pretty bad, my own relatives included.

> The God who made New Hampshire
> Taunted the lofty land
> With little men;—

And if I may be further reminiscent parenthetically, my friend Amy Lowell hadn't much use for them either. "I have left New Hampshire," she told me. Why in the world? She couldn't stand the people. What's the matter with the people? "Read your own books and find out." They really differ from other New Englanders, or did in the days of Franklin Pierce.

But now to return to the speech that was his admiration and mine in a burst of poetry in "Monadnock":

> Yet wouldst thou learn our ancient speech
> These the masters that can teach
> Fourscore or a hundred words
> All their vocal muse affords.
> Yet they turn them in a fashion
> Past the statesman's art and passion.
> Rude poets of the tavern hearth
> Squandering your unquoted mirth,
> That keeps the ground and never soars,
> While Jake retorts and Reuben roars.
> Scoff of yeoman, strong and stark,
> Goes like bullet to the mark,
> And the solid curse and jeer
> Never balk the waiting ear.

Fourscore or a hundred is seven hundred less than my friend Ivor Richard's basic eight hundred. I used to climb on board a load of shooks (boxes that haven't been set up) just for the pleasure I had in the driver's good use of his hundred-word limit. This at the risk of liking it so much as to lose myself in mere picturesqueness. I was always in favor of the solid curse as one of the most beautiful of figures. We were warned against it in school for its sameness. It depends for variety on the tones of saying it and the situations.

I had a talk with John Erskine, the first time I met him, on this subject of sentences that may look tiresomely alike, short and with short words, yet turn out as calling for all sorts of ways of being said aloud or in the mind's ear, Horatio. I took Emerson's prose and verse as my illustration. Writing is unboring to the extent that it is dramatic.

In a recent preface to show my aversion to being interrupted with notes in reading a poem, I find myself resorting to Emerson again. I wanted to be too carried away for that. There was much of "Brahma" that I didn't get to begin with but I got enough to make me sure I would be back there reading it again some day when I had read more and lived more; and sure enough, without help from dictionary or encyclopedia I can now understand every line in it but one or two. It is a long story of many experiences that let me into the secret of:

> But thou, meek lover of the good!
> Find me, and turn thy back on heaven.

What baffled me was the Christianity in "meek lover of the good." I don't like obscurity and obfuscation, but I do like dark sayings I must leave the clearing of to time. And I don't want to be robbed of the pleasure of fathoming depths for myself. It was a moment for me when I saw how Shakespeare set bounds to science when he brought in the North Star, "whose worth's unknown although his height be taken." Of untold worth: it brings home some that should and some that shouldn't come. Let the psychologist take notice how unsuccessful he has to be.

I owe more to Emerson than anyone else for troubled thoughts about freedom. I had the hurt to get over when I first heard us made fun of by foreigners as the land of the free and the home of the brave. Haven't we won freedom? Is there no such thing as freedom? Well, Emerson says God

> Would take the sun out of the skies
> Ere freedom out of a man.

and there rings the freedom I choose.

Never mind how and where Emerson disabused me of my notion I may have been brought up to that the truth would make me free. My truth will bind you slave to me. He didn't want converts and followers. He was a Unitarian. I am on record as saying that freedom is nothing but departure—setting forth—leaving things behind, brave origination of the courage to be new. We may not want freedom. But let us not deceive ourselves about what we don't want. Freedom is one jump ahead of formal laws, as in planes and even automobiles right now. Let's see the law catch up with us very soon.

Emerson supplies the emancipating formula for giving an attachment up for an attraction, one nationality for another nationality, one love for another love. If you must break free,

> Heartily know,
> When half-gods go
> The gods arrive.

I have seen it invoked in *Harper's Magazine* to excuse disloyalty to our democracy in a time like this. But I am not sure of the reward promised. There is such a thing as getting too transcended. There are limits. Let's not talk socialism. I feel projected out from politics with lines like:

> Musketaquit, a goblin strong,
> Of shards and flints makes jewels gay;
> They lose their grief who hear his song,
> And where he winds is the day of day.
>
> So forth and brighter fares my stream,—
> Who drink it shall not thirst again;
> No darkness stains its equal gleam,
> And ages drop in it like rain.

Left to myself, I have gradually come to see what Emerson was meaning in "Give all to Love" was, Give all to Meaning. The freedom is ours to insist on meaning.

The kind of story Steinbeck likes to tell is about an old labor hero punch-drunk from fighting the police in many strikes, beloved by everybody at headquarters as the greatest living hater of tyranny. I take it that the production line was his grievance. The only way he could make it mean anything was to try to ruin it. He took arms and fists against it. No one could have given him that kind of freedom. He saw it as his to seize. He was no freedman; he was a free man. The one inalienable right is to go to destruction in your own way. What's worth living for is worth dying for. What's worth succeeding in is worth failing in.

If you have piled up a great rubbish heap of oily rags in the basement for your doctor's thesis and it won't seem to burst into flame spontaneously, come away quickly and without declaring rebellion. It will cost you only your Ph.D. union card and the respect of the union. But it will hardly be noticed even to your credit in the world. All you have to do is to amount to something anyway. The only reprehensible materiality is the materialism of getting lost in your material so you can't find out yourself what it is all about.

A young fellow came to me to complain of the department of philosophy in his university. There wasn't a philosopher in it. "I can't stand it." He was really complaining of his situation. He wasn't where he could feel real. But I didn't tell him so I didn't go into that. I agreed with him that there wasn't a philosopher in his university—there was hardly ever more than one at a time in the world—and I advised him to quit. Light out for somewhere. He hated to be a quitter. I told him the Bible says, "Quit ye, like men." "Does it," he said. "Where would I go?" Why anywhere almost. Kamchatka, Madagascar, Brazil. I found him doing well in the educational department of Rio when I was sent on an errand down there by our government several years later. I had taken too much responsibility for him when I sent him glimmering like that. I wrote to him with troubled conscience and got no answer for two whole years. But the story has a happy ending. His departure was not suicidal. I had a post card from him this Christmas to tell me he was on Robinson Crusoe's island Juan Fernandez on his way to Easter Island that it had always been a necessity for him some day to see. I would next hear from him in Chile where he was to be employed in helping restore two colleges. Two! And the colleges were universities!

No subversive myself, I think it very Emersonian of me that I am so sympathetic with subversives, rebels, runners out, runners out ahead, eccentrics, and radicals. I don't care how extreme their enthusiasm so long as it doesn't land them in the Russian camp. I always wanted one of them teaching in the next room to me so my work would be cut out for me warning the children taking my courses not to take his courses.

I am disposed to cheat myself and others in favor of any poet I am in love with. I hear people say the more they love anyone the more they see his faults. Nonsense. Love is blind and should be left so. But it hasn't been hidden in what I have said that I am not quite satisfied with the easy way Emerson takes disloyalty. He didn't know or ignored his Blackstone. It is one thing for the deserter and another for the deserted. Loyalty is that for the lack of which your gang will shoot you without benefit of trial by jury. And serves you right. Be as treacherous as you must be for your ideals, but don't expect to be kissed good-by by the idol you go back on. We don't want to look too foolish, do we? And probably Emerson was too Platonic about evil. It was a mere Τὸ *μὴ οὔ* that could be disposed of like the butt of a cigarette. In a poem I have called the best Western poem yet he says:

Unit and universe are round.

Another poem could be made from that, to the effect that ideally in thought only is a circle round. In practice, in nature, the circle becomes an oval. As a circle it has one center—Good. As an oval it has two centers—Good and Evil. Thence Monism versus Dualism.

Emerson was a Unitarian because he was too rational to be superstitious and too little a storyteller and lover of stories to like gossip and pretty scandal. Nothing very religious can be done for people lacking in superstition. They usually end up abominable agnostics. It takes superstition and the prettiest scandal story of all to make a good Trinitarian. It is the first step in the descent of the spirit into the material-human at the risk of the spirit.

But if Emerson had left us nothing else he would be remembered longer than the Washington Monument for the monument at Concord that he glorified with lines surpassing any other ever written about soldiers:

By the rude bridge that arched the flood
Their flag to April breeze unfurled
Here once the embattled farmers stood
And fired the shot heard round the world.

Not even Thermopylae has been celebrated better. I am not a shriner, but two things I never happen on unmoved: one, this poem on stone; and the other, the tall shaft seen from Lafayette Park across the White House in Washington.

# Address at the Emerson Centenary in Concord

## *by William James*

The pathos of death is this, that when the days of one's life are ended, those days that were so crowded with business and felt so heavy in their passing, what remains of one in memory should usually be so slight a thing. The phantom of an attitude, the echo of a certain mode of thought, a few pages of print, some invention, or some victory we gained in a brief critical hour, are all that can survive the best of us. It is as if the whole of a man's significance had now shrunk into the phantom of an attitude, into a mere musical note or phrase suggestive of his singularity—happy are those whose singularity gives a note so clear as to be victorious over the inevitable pity of such a diminution and abridgment.

An ideal wraith like this, of Emerson's personality, hovers over all Concord to-day, taking, in the minds of those of you who were his neighbors and intimates a somewhat fuller shape, remaining more abstract in the younger generation, but bringing home to all of us the notion of a spirit indescribably precious. The form that so lately moved upon these streets and country roads, or awaited in these fields and woods the beloved Muse's visits, is now dust; but the soul's note, the spiritual voice, rises strong and clear above the uproar of the times, and seems securely destined to exert an ennobling influence over future generations.

What gave a flavor so matchless to Emerson's individuality was, even more than his rich mental gifts, their singularly harmonious combination. Rarely has a man so accurately known the limits of his genius or so unfailingly kept within them. "Stand by your order," he used to say to youthful students; and perhaps the paramount impression one gets of his life is of his loyalty to his own personal type and mission. The type was that of what he liked to call the scholar, the perceiver of pure truth; and the mission was that of the reporter in worthy form of each

"Address at the Emerson Centenary in Concord." From *Memories and Studies* (London: Longmans, Green & Co., 1911). Copyright 1903 by William James. Reprinted by permission of Paul R. Reynolds & Son.

perception. The day is good, he said, in which we have the most perceptions. There are times when the cawing of a crow, a weed, a snowflake, or a farmer planting in his field become symbols to the intellect of truths equal to those which the most majestic phenomena can open. Let me mind my own charge, then, walk alone, consult the sky, the field and forest, sedulously waiting every morning for the news concerning the structure of the universe which the good Spirit will give me.

This was the first half of Emerson, but only half; for genius, as he said, is insatiate for expression, and truth has to be clad in the right verbal garment. The form of the garment was so vital with Emerson that it is impossible to separate it from the matter. They form a chemical combination—thoughts which would be trivial expressed otherwise, are important through the nouns and verbs to which he married them. The style is the man, it has been said; the man Emerson's mission culminated in his style, and if we must define him in one word, we have to call him Artist. He was an artist whose medium was verbal and who wrought in spiritual material.

This duty of spiritual seeing and reporting determined the whole tenor of his life. It was to shield this duty from invasion and distraction that he dwelt in the country, that he consistently declined to entangle himself with associations or to encumber himself with functions which, however he might believe in them, he felt were duties for other men and not for him. Even the care of his garden, "with its stoopings and fingerings in a few yards of space," he found "narrowing and poisoning," and took to long free walks and saunterings instead, without apology. "Causes" innumerable sought to enlist him as their "worker"—all got his smile and word of sympathy, but none entrapped him into service. The struggle against slavery itself, deeply as it appealed to him, found him firm:

> God must govern his own world, and knows his way out of this pit without my desertion of my post, which has none to guard it but me. I have quite other slaves to face than those Negroes, to wit, imprisoned thoughts far back in the brain of man, and which have no watchman or lover or defender but me.

This in reply to the possible questions of his own conscience. To hot-blooded moralists with more objective ideas of duty, such a fidelity to the limits of his genius must often have made him seem provokingly remote and unavailable; but we, who can see things in more liberal perspective, must unqualifiably approve the results. The faultless tact with which he kept his safe limits while he so dauntlessly asserted himself within them, is an example fitted to give heart to other theorists and artists the world over.

The insight and creed from which Emerson's life followed can be best summed up in his own verses:

So nigh is grandeur to our dust,
So near is God to man!

Through the individual fact there ever shone for him the effulgence of the Universal Reason. The great Cosmic Intellect terminates and houses itself in mortal men and passing hours. Each of us is an angle of its eternal vision, and the only way to be true to our Maker is to be loyal to ourselves. "O rich and various Man!" he cries, "thou palace of sight and sound, carrying in thy senses the morning and the night and the unfathomable galaxy; in thy brain the geometry of the city of God; in thy heart the bower of love and the realms of right and wrong."

If the individual open thus directly into the Absolute, it follows that there is something in each and all of us, even the lowliest, that ought not to consent to borrowing traditions and living at second hand. "If John was perfect, why are you and I alive?" Emerson writes; "As long as any man exists there is some need of him: let him fight for his own." This faith that in a life at first hand there is something sacred is perhaps the most characteristic note in Emerson's writings. The hottest side of him is this non-conformist persuasion, and if his temper could ever verge on common irascibility, it would be by reason of the passionate character of his feelings on this point. The world is still new and untried. In seeing freshly, and not in hearing of what others saw, shall a man find what truth is. "Each one of us can bask in the great morning which rises out of the Eastern Sea, and be himself one of the children of the light." "Trust thyself, every heart vibrates to that iron string. There is a time in each man's education when he must arrive at the conviction that imitation is suicide; when he must take himself for better or worse as his portion; and know that though the wide universe is full of good, no kernel of nourishing corn can come to him but through his toil bestowed on that plot of ground which it was given him to till."

The matchless eloquence with which Emerson proclaimed the sovereignty of the living individual electrified and emancipated his generation, and this bugle-blast will doubtless be regarded by future critics as the soul of his message. The present man is the aboriginal reality, the Institution is derivative, and the past man is irrelevant and obliterate for present issues. "If anyone would lay an axe to your tree with a text from I John, vs. 7, or a sentence from Saint Paul, say to him," Emerson wrote, " 'My tree is Yggdrasil, the tree of life.' Let him know by your security that your conviction is clear and sufficient, and, if he were Paul himself, that you also are here and with your Creator." "Cleave ever to God," he insisted, "against the name of God";—and so, in spite of the intensely religious character of his total thought, when he began his career it seemed to many of his brethren in the clerical profession that he was little more than an iconoclast and desecrator.

Emerson's belief that the individual must in reason be adequate to the vocation for which the Spirit of the world has called him into being, is the source of those sublime pages, hearteners, and sustainers of our youth, in which he urges his hearers to be incorruptibly true to their own private conscience. Nothing can harm the man who rests in his appointed place and character. Such a man is invulnerable; he balances the universe, balances it as much by keeping small when he is small, as by being great and spreading when he is great. "I love and honor Epaminondas," said Emerson, "but I do not wish to be Epaminondas. I hold it more just to love the world of this hour than the world of his hour. Nor can you, if I am true, excite me to the least uneasiness by saying, 'He acted and thou sittest still.' I see action to be good when the need is, and sitting still to be also good. Epaminondas, if he was the man I take him for, would have sat still with joy and peace, if his lot had been mine. Heaven is large, and affords space for all modes of love and fortitude." "The fact that I am here certainly shows me that the Soul has need of an organ here, and shall I not assume the post?"

The vanity of all superserviceableness and pretence was never more happily set forth than by Emerson in the many passages in which he develops this aspect of his philosophy. Character infallibly proclaims itself. "Hide your thoughts!—hide the sun and moon. They publish themselves to the universe. They will speak through you though you were dumb. They will flow out of your actions, your manners and your face. . . . Don't say things: What you are stands over you the while and thunders so that I cannot hear what you say to the contrary. . . . What a man *is* engraves itself upon him in letters of light. Concealment avails him nothing, boasting nothing. There is confession in the glances of our eyes; in our smiles; in salutations; and the grasp of hands. His sin bedaubs him, mars all his good impression. Men know not why they do not trust him, but they do not trust him. His vice glasses the eye, casts lines of mean expression in the cheek, pinches the nose, sets the mark of the beast upon the back of the head, and writes, O fool! fool! on the forehead of a king. If you would not be known to do a thing, never do it; a man may play the fool in the drifts of a desert, but every grain of sand shall seem to see—How can a man be concealed? How can he be concealed?"

On the other hand, never was a sincere word or a sincere thought utterly lost. "Never a magnanimity fell to the ground but there is some heart to greet and accept it unexpectedly. . . . The hero fears not that if he withstood the avowal of a just and brave act, it will go unwitnessed and unloved. One knows it,—himself—and is pledged by it to sweetness of peace and to nobleness of aim, which will prove in the end a better proclamation than the relating of the incident."

The same indefeasible right to be exactly what one is, provided one only be authentic, spreads itself, in Emerson's way of thinking, from persons to things and to times and places. No date, no position is insignificant, if the life that fills it out be only genuine:

> In solitude, in a remote village, the ardent youth loiters and mourns. With inflamed eye, in this sleeping wilderness, he has read the story of the Emperor, Charles the Fifth, until his fancy has brought home to the surrounding woods the faint roar of cannonades in the Milanese, and marches in Germany. He is curious concerning that man's day. What filled it? The crowded orders, the stern decisions, the foreign despatches, the Castilian etiquette? The soul answers—Behold his day here! In the sighing of these woods, in the quiet of these gray fields, in the cool breeze that sings out of these northern mountains; in the workmen, the boys, the maidens you meet, —in the hopes of the morning, the ennui of noon, and sauntering of the afternoon; in the disquieting comparisons; in the regrets at want of vigor; in the great idea and the puny execution,—behold Charles the Fifth's day; another, yet the same; behold Chatham's, Hampden's, Bayard's, Alfred's, Scipio's, Pericles's day,—day of all that are born of women. The difference of circumstance is merely costume. I am tasting the selfsame life,—its sweetness, its greatness, its pain, which I so admire in other men. Do not foolishly ask of the inscrutable, obliterated past what it cannot tell,—the details of that nature, of that day, called Byron or Burke;—but ask it of the enveloping Now. . . . Be lord of a day, and you can put up your history books.

"The deep to-day which all men scorn" receives thus from Emerson superb revindication. "Other world! there is no other world." All God's life opens into the individual particular, and here and now, or nowhere, is reality. "The present hour is the decisive hour, and every day is doomsday."

Such a conviction that Divinity is everywhere may easily make of one an optimist of the sentimental type that refuses to speak ill of anything. Emerson's drastic perception of differences kept him at the opposite pole from this weakness. After you have seen men a few times, he could say, you find most of them as alike as their barns and pantries, and soon as musty and as dreary. Never was such a fastidious lover of significance and distinction, and never an eye so keen for their discovery. His optimism had nothing in common with that indiscriminate hurrahing for the Universe with which Walt Whitman has made us familiar. For Emerson, the individual fact and moment were indeed suffused with absolute radiance, but it was upon a condition that saved the situation—they must be worthy specimens,—sincere, authentic, archetypal; they must have made connection with what he calls the Moral Sentiment, they must in some way act as symbolic mouthpieces of the Universe's meaning. To know just which thing does act in this way, and which thing fails to make the true connection, is the secret (somewhat incommunicable, it must be confessed) of seership, and doubtless we must not expect of the seer too rigorous a consistency. Emerson himself was a real seer. He could perceive the full squalor of the individual fact, but he could also see the transfiguration. He might easily have found himself saying of some present-day agitator against our Philippine conquest what he said of this or that reformer of his own time. He might have called him, as a private person, a tedious bore and canter. But he would infallibly have added what he then added: "It is strange and horrible to say this, for I feel that under him and his partiality and exclusiveness is the earth and the sea, and all that in them is, and the axis round which the Universe revolves passes through his body where he stands."

Be it how it may, then, this is Emerson's revelation: The point of any pen can be an epitome of reality; the commonest person's act, if genuinely actuated, can lay hold on eternity. This vision is the head-spring of all his outpourings; and it is for this truth, given to no previous literary artist to express in such penetratingly persuasive tones, that posterity will reckon him a prophet, and, perhaps neglecting other pages, piously turn to those that convey this message. His life was one long conversation with the invisible divine, expressing itself through individuals and particulars: "So nigh is grandeur to our dust, so near is God to man!"

I spoke of how shrunken the wraith, how thin the echo, of men is after they are departed. Emerson's wraith comes to me now as if it were but the very voice of this victorious argument. His words to this effect are certain to be quoted and extracted more and more as time goes on, and to take their place among the Scriptures of humanity. " 'Gainst death and all oblivious enmity, shall you pace forth," beloved Master. As long as our English language lasts men's hearts will be cheered and their souls strengthened and liberated by the noble and musical pages with which you have enriched it.

# Ralph Waldo Emerson

### *by John Dewey*

It is said that Emerson is not a philosopher. I find this denegation false or true according as it is said in blame or praise—according to the reasons proffered. When the critic writes of lack of method, of the absence of continuity, of coherent logic, and, with the old story of the string of pearls loosely strung, puts Emerson away as a writer of maxims and proverbs, a recorder of brilliant insights and abrupt aphorisms, the critic, to my mind, but writes down his own incapacity to follow a logic that is finely wrought.

> We want in every man a logic; we cannot pardon the absence of it, but it must not be spoken. Logic is the procession or proportionate unfolding of the intuition; but its virtue is as silent method; the moment it would appear as propositions and have a separate value, it is worthless.

Emerson fulfills his own requisition. The critic needs the method separately propounded, and not finding his wonted leading-string is all lost. Again, says Emerson, "There is no compliment like the addressing to the human being thoughts out of certain heights and presupposing his intelligence"—a compliment which Emerson's critics have mostly hastened to avert. But to make this short, I am not acquainted with any writer, no matter how assured his position in treatises upon the history of philosophy, whose movement of thought is more compact and unified, nor one who combines more adequately diversity of intellectual attack with concentration of form and effect. I recently read a letter from a gentleman, himself a distinguished writer of philosophy, in which he remarked that philosophers are a stupid class, since they want every reason carefully pointed out and labelled, and are incapable of taking anything for granted. The condescending patronage by literary critics of Emerson's lack of cohesiveness may remind us that philosophers have no monopoly of this particular form of stupidity.

"Ralph Waldo Emerson." From *Characters and Events,* Vol. I, edited by John Dewey and Joseph Ratner (New York: Holt, Rinehart & Winston, Inc., 1929). 

Perhaps those are nearer right, however, who deny that Emerson is a philosopher, because he is more than a philosopher. He would work, he says, by art, not by metaphysics, finding truth "in the sonnet and the play." "I am," to quote him again, "in all my theories, ethics and politics, a poet"; and we may, I think, safely take his word for it that he meant to be a maker rather than a reflector. His own preference was to be ranked with the seers rather than with the reasoners of the race, for he says, "I think that philosophy is still rude and elementary; it will one day be taught by poets. The poet is in the right attitude; he is believing; the philosopher, after some struggle, having only reasons for believing." Nor do I regard it as impertinent to place by the side of this utterance, that other in which he said "We have yet to learn that the thing uttered in words is not therefore affirmed. It must affirm itself or no forms of grammar and no plausibility can give it evidence and no array of arguments." To Emerson, perception was more potent than reasoning; the deliverances of intercourse more to be desired than the chains of discourse; the surprise of reception more demonstrative than the conclusions of intentional proof. As he said "Good as is discourse, silence is better, and shames it. The length of discourse indicates the distance of thought betwixt the speaker and the hearer." And again, "If I speak, I define and confine, and am less." "Silence is a solvent that destroys personality and gives us leave to be great and universal."

I would not make hard and fast lines between philosopher and poet, yet there is some distinction of accent in thought and of rhythm in speech. The desire for an articulate, not for silent, logic is intrinsic with philosophy. The unfolding of the perception must be stated, not merely followed and understood. Such conscious method is, one might say, the only thing of ultimate concern to the abstract thinker. Not thought, but reasoned thought, not things, but the ways of things, interest him; not even truth, but the paths by which truth is sought. He construes elaborately the symbols of thinking. He is given over to manufacturing and sharpening the weapons of the spirit. Outcomes, interpretations, victories, are indifferent. Otherwise is it with art. That, as Emerson says, is "the path of the Creator to his work"; and again "a habitual respect to the whole by an eye loving beauty in detail." Affection is towards the meaning of the symbol, not to its constitution. Only as he wields them, does the artist forge the sword and buckler of the spirit. His affair is to uncover rather than to analyze; to discern rather than to classify. He reads but does not compose.

One, however, has no sooner drawn such lines than one is ashamed and begins to retract. Euripides and Plato, Dante and Bruno, Bacon and Milton, Spinoza and Goethe, rise in rebuke. The spirit of Emerson rises to protest against exaggerating his ultimate value by trying to place him upon a plane of art higher than a philosophic platform. Literary critics admit his philosophy and deny his literature. And if philosophers extol his keen, calm art and speak with some depreciation of his metaphysic, it also is perhaps because Emerson knew something deeper than our conventional definitions. It is indeed true that reflective thinkers have taken the way to truth for their truth; the method of life for the conduct of life —in short, have taken means for end. But it is also assured that in the completeness of their devotion, they have expiated their transgression; means become identified with end, thought turns to life, and wisdom is justified not of herself but of her children. Language justly preserves the difference between philosopher and sophist. It is no more possible to eliminate love and generation from the definition of the thinker than it is to eliminate thought and limits from the conception of the artist. It is interest, concern, caring, which makes the one as it makes the other. It is significant irony that the old quarrel of philosopher and poet was brought off by one who united in himself more than has another individual the qualities of both artist and metaphysician. At bottom the quarrel is not one of objectives nor yet of methods, but of the affections. And in the divisions of love, there always abides the unity of him who loves. Because Plato was so great he was divided in his affections. A lesser man could not brook that torn love, because of which he set poet and philosopher over against one another. Looked at in the open, our fences between literature and metaphysics appear petty—signs of an attempt to affix the legalities and formularies of property to the things of the spirit. If ever there lived not only a metaphysician but a professor of metaphysics it was Immanuel Kant. Yet he declares that he should account himself more unworthy than the day laborer in the field if he did not believe that somehow, even in his technical classifications and remote distinctions, he too, was carrying forward the struggle of humanity for freedom—that is for illumination.

And for Emerson of all others, there is a one-sidedness and exaggeration, which he would have been the first to scorn, in exalting overmuch his creative substance at the expense of his reflective procedure. He says in effect somewhere that the individual man is only a method, a plan of arrangement. The saying is amply descriptive of Emerson. His idealism is the faith of the thinker in his thought raised to its *nth* power. "History," he says, "and the state of the world at any one time is directly dependent on the intellectual classification then existing in the minds of men." Again, "Beware when the great God lets loose a thinker on this planet. Then all things are at risk. The very hopes of man, the thoughts of his heart, the religion of nations, the manner and morals of mankind are all at the mercy of a new generalization." And again, "Everything looks permanent until its secret is known. Nature looks provokingly stable and secular, but it has a cause like all the rest; and when once I comprehend that, will these fields stretch so immovably wide, these leaves hang so individually considerable?" And finally, "In history an idea always overhangs like a moon and rules the tide which rises simultaneously in all the souls of a generation." There are times, indeed, when one is inclined to regard

Emerson's whole work as a hymn to intelligence, a pæon to the all-creating, all-disturbing power of thought.

And so, with an expiatory offering to the Manes of Emerson, one may proceed to characterize his thought, his method, yea, even his system. I find it in the fact that he takes the distinctions and classifications which to most philosophers are true in and of and because of their systems, and makes them true of life, of the common experience of the everyday man. To take his own words for it,

> There are degrees in idealism. We learn first to play with it academically, as the magnet was once a toy. Then we see, in the heyday of youth and poetry, that it may be true, that it is true in gleams and fragments. Then, its countenance waxes stern and grand, and we see that it must be true. It now shows itself ethical and practical.

The idealism which is a thing of the academic intellect to the professor, a hope to the generous youth, an inspiration to the genial projector, is to Emerson a narrowly accurate description of the facts of the most real world in which all earn their living.

Such reference to the immediate life is the text by which he tries every philosopher. "Each new mind we approach seems to require," he says, "an abdication of all our past and present possessions. A new doctrine seems at first a subversion of all our opinions, tastes and manner of living." But while one gives himself "up unreservedly to that which draws him, because that is his own, he is to refuse himself to that which draws him not, because it is not his own. I were a fool not to sacrifice a thousand Aeschyluses to my intellectual integrity. Especially take the same ground in regard to abstract truth, the science of the mind. The Bacon, the Spinoza, the Hume, Schelling, Kant, is only a more or less awkward translator of things in your consciousness. Say, then, instead of too timidly poring into his obscure sense, that he has not succeeded in rendering back to you your consciousness. Anyhow, when at last, it is done, you will find it is not recondite, but a simple, natural state which the writer restores to you." And again, take this other saying, "Aristotle or Bacon or Kant propound some maxim which is the keynote of philosophy thenceforward, but I am more interested to know that when at last they have hurled out their grand word, it is only some familiar experience of every man on the street." I fancy he reads the so-called eclecticism of Emerson wrongly who does not see that it is reduction of all the philosophers of the race, even the prophets like Plato and Proclus whom Emerson holds most dear, to the test of trial by the service rendered the present and immediate experience. As for those who contemn Emerson for superficial pedantry because of the strings of names he is wont to flash like beads before our eyes, they but voice their own pedantry, not seeing, in their literalness, that all such things are with Emerson symbols of various uses administered to the common soul.

As Emerson treated the philosophers, so he treats their doctrines. The Platonist teaches the immanence of absolute ideas in the World and in Man, that every thing and every man participates in an absolute Meaning, individualized in him and through which one has community with others. Yet by the time this truth of the universe has become proper and fit for teaching, it has somehow become a truth of philosophy, a truth of private interpretation, reached by some men, not others, and consequently true for some, but not true for all, and hence not wholly true for any. But to Emerson all "truth lies on the highway." Emerson says, "We lie in the lap of immense intelligence which makes us organs of its activity and receivers of its truth," and the Idea is no longer either an academic toy nor even a gleam of poetry, but a literal report of the experience of the hour as that is enriched and reinforced for the individual through the tale of history, the appliance of science, the gossip of conversation and the exchange of commerce. That every individual is at once the focus and the channel of mankind's long and wide endeavor, that all nature exists for the education of the human soul—such things, as we read Emerson, cease to be statements of a separated philosophy and become natural transcripts of the course of events and of the rights of man.

Emerson's philosophy has this in common with that of the transcendentalists; he prefers to borrow from them rather than from others certain pigments and delineations. But he finds truth in the highway, in the untaught endeavor, the unexpected idea, and this removes him from their remotenesses. His ideas are not fixed upon any Reality that is beyond or behind or in any way apart, and hence they do not have to be bent. They are versions of the Here and the Now, and flow freely. The reputed transcendental worth of an overweening Beyond and Away, Emerson, jealous for spiritual democracy, finds to be the possession of the unquestionable Present. When Emerson, speaking of the chronology of history, designated the There and Then as "wild, savage, and preposterous," he also drew the line which marks him off from transcendentalism—which is the idealism of a Class. In sorry truth, the idealist has too frequently conspired with the sensualist to deprive the pressing and so the passing Now of value which is spiritual. Through the joint work of such malign conspiracy, the common man is not, or at least does not know himself for, an idealist. It is such disinherited of the earth that Emerson summons to their own. "If man is sick, is unable, is mean-spirited and odious, it is because there is so much of his nature which is unlawfully withholden from him."

Against creed and system, convention and institution, Emerson stands for restoring to the common man that which in the name of religion, of philosophy, of art, and of morality, has been embezzled from the common store and appropriated to sectarian and class use. Beyond any one we know of, Emerson has comprehended and declared how such malversation makes truth decline from its simplicity, and in becoming partial and owned, become a puzzle of and trick for theologian, metaphysician and litterateur—a puzzle of an imposed law, of an unwished for and refused goodness, of a romantic ideal gleaming only from afar, and a trick of manipular skill, of specialized performance.

For such reasons, the coming century may well make evident what is just now dawning, that Emerson is not only a philosopher, but that he is the Philosopher of Democracy. Plato's own generation would, I think, have found it difficult to class Plato. Was he an inept visionary or a subtle dialectician? A political reformer or a founder of the new type of literary art? Was he a moral exhorter, or an instructor in an Academy? Was he a theorist upon education, or the inventor of a method of knowledge? We, looking at Plato through the centuries of exposition and interpretation, find no difficulty in placing Plato as a philosopher and in attributing to him a system of thought. We dispute about the nature and content of this system, but we do not doubt it is there. It is the intervening centuries which have furnished Plato with his technique and which have developed and wrought Plato to a system. One century bears but a slender ratio to twenty-five; it is not safe to predict. But at least, thinking of Emerson as the one citizen of the New World fit to have his name uttered in the same breath with that of Plato, one may without presumption believe that even if Emerson has no system, none the less he is the prophet and herald of any system which democracy may henceforth construct and hold by, and that when democracy has articulated itself, it will have no difficulty in finding itself already proposed in Emerson. It is as true today as when he said it: "It is not propositions, not new dogmas and the logical exposition of the world that are our first need, but to watch and continually cherish the intellectual and moral sensibilities and woo them to stay and make their homes with us. Whilst they abide with us, we shall not think amiss." We are moved to say that Emerson is the first and as yet almost the only Christian of the Intellect. From out such reverence for the instinct and impulse of our common nature shall emerge in their due season propositions, systems, and logical expositions of the world. Then shall we have a philosophy which religion has no call to chide and which knows its friendship with science and with art.

Emerson wrote of a certain type of mind: "This tranquil, well-founded, wide-seeing soul is no express-rider, no attorney, no magistrate. It lies in the sun and broods on the world." It is the soul of Emerson which these words describe. Yet this is no private merit nor personal credit. For thousands of earth's children, Emerson has taken away the barriers that shut out the sun and has secured the unimpeded, cheerful circulation of the light of heaven, and the wholesome air of day. For such, content to endure without contriving and contending, at the last all express-riders journey, since to them comes the final service of all commodity. For them, careless to make out their own case, all attorneys plead in the day of final judgment; for though falsehoods pile mountain high, truth is the only deposit that nature tolerates. To them who refuse to be called "master, master," all magistracies in the end defer, for theirs is the common cause for which dominion, power and principality is put under foot. Before such successes, even the worshipers of that which today goes by the name of success, those who bend to millions and incline to imperialisms, may lower their standard, and give at least a passing assent to the final word of Emerson's philosophy, the identity of Being, unqualified and immutable, with Character.

# Emerson

*by George Santayana*

Those who knew Emerson, or who stood so near to his time and to his circle that they caught some echo of his personal influence, did not judge him merely as a poet or philosopher, nor identify his efficacy with that of his writings. His friends and neighbors, the congregations he preached to in his younger days, the audiences that afterward listened to his lectures, all agreed in a veneration for his person which had nothing to do with their understanding or acceptance of his opinions. They flocked to him and listened to his word, not so much for the sake of its absolute meaning as for the atmosphere of candor, purity, and serenity that hung about it, as about a sort of sacred music. They felt themselves in the presence of a rare and beautiful spirit, who was in communion with a higher world. More than the truth his teaching might express, they valued the sense it gave them of a truth that was inexpressible. They became aware, if we may say so, of the ultra-violet rays of his spectrum, of the inaudible highest notes of his gamut, too pure and thin for common ears.

This effect was by no means due to the possession on the part of Emerson of the secret of the universe, or even of a definite conception of ultimate truth. He was not a prophet who had once for all climbed his Sinai or his Tabor, and having there beheld the transfigured reality, descended again to make authoritative report of it to the world. Far from it. At bottom he had no doctrine at all. The deeper he went and the more he tried to grapple with fundamental conceptions, the vaguer and more elusive they became in his hands. Did he know what he meant by Spirit or the "Over-Soul"? Could he say what he understood by the terms, so constantly on his lips, Nature, Law, God, Benefit, or Beauty? He could not, and the consciousness of that incapacity was so lively within him that he never attempted to give articulation to his philosophy. His finer instinct kept him from doing that violence to his inspiration.

"Emerson." From *Interpretations of Poetry and Religion* (New York: Charles Scribner's Sons, 1900). Reprinted by permission of Charles Scribner's Sons and Constable & Co., Ltd.

The source of his power lay not in his doctrine, but in his temperament, and the rare quality of his wisdom was due less to his reason than to his imagination. Reality eluded him; he had neither diligence nor constancy enough to master and possess it; but his mind was open to all philosophic influences, from whatever quarter they might blow; the lessons of science and the hints of poetry worked themselves out in him to a free and personal religion. He differed from the plodding many, not in knowing things better, but in having more ways of knowing them. His grasp was not particularly firm, he was far from being, like a Plato or an Aristotle, past master in the art and the science of life. But his mind was endowed with unusual plasticity, with unusual spontaneity and liberty of movement—it was a fairyland of thoughts and fancies. He was like a young god making experiments in creation: he blotched the work, and always began again on a new and better plan. Every day he said, "Let there be light," and every day the light was new. His sun, like that of Heraclitus, was different every morning.

What seemed, then, to the more earnest and less critical of his hearers a revelation from above was in truth rather an insurrection from beneath, a shaking loose from convention, a disintegration of the normal categories of reason in favor of various imaginative principles, on which the world might have been built, if it had been built differently. This gift of revolutionary thinking allowed new aspects, hints of wider laws, premonitions of unthought-of fundamental unities to spring constantly into view. But such visions were necessarily fleeting, because the human mind had long before settled its grammar, and discovered, after much groping and many defeats, the general forms in which experience will allow itself to be stated. These general forms are the principles of common sense and positive science, no less imaginative in their origin than those notions which we now call transcendental, but grown prosaic, like the metaphors of common speech, by dint of repetition.

Yet authority, even of this rational kind, sat lightly upon Emerson. To reject tradition and think as one might have thought if no man had ever existed before was indeed the aspiration of the Transcendentalists, and although Emerson hardly regarded himself as a member of that school, he largely shared its tendency and passed for its spokesman. Without protesting against tradition, he smilingly eluded it in his thoughts, untamable in their quiet irresponsibility. He fled to his woods or to his "pleachèd garden," to be the creator of his own worlds in solitude and freedom. No wonder that he brought thence to the tightly conventional minds of his contemporaries a breath as if from paradise. His simplicity in novelty, his profundity, his ingenuous ardor must have seemed to them something heavenly, and they may be excused if they thought they detected inspiration even in his occasional thin paradoxes and guileless whims. They were stifled with conscience and he brought them a breath of Nature; they were surfeited with shallow controversies and he gave them poetic truth.

Imagination, indeed, is his single theme. As a preacher might under every text enforce the same lessons of the gospel, so Emerson traces in every sphere the same spiritual laws of experience—compensation, continuity, the self-expression of the Soul in the forms of Nature and of society, until she finally recognizes herself in her own work and sees its beneficence and beauty. His constant refrain is the omnipotence of imaginative thought; its power first to make the world, then to understand it, and finally to rise above it. All Nature is an embodiment of our native fancy, all history a drama in which the innate possibilities of the spirit are enacted and realized. While the conflict of life and the shocks of experience seem to bring us face to face with an alien and overwhelming power, reflection can humanize and rationalize that power by conceiving its laws; and with this recognition of the rationality of all things comes the sense of their beauty and order. The destruction which Nature seems to prepare for our special hopes is thus seen to be the victory of our impersonal interests. To awaken in us this spiritual insight, an elevation of mind which is at once an act of comprehension and of worship, to substitute it for lower passions and more servile forms of intelligence—that is Emerson's constant effort. All his resources of illustration, observation, and rhetoric are used to deepen and clarify this sort of wisdom.

Such thought is essentially the same that is found in the German romantic or idealistic philosophers, with whom Emerson's affinity is remarkable, all the more as he seems to have borrowed little or nothing from their works. The critics of human nature, in the eighteenth century, had shown how much men's ideas depend on their predispositions, on the character of their senses and the habits of their intelligence. Seizing upon this thought and exaggerating it, the romantic philosophers attributed to the spirit of man the omnipotence which had belonged to God, and felt that in this way they were reasserting the supremacy of mind over matter and establishing it upon a safe and rational basis.

The Germans were great system-makers, and Emerson cannot rival them in the sustained effort of thought by which they sought to reinterpret every sphere of being according to their chosen principles. But he surpassed them in an instinctive sense of what he was doing. He never represented his poetry as science, nor countenanced the formation of a new sect that should nurse the sense of a private and mysterious illumination, and re-light the fagots of passion and prejudice. He never tried to seek out and defend the universal implications of his ideas, and never wrote the book he had once planned on the law of compensation, foreseeing, we may well believe, the sophistries in which he would have been directly involved. He fortunately preferred a fresh statement on a fresh subject. A suggestion once given, the spirit once aroused to speculation, a glimpse once gained of some ideal harmony, he chose to descend again to common sense and to touch the earth for a moment before another flight. The faculty of idealization was itself what he valued. Philosophy for him was rather a moral energy flowering into sprightliness of thought than a body of serious and defensible doctrines. In practicing transcendental speculation only in this poetic and sporadic fashion, Emerson retained its true value and avoided its greatest danger. He secured the freedom and fertility of his thought and did not allow one conception of law or one hint of harmony to sterilize the mind and prevent the subsequent birth within it of other ideas, no less just and imposing than their predecessors. For we are not dealing at all in such a philosophy with matters of fact or with such verifiable truths as exclude their opposites. We are dealing only with imagination, with the art of conception, and with the various forms in which reflection, like a poet, may compose and recompose human experience.

A certain disquiet mingled, however, in the minds of Emerson's contemporaries with the admiration they felt for his purity and genius. They saw that he had forsaken the doctrines of the Church; and they were not sure whether he held quite unequivocally any doctrine whatever. We may not all of us share the concern for orthodoxy which usually caused this puzzled alarm: we may understand that it was not Emerson's vocation to be definite and dogmatic in religion any more than in philosophy. Yet that disquiet will not, even for us, wholly disappear. It is produced by a defect which naturally accompanies imagination in all but the greatest minds. I mean disorganization. Emerson not only conceived things in new ways, but he seemed to think the new ways might cancel and supersede the old. His imagination was to invalidate the understanding. That inspiration which should come to fulfil seemed too often to come to destroy. If he was able so constantly to stimulate us to fresh thoughts, was it not because he demolished the labor of long ages of reflection? Was not the startling effect of much of his writing due to its contradiction to tradition and to common sense?

So long as he is a poet and in the enjoyment of his poetic license, we can blame this play of mind only by a misunderstanding. It is possible to think otherwise than as common sense thinks; there are other categories beside those of science. When we employ them we enlarge our lives. We add to the world of fact any number of worlds of the imagination in which human nature and the eternal relations of ideas may be nobly expressed. So far our imaginative fertility is only a benefit: it surrounds us with the congenial and necessary radiation of art and religion. It manifests our moral vitality in the bosom of Nature.

But sometimes imagination invades the sphere of understanding and seems to discredit its indispensable work. Common sense, we are allowed to infer, is a shallow affair: true insight changes all that. When so applied, poetic activity is not an unmixed good. It loosens our hold on fact and confuses our intelligence, so that we forget that intelligence has itself every prerogative of imagination, and has besides the sanction of practical validity. We are made to believe that since the understanding is something human and conditioned, something which might have been different, as the senses might have been different, and which we may yet, so to speak, get behind—therefore the understanding ought to be abandoned. We long for higher faculties, neglecting those we have, we yearn for intuition, closing our eyes upon experience. We become mystical.

Mysticism, as we have said, is the surrender of a category of thought because we divine its relativity. As every new category, however, must share this reproach, the mystic is obliged in the end to give them all up, the poetic and moral categories no less than the physical, so that the end of his purification is the atrophy of his whole nature, the emptying of his whole heart and mind to make room, as he thinks, for God. By attacking the authority of the understanding as the organon of knowledge, by substituting itself for it as the herald of a deeper truth, the imagination thus prepares its own destruction. For if the understanding is rejected because it cannot grasp the absolute, the imagination and all its works —art, dogma, worship—must presently be rejected for the same reason. Common sense and poetry must both go by the board, and conscience must follow after: for all these are human and relative. Mysticism will be satisfied only with the absolute, and as the absolute, by its very definition, is not representable by any specific faculty, it must be approached through the abandonment of all. The lights of life must be extinguished that the light of the absolute may shine, and the possession of everything in general must be secured by the surrender of everything in particular.

The same diffidence, however, the same constant renewal of sincerity which kept Emerson's flights of imagination near to experience, kept his mysticism also within bounds. A certain mystical tendency is pervasive with him, but there are only one or two subjects on which he dwells with enough constancy and energy of attention to make his mystical treatment of them pronounced. One of these is the question of the unity of all minds in the single soul of the universe, which is the same in all creatures; another is the question of evil and of its evaporation in the universal harmony of things. Both these ideas suggest themselves at certain turns in every man's experience, and might receive a rational formulation. But they are intricate subjects, obscured by many emotional prejudices, so that the labor, impartiality, and precision which would be needed to elucidate them are to be looked for in scholastic rather than in inspired thinkers, and in Emerson least of all. Before these problems he is alternately ingenuous and rhapsodical, and in both moods equally helpless. Individuals no doubt exist, he says to himself. But, ah! Napoleon is in every schoolboy. In every squatter in the western prairies we shall find an owner—

> Of Caesar's hand and Plato's brain,
> Of Lord Christ's heart, and Shakespeare's strain.

But how? we may ask. Potentially? Is it because any mind, were it given the right body and the right experience, were it made over, in a word, into another mind, would resemble that other mind to the point of identity? Or is it that our souls are already so largely similar that we are subject to many kindred promptings and share many ideals unrealizable in our particular circumstances? But then we should simply be saying that if what makes men different were removed, men would be indistinguishable, or that, in so far as they are now alike, they can understand one another by summoning up their respective experiences in the fancy. There would be no mysticism in that, but at the same time, alas, no eloquence, no paradox, and, if we must say the word, no nonsense.

On the question of evil, Emerson's position is of the same kind. There is evil, of course, he tells us. Experience is sad. There is a crack in everything that God has made. But, ah! the laws of the universe are sacred and beneficent. Without them nothing good could arise. All things, then, are in their right places and the universe is perfect above our querulous tears. Perfect? we may ask. But perfect from what point of view, in reference to what ideal? To its own? To that of a man who renouncing himself and all naturally dear to him, ignoring the injustice, suffering, and impotence in the world, allows his will and his conscience to be hypnotized by the spectacle of a necessary evolution, and lulled into cruelty by the pomp and music of a tragic show? In that case the evil is not explained, it is forgotten; it is not cured, but condoned. We have surrendered the category of the better and the worse, the deepest foundation of life and reason; we have become mystics on the one subject on which, above all others, we ought to be men.

Two forces may be said to have carried Emerson in this mystical direction; one, that freedom of his imagination which we have already noted, and which kept him from the fear of self-contradiction; the other the habit of worship inherited from his clerical ancestors and enforced by his religious education. The spirit of conformity, the unction, the loyalty even unto death inspired by the religion of Jehovah, were dispositions acquired by too long a discipline and rooted in too many forms of speech, of thought, and of worship for a man like Emerson, who had felt their full force, ever to be able to lose them. The evolutions of his abstract opinions left that habit unchanged. Unless we keep this circumstance in mind, we shall not be able to understand the kind of elation and sacred joy, so characteristic of his eloquence, with which he propounds laws of Nature and aspects of experience which, viewed in themselves, afford but an equivocal support to moral enthusiasm. An optimism so persistent and unclouded as his will seem at variance with the description he himself gives of human life, a description colored by a poetic idealism, but hardly by an optimistic bias.

We must remember, therefore, that this optimism is a pious tradition, originally justified by the belief in a personal God and in a providential government of affairs for the ultimate and positive good of the elect, and that the habit of worship survived in Emerson as an instinct after those positive beliefs had faded into a recognition of "spiritual laws." We must remember that Calvinism had known how to combine an awestruck devotion to the Supreme Being with no very roseate picture of the destinies of mankind, and for more than two hundred years had been breeding in the stock from which Emerson came a willingness to be, as the phrase is, "damned for the glory of God."

What wonder, then, that when, for the former inexorable dispensation of Providence, Emerson substituted his general spiritual and natural laws, he should not have felt the spirit of worship fail within him? On the contrary, his thought moved in the presence of moral harmonies which seemed to him truer, more beautiful, and more beneficent than those of the old theology. An independent philosopher would not have seen in those harmonies an object of worship or a sufficient basis for optimism. But he was not an independent philosopher, in spite of his belief in independence. He inherited the problems and the preoccupations of the theology from which he started, being in this respect like the German idealists, who, with all their pretence of absolute metaphysics, were in reality only giving elusive and abstract forms to traditional theology. Emerson, too, was not primarily a philosopher, but a Puritan mystic with a poetic fancy and a gift for observation and epigram, and he saw in the laws of Nature, idealized by his imagination, only a more intelligible form of the divinity he had always recognized and adored. His was not a philosophy passing into a religion, but a religion expressing itself as a philosophy and veiled, as at its setting it descended the heavens, in various tints of poetry and science.

If we ask ourselves what was Emerson's relation to the scientific and religious movements of his time, and what place he may claim in the history of opinion, we must answer that he belonged very little to the past, very little to the present, and almost wholly to that abstract sphere into which mystical or philosophic aspiration has carried a few men in all ages. The religious tradition in which he was reared was that of Puritanism, but of a Puritanism which, retaining its moral intensity and metaphysical abstraction, had minimized its doctrinal expression and become Unitarian. Emerson was indeed the Psyche of Puritanism, "the latest-born and fairest vision far" of all that "faded hierarchy." A Puritan whose religion was all poetry, a poet whose only pleasure was thought, he showed in his life and personality the meagerness, the constraint, the frigid and conscious consecration which belonged to his clerical ancestors, while his inmost impersonal spirit ranged abroad over the fields of history and Nature, gathering what ideas it might, and singing its little snatches of inspired song.

The traditional element was thus rather an external and unessential contribution to Emerson's mind; he had the professional tinge, the decorum, the distinction of an old-fashioned divine; he had also the habit of writing sermons, and he had the national pride and hope of a religious people that felt itself providentially chosen to establish a free and godly commonwealth in a new world. For the rest, he separated himself from the ancient creed of the community with a sense rather of relief than of regret. A literal belief in Christian doctrines repelled him as unspiritual, as manifesting no understanding of the meaning which, as allegories, those doctrines might have to a philosophic and poetical spirit. Although as a clergyman he was at first in the habit of referring to the Bible and its lessons as to a supreme authority, he had no instinctive sympathy with the inspiration of either the Old or the New Testament; in Hafiz or Plutarch, in Plato or Shakespeare, he found more congenial stuff.

While he thus preferred to withdraw, without rancor and without contempt, from the ancient fellowship of the church, he assumed an attitude hardly less cool and deprecatory toward the enthusiasms of the new era. The national ideal of democracy and freedom had his entire sympathy; he allowed himself to be drawn into the movement against slavery; he took a curious and smiling interest in the discoveries of natural science and in the material progress of the age. But he could go no farther. His contemplative nature, his religious training, his dispersed reading, made him stand aside from the life of the world, even while he studied it with benevolent attention. His heart was fixed on eternal things, and he was in no sense a prophet for his age or country. He belonged by nature to that mystical company of devout souls that recognize no particular home and are dispersed throughout history, although not without intercommunication. He felt his affinity to the Hindus and the Persians, to the Platonists and the Stoics. Like them he remains "a friend and aider of those who would live in the spirit." If not a star of the first magnitude, he is certainly a fixed star in the firmament of philosophy. Alone as yet among Americans, he may be said to have won a place there, if not by the originality of his thought, at least by the originality and beauty of the expression he gave to thoughts that are old and imperishable.

# Emerson's Tragic Sense

*by Stephen E. Whicher*

There is something enigmatic about most American authors. Poe, Hawthorne, Melville, Thoreau, Whitman, Mark Twain, Emily Dickinson, Henry Adams, Henry James, Frost, Faulkner—each has his secret space, his halls of Thermes, his figure in the carpet, which is felt most strongly in his best work and yet eludes definition. Sometimes it is quite opposed to what its possessor thinks he is or wants to be: for example, Hawthorne, envying Trollope his sunshine and his sales, whose best story was "positively hell-fired"; or Whitman, affirmer of life, whose poetry is never more powerful than when it treats of death; Poe, who liked to think himself icily logical and who wrote best from a haunted fantasy; Mark Twain, professional joker and amateur pessimist; or Frost, tough and humorous individualist, whose best poems are often his saddest. Generally this is linked with an obscure fear or grief, even despair: American literature, closely read, can seem one of the least hopeful of literatures.

To all this, Emerson, representative American author that he is, is no exception. The more we know him, the less we know him. He can be summed up in a formula only by those who know their own minds better than his. We hear his grand, assuring words, but where is the man who speaks them? We know the part he played so well; we feel his powerful charm: we do not know the player. He is, finally, impenetrable, for all his forty-odd volumes.

Yet no man can write so much and so honestly and not reveal himself in some measure. We can see enough to sense in him an unusually large gap, even a contradiction, between his teachings and his experience. He taught self-reliance and felt self-distrust, worshipped reality and knew illusion, proclaimed freedom and submitted to fate. No one has expected more of man; few have found him less competent. There is an Emersonian tragedy and an Emersonian sense of tragedy, and we begin to know him when we feel their presence underlying his impressive confidence.

"Emerson's Tragic Sense." From *Interpretations of American Literature,* edited by Charles Feidelson, Jr. and Paul Brodtkorb, Jr. (New York: Oxford University Press, 1959). 

Of course I must stress the word "Emersonian" here. As Mark Van Doren has remarked, "Emerson had no theory of tragedy," unless to deny its existence is a theory. His oblivion can be prodigious.

> The soul will not know either deformity or pain. If, in the hours of clear reason, we should speak the severest truth, we should say that we had never made a sacrifice. In these hours the mind seems so great, that nothing can be taken from us that seems much. All loss, all pain, is particular; the universe remains to the heart unhurt. Neither vexations nor calamities abate our trust. No man ever stated his griefs as lightly as he might.

As he explained in his lecture on "The Tragic," the man who is grounded in the divine life will transcend suffering in a flight to a region "whereunto these passionate clouds of sorrow cannot rise."

Such transcendence of suffering is one of the great historic answers to tragedy and commands respect. To be valid, however, it must "cost not less than everything." Emerson seems to pay no such price. When, in the same lecture on "The Tragic," he tells the "tender American girl," horrified at reading of the transatlantic slave trade, that these crucifixions were not horrid to the obtuse and barbarous blacks who underwent them, "but only a little worse than the old sufferings," we wonder if he paid anything at all for his peace. The only coin in which we can discharge our debt to suffering is attention to it, but Emerson seems to evade this obligation.

Yet this chilling idealism is not simple insensitivity. Emerson is teaching his tested secret of insulation from calamity: Live in the Soul. His famous assertion in *Experience* of the unreality of his devasting grief for his son is an impressive illustration of the necessity he was under to protect, at whatever human cost, his hard-won security. Yeats has said somewhere that we begin to live when we have conceived life as tragedy. The opposite was true of Emerson. Only as he refused to conceive life as tragedy could he find the courage to live.

By denying man's fate, however, Emerson did not escape it. His urgent need to deny it shows that his confidence was more precarious than he would admit. Who has not felt the insistence, the over-insistence, in such radical claims to freedom and power as *Self-Reliance*?

> Trust thyself: every heart vibrates to that iron string. Accept the place the divine providence has found for you, the society of your contemporaries, the connection of events. Great men have always done so, and confided themselves childlike to the genius of their age, betraying their perception that the absolutely trustworthy was seated at their heart, working through their hands, predominating in all their being. And we are now men, and must accept in the highest mind the same transcendent destiny; and not minors and invalids in a protected corner, not cowards fleeing before a revolution, but guides, redeemers, and benefactors, obeying the Almighty effort, and advancing on Chaos and the Dark.

What speaks here is self-*dis*trust, a distrust so pervasive that it must find an "absolutely trustworthy" seated at the heart before it can trust at all. Self-reliance, in the oft-cited phrase, is God-reliance, and therefore not self-reliance. Contrast the accent of a genuine individualist like Ibsen: "The strongest man in the world is he who stands most alone." Or recall a truly self-reliant American: "It was about this time I conceiv'd the bold and arduous project of arriving at moral perfection. I wish'd to live without committing any fault at any time; I would conquer all that either natural inclination, custom, or company might lead me into. As I knew, or thought I knew, what was right and wrong, I did not see why I might not always do the one and avoid the other. . . . For this purpose I therefore contrived the following method. . . ." The free and easy assurance of Franklin is just what is missing in Emerson.

Certainly the first thirty years or so showed no great self-trust. A tubercular, like many in his family (two brothers died of the disease), he was engaged throughout his twenties in a serious battle of life and death in which he was not at all sure of winning. With his poor health went a disheartening self-criticism. He imagined he was incurably idle and self-indulgent, without force or worldly competence, constrained in the company of others, unresponsive in his affections. Though his early journals often show a manly courage and good sense, the dominant mood is a sense of impotence. He lacks all power to realize his larger ambitions and feels himself drifting, sometimes in humiliation, sometimes in wry amusement, before the inexorable flowing of time. He was the servant more than the master of his fate, he found in 1824; and later, in the depths of his illness, it seemed to him that he shaped his fortunes not at all. In all his life, he wrote, he obeyed a strong necessity.

The electrifying release of power brought to him by the amazing discovery, the start of his proper career, that God was within his own soul is understandable only against this early—indeed, this lifelong submission to a strong necessity. His subjection bred a longing for self-direction, all the stronger for his underlying sense of its impossibility. The force of his transcendental faith, and its almost willful extravagance, sprang from his need to throw off, against all probability and common sense, his annihilating dependence. He welcomed the paradoxical doctrine that "God dwells in thee" with uncritical delight, as the solution to all the doubts that oppressed him, and rushed in a Saturnalia of faith to spell out its revolutionary consequences for the solitary soul:

> . . . The world is nothing, the man is all; . . . in yourself slumbers the whole of Reason; it is for you to know all, it is for you to dare all. . . .
>
> . . . The height, the deity of man is, to be self-sustained, to need no gift, no foreign force. . . . All that you call the world is the shadow of that substance which you are, the perpetual creation of the powers of thought, of those that are dependent and of those that are independent of your will.

> . . . You think me the child of my circumstances: I make my circumstance. . . .
>
> . . . Every rational creature has all nature for his dowry and estate. It is his, if he will. He may divest himself of it; he may creep into a corner, and abdicate his kingdom, as most men do, but he is entitled to the world by his constitution. . . .

Yet this proclamation of the kingdom of man was always what he soon came to call it, a romance. He retained a common-sense awareness (and so retains our respect) that experience did not support it. Not merely were all manipular attempts to realize his kingdom premature and futile. The Power within, from which all capacity stemmed, was itself wayward. The individual relying on it was a mere pipe for a divine energy that came and went as it willed. With this hidden life within him, man was no longer hopeless, but he was still helpless. "I would gladly," Emerson wrote at the age of forty-one, ". . . allow the most to the will of man, but I have set my heart on honesty in this chapter, and I can see nothing at last, in success or failure, than more or less of vital force supplied from the Eternal."

When Emerson wrote *The American Scholar,* seven years earlier, his imagination had kindled to a blaze at the thought of the divine power latent in the soul. Give way to it, let it act, and the conversion of the world will follow. As this millennial enthusiasm inevitably waned, the old helplessness it had contradicted emerged unaltered from the flames. The result was a head-on clash of belief and fact. His vision of man as he might be only intensified the plight of man as he was. Something resembling the Fall of Man, which he had so ringingly denied, reappears in his pages.

It is not sin now that troubles him, but "the incompetency of power." One may accuse Providence of a certain parsimony.

> It has shown the heaven and earth to every child, and filled him with a desire for the whole; a desire raging, infinite; a hunger, as of space to be filled with planets; a cry of famine, as of devils for souls. Then for the satisfaction,—to each man is administered a single drop, a bead of dew of vital power, *per day,*—a cup as large as space, and one drop of the water of life in it. Each man woke in the morning with an appetite that could eat the solar system like a cake; a spirit for action and passion without bounds; he could lay his hand on the morning star; he could try conclusions with gravitation or chemistry; but, on the first motion to prove his strength,—hands, feet, senses, gave way, and would not serve him. He was an emperor deserted by his states, and left to whistle by himself, or thrust into a mob of emperors, all whistling: and still the sirens sang, "The attractions are proportioned to the destinies." In every house, in the heart of each maiden and of each boy, in the soul of the soaring saint, this chasm is found,—between the largest promise of ideal power and the shabby experience.

This chasm is the Emersonian tragedy, a tragedy of incapacity. Man's reach must exceed his grasp, of course; that is not tragic. Emerson's chasm cuts deeper: between a vision that claims all power now, and an experience that finds none. Emerson's thought of the self was split between a total Yes and a total No, which could not coexist, could not be reconciled, and yet were both true. "Alas for this infirm faith, this will not strenuous, this vast ebb of a vast flow! I am God in nature; I am a weed by the wall."

There is an Emersonian skepticism as well as an Emersonian faith. Of the seven "lords of life" he distinguishes in his key essay, *Experience,* five are principles of weakness. A man is slave to his moods and his temperament, swept like a bubble down the stream of time, blinded and drugged with illusion, the captive of his senses—in a word, the creature of a strong necessity. To be sure, the God is a native of the bleak rocks of his isolation, and can at any moment surprise and cheer him with new glimpses of reality. But for all this miraculous consolation, he has no will or force of his own; self-reliant is precisely what he can never be. *The American Scholar's* assurance of the unsearched might of man is a feat of faith in view of the actual humiliating human predicament, "with powers so vast and unweariable ranged on one side, and this little, conceited, vulnerable popinjay that a man is, bobbing up and down into every danger, on the other."

It goes without saying that one can easily overstate the case for a tragic sense in Emerson. *Experience,* for instance, is not a tragic-sounding essay. Perhaps "sense of limitation" would be more accurate; I have deliberately chosen a controversial term, in order to stress a side of Emerson often overlooked. For all his loss of millennial hope, Emerson in fact came to allow much to the will of man, as any reader of *The Conduct of Life* can see. Nor do I mean to suggest that he did not find the secret of a serene and affirmative life. The evidence is overwhelming that he did. My point is that his serenity was a not unconscious *answer* to his experience of life, rather than an inference from it (even when presented as such). It was an act of faith, forced on him by what he once called "the ghastly reality of things." Only as we sense this tension of faith and experience in him can we catch the quality of his affirmation. He *had* to ascribe more reality to his brief moments of "religious sentiment" than to the rest of life, or he could not live.

The way he did so altered sensibly, as his first excess of faith in man diminished. A gentle resignation came to settle over his thought of human nature, an elegiac recognition that life perpetually promises us a glory we can never realize. As it did so, the center of his faith traveled imperceptibly from man to the order that included him. In moments of faith, as he explained even in the midst of his essay on *Self-Reliance,* "The soul raised over passion beholds identity and eternal causation, perceives the self-existence of Truth and Right, and calms itself with knowing that all things go well." Such dogmatic optimism, always a part of his faith, became more and more its sole content as his first dream of a kingdom of Man dwindled into reasonableness.

Emerson the optimist said some shallow and callous things, as he did in his lecture on "The Tragic." To restore our sympathy with his humanity, we must glimpse the prisoner that now and then looked out of the eyes above the smile. Within, he was sovereign, a guide, redeemer, and benefactor; without, he was a lecturing and publishing old gentleman. Each time his inner promise of ideal power came up against the narrow limits of his experience, the response could only be the same—a renewed surrender to the Power that planned it that way.

He did not surrender to necessity because he found it good, so much as he found it good because he surrendered. Recurrently the Good he recognizes is more conspicuous for power than for goodness, a "deaf, unimplorable, immense fate," to which all man-made distinctions of good and ill are an impertinence. In some of his poems, particularly, those that have eyes to see may watch him swept into entranced submission to "the over-god" by the compulsion of his personal problems. This is how he meets the impossible challenge of social action, in the "Ode" to Channing. So the teasing evanescence of his moments of insight into reality is submerged in "The World-Soul." He bows to the same power for a bleak consolation in his "Threnody" for his son:

> Silent rushes the swift Lord
> Through ruined systems still restored,
> Broadsowing, bleak and void to bless,
> Plants with worlds the wilderness;
> Waters with tears of ancient sorrow
> Apples of Eden ripe to-morrow.
> House and tenant go to ground,
> Lost in God, in Godhead found.

In such poems we feel the hunger for strength that sent him first to his grand doctrine of Self-Reliance, and then swung him to its polar opposite, a worship of the Beautiful Necessity.

Like all puritans, Emerson was an extremist: he had to have entire assurance, or he had none at all. Though we have a tradition of mature tragedy in our literature, American authors have typically made the same demand. Either they have risen to his transcendental trust, like Thoreau and Whitman; or they have accepted shoddy substitutes, like Norris or Sandburg or Steinbeck; or they have dropped into blackness, like Henry Adams or Jeffers. Emerson himself teetered on the edge of this drop, as did Thoreau and Whitman too, sustained by little more than their own power of belief. Since then the impulse to believe has become progressively feebler and the drop quicker and harder, until now, John Aldridge tells us, our honest writers *start* in the pit. If we are ever to have a great literature again, one would conclude, it will not be until we can break decisively with the whole extremist Emersonian pattern and find some means to face this world without either transcendence or despair.

# The House of Pain

*by Newton Arvin*

No one knew better than Emerson that every generation goes through a necessary and proper ritual-slaying of its parents; that Zeus, as he would say, is forever destroying his father Cronos; and that, if the writers of one age reject, with a kind of sacrificial solemnity, the writers who have just preceded them, this is quite as it ought to be—is the Method of Nature herself. "Our life," he said, "is an apprenticeship to the truth that around every circle another can be drawn; that there is no end in nature, but every end is a beginning; that there is always another dawn risen on mid-noon, and under every deep a lower deep opens." He could not have been surprised, therefore, and probably he would not even have been much disturbed, if his sons, or his son's sons, turned upon him, metaphorically speaking, and put him to the knife on the reeking altar of literary and intellectual change. Certainly this is what happened. Emerson had been the Socrates and even the Zoroaster of the generation of young men and women for whom he first spoke, and to tell the truth, it was not until a third age had arrived that the Imitation of Emerson was followed by his Immolation.

This rite was performed by the literary leaders of the period of the First World War. Almost forty years ago Mr. T. S. Eliot, whose voice was rightly to carry so far, remarked that "the essays of Emerson are already an encumbrance." Three or four years later D. H. Lawrence expressed a somewhat less drastic but in its implications almost equally repudiative view: "I like Emerson's real courage," he said. "I like his wild and genuine belief in the Oversoul and the inrushes he got from it. But it is a museum-interest. Or else it is a taste of the old drug to the old spiritual dope-fiend in me." Emerson, not as a tonic, but as a narcotic—this is the Emerson who came more and more to serve as an image of the man for the new era. The greatest poet of that generation put the case against him with almost filial finality. Speaking, in his autobiography, of his friend, the Irish poet AE, William Butler Yeats observed that he some-

"The House of Pain: Emerson and the Tragic Sense." From *The Hudson Review,* Vol. XII, No. 1 (Spring, 1959), 37-53. 

times wondered what AE "would have been had he not met in early life the poetry of Emerson and Walt Whitman, writers who have begun to seem superficial," said Yeats, "because they lack the Vision of Evil."

There was much in Emerson's writings, Heaven knows, to account for these rejections; but the ground on which Yeats put *his* was the most serious and the most fundamental—the deficiency in Emerson of what a Spanish writer of that period called famously the Tragic Sense of Life. And indeed it did not have to be left to the age of Eliot and Yeats to express a dissatisfaction with this blindness of Emerson's. There were writers, as there were doubtless readers, of his own time who found him terribly wanting in any true awareness of what one of them called the Power of Blackness. Hawthorne, who was his neighbor in Concord, had a due respect for Emerson as a man; but Emerson the transcendental optimist addressed no word of authority to the ear of Hawthorne—who described him as "Mr. Emerson—the mystic, stretching his hand out of cloudland, in vain search for something real." And Hawthorne's younger contemporary Melville could be even more severe; in the margin of his copy of Emerson's essays, adjoining a particularly cheerful passage in the essay on "Prudence," Melville wrote: "To one who has weathered Cape Horn as a common sailor, what stuff all this is." A much younger man than either Hawthorne or Melville, Henry James, would not have spoken of Mr. Emerson, his father's friend, in just this vein of disrespectful impatience, but he too could not refrain from remarking that there was a side of life as to which Emerson's eyes were thickly bandaged. "He had no great sense of wrong," said James—"a strangely limited one, indeed, for a moralist—no sense of the dark, the foul, the base."

They all mount up—judgments like these, and there are a hundred of them—to what sometimes seems like not only a damaging but a fatal indictment of Emerson as a writer whom we can ever again listen to with the old reverential attention. A writer who lacks the Vision of Evil, who has no great sense of wrong—how can he be read with respect, or perhaps read at all, in a time when we all seem agreed that anguish, inquietude, the experience of guilt, and the knowledge of the Abyss are the essential substance of which admissible literature is made? It is a painful question to any reader who cannot suppress his sense of a deep debt to Emerson. But it is a question that must be asked, and one has to confess that, as one turns the pages of his essays, the reasons stare one in the face why Hawthorne and Melville, Eliot and Yeats, should have answered it so negatively.

Certainly it is hard to understand how a writer of even the least seriousness could dispose so jauntily as Emerson sometimes does of the problem of moral evil—genially denying, in fact, or seeming to, that it is a problem at all. Are we really listening to a moralist who expects to be heard respectfully when we find Emerson saying, apropos of young people who are troubled by the problems of original sin, the origin of evil, and the like: "These never presented a practical difficulty to any man,—never darkened across any man's road who did not go out of his way to seek them. These are the soul's mumps and measles and whooping-coughs. . . . A simple mind will not know these enemies"? We rub our eyes as we read, and then open another volume and find the same sage and seer reassuring us even more blandly that "The less we have to do with our sins the better. No man can afford to waste his moments in compunctions."

Did any writer on morals, we are tempted to ask at such moments, ever go farther than this toward inculcating a hard complacency, a shallow self-righteousness, in his readers? The feeling of unreality that rises in us at these times is almost dreamlike, and so it is on at least some of the occasions when Emerson turns his gaze reluctantly to what used to be called natural evil—to the facts of human misery and suffering—to the Tragic. Is it possible to recognize, in the sun-warmed landscape of the Emersonian center, the terribly familiar world of primordial human experience—that world in which sunshine and warmth have alternated, for most men, with bitter cold and darkness? It is easy to get the mistaken impression that, for Emerson, there were indeed no Cape Horns in experience, no jungles, no Arctic nights, no shark-infested seas; only the amiable rustic landscape of the Concord fields and wood-lots. "I could never give much reality to evil and pain," he wrote in his late fifties, and though he had also said quite different things from this, it is true that at the *center* of his mind the space was wholly free from either pain or evil. His thought may be in some sense on the hither side of the tragic; it may be in another sense beyond the tragic; *non*-tragic it undeniably is. He himself was quite clear about this. "And yet," he writes in a characteristic poem,

> And yet it seemeth not to me
> That the high gods love tragedy.

Nor did he love it himself. I am speaking now not of the literary form but of tragedy as an aspect of experience—a subject to which only once in his mature career did Emerson give sustained attention. This was in a short essay he contributed to the *Dial,* an essay called "The Tragic" that was based in part on a lecture he had given a little earlier. It is true that Emerson published this essay in a magazine, but characteristically he never reprinted it, and it was left for his literary executors to include it in a posthumous volume. The theme of this piece is that, after everything has been said that may be said on the topic of human misery, in the end one returns to the knowledge that suffering is a kind of illusion, that it has no absolute or ultimate reality. All sorrow, says Emerson, "is superficial; for the most part fantastic, or in the appearance and not in things . . . For all melancholy, as all passion, belongs to the exterior life. . . . Most suffering is only apparent." And he goes on to speak of the self-operating compensations for suffering in a passage about the horrors of the slave-trade that tempts one, for a moment, to throw his book into the fire, as Whittier is said to have thrown *Leaves of Grass.*

To fix one's attention on passages such as this is to wonder how it is humanly possible for a man to have so weak a memory of his own sorrows or so little compassion for those of other men. Along with this there is that other strain in Emerson that has driven so many readers away from him—the strain in which he seems to be saying that progress, amelioration, an upward movement of things is a law of nature, like gravitation or natural selection, and that the painful human will is very little engaged in it. "Gentlemen," he said to one audience, "there is a sublime and friendly Destiny by which the human race is guided . . . to results affecting masses and ages. Men are narrow and selfish, but the Genius or Destiny is not narrow, but beneficent. . . . Only what is inevitable interests us, and it turns out that love and good are inevitable, and in the course of things." This is the very lotus-dream of progress, you will say, and so is that Emersonian conviction that good ends are always served whether by good men or bad; that rogues and savages are as effectual in the process as prophets and saints. "The barbarians who broke up the Roman Empire," he says, "did not arrive a day too soon." This apparently effortless emergence of good from evil, we are told, is a law not only of nature but of history. "Through the years and the centuries," says Emerson, "through evil agents, through toys and atoms, a great and beneficent tendency irresistibly streams."

"Irresistibly," did you say? Did you say that "love and good are *inevitable*"? Are we to understand that the Destiny that guides human history is simply "friendly" and "beneficient"? To the ears of contemporary men there is a mockery of unreality in such language that makes the language of the Arabian Nights seem to ring with the strong accents of realism. In the fearful light of what has happened in history since Emerson said these things—not to speak of what happened before—can one be merely indignant if some thoughtful men have long since settled it that Emerson is not for them? Can one even be wholly surprised if he has sometimes been relegated to the shabby company of faddists and faith healers, or the equally questionable company of those who have preached the gospel of success, the strenuous life, or the power of positive thinking? The truth is, these charlatans have often drawn, either directly or indirectly, on Emerson himself, and, alas, one can only too easily see why. Let us face it. If Emerson has been coarsened and vulgarized by these people, it is because there are aspects of his thought that have lent themselves to this process. And it is as certain as any human forecast can be that no writer of comparable scope and authority will ever again tell us *in just those tones* that moral evil is negligible and that suffering is a mere illusion.

Yet no one in his senses supposes for a moment that Emerson really belongs in the company of Bruce Barton or Dale Carnegie any more than Plato belongs in the company of Norman Vincent Peale. A powerful instinct tells us that, as he himself remarked of Channing, Emerson is still in some sense our bishop, and that we have not done with him yet. There is no danger of our ever having too many guides or fortifiers, and we know perfectly well that, though we are determined to hold on to Hawthorne and Melville, we cannot afford to dispense with Emerson either. We can afford to dispense with him so little that I suppose most of us are willing now to look at the whole of his work dispassionately and raise for ourselves the question whether his essays are really, after all, a mere encumbrance—or drug. If there proves to be more than this to say, we can hardly be losers. And the more critically one looks at his work, the more it becomes clear that there is a good deal more to be said. No great writer is ever rectilinear—is ever unequivocal or free from contradictions—and Emerson, who consciously disbelieved in straight lines and single poles, is at least as resistant to simple formulas as most. Not only so, but, after all, the problem of evil—the tragic question—is hardly a simple one itself, and the truth is that men have given more than one answer to it. It is a matter of elementary critical justice, surely, to try to arrive at a view of Emerson not only in the flat but in depth.

To tell the truth, there is a greater willingness nowadays to work toward such a view than there was thirty or forty years ago. It has become more usual than it once was to recognize that that celebrated optimism of Emerson's was somewhat less the product of good fortune or of a natively happy temper than it was an achievement both of intellectual and emotional discipline. It was a conviction he had arrived at after youthful years during which he had as good reasons as most men—poverty, ill health, bereavement, anxiety—for questioning the absolute rightness of things. No one who has read his early letters and journals can fail to be conscious of the minor strain that runs through them—the strain of sadness, apprehension, and doubtfulness of the goods of existence. The young Emerson can sound strangely like the mature Melville. He was only twenty, and a year or two out of college, when he wrote in his journal: "There *is* a huge and disproportionate abundance of *evil* on earth. Indeed the good that is here is but a little island of light amidst the unbounded ocean." Three or four years after this, forced by his alarming physical weakness, he gave up preaching temporarily and went South in search of recovery. It was a period of dire low spirits and anxiety for him, and one can understand his writing from St. Augustine to his aunt, Mary Moody Emerson: "He has seen but half the Universe who never has been shown the house of Pain. Pleasure and Peace are but indifferent teachers of what it is life to know." One might suppose that this outcry was only the bitter expression of a passing state of physical and emotional misery; but it was more than that. A dozen years had elapsed after his stay in the South when he contributed to the *Dial* the essay on "The Tragic" I have already alluded to. That essay, oddly enough, begins with one of the sentences from the old letter to his aunt; let me quote it again: "He has seen but half the Universe who never has been shown the house of Pain." And he goes on at once, in the essay, to say: "As the salt sea covers more than two thirds of the surface of the globe, so sorrow encroaches in man on felicity."

Whatever his theory of suffering may have come to be, Emerson cannot be accused, at least in his earlier years, of having denied to it a kind of reality. On the contrary, there are passages in the sermons he preached as a young minister that remind one much more of the sombre Calvinist homilies of his forebears than of the characteristically hopeful and cheerful Unitarians in whose ranks he was for a time enlisted. A few weeks after he returned from St. Augustine, in 1827, he preached a sermon on the theme of change and mortality that strikes an even Biblical note of sorrow and affliction. "Have we brought in our hands," he asks, like a kind of Unitarian Job—"Have we brought in our hands any safe conduct to show to our ghastly enemies, Pain and Death? Shall we not, my brethren, be sufferers as all our fathers were? Shall we not be sick? Shall we not die?" And a little later in the same sermon he alludes, in a phrase that suggests Hawthorne rather than the familiar Emerson, to "the dark parable of human existence."

It is quite true that these Old Testament accents become less and less characteristic of him as he approaches the maturity of his powers, and that the Emerson of the great middle period—of the famous addresses at Harvard, Dartmouth, and Waterville, and of all the best-known essays —is the Emerson whom we have to think of as the Orpheus of Optimism. But, even in this period, and certainly later, there is another tone, an undertone, in his writings which we should listen to if we wish to sensitize ourselves to the complex harmony of his total thought. That thought, to change the image, is a polarized thought, and if at one pole we find a celebration of the powers of the human will, at the other pole we find an insistence on its limitations—on the forces in nature that are not friendly but hostile and even destructive to human wishes, and on the discrepancy between what a man aspires to do and what nature and circumstance allow him to do. "The word Fate, or Destiny," he says in the essay on Montaigne, "expresses the sense of mankind, in all ages, that the laws of the world do not always befriend, but often hurt and crush us. Fate, in the shape of . . . nature, grows over us like grass. . . . What front can we make against these unavoidable, victorious, maleficent forces?"

Are there, then, along with, or running counter to, the "great and beneficent tendency," forces of immense potency in nature which are not amiable but fierce and ruinous? Yes, so Emerson tells us—not only in this essay of the forties but in a lecture he delivered several times in the fifties and at last published as the essay on "Fate" in *The Conduct of Life*. It is an essay that should be read by everyone who imagines that for Emerson there were not really any Cape Horns in experience. "No picture of life," he says, "can have any veracity that does not admit the odious facts." And he lays himself out to suggest what those facts are—the facts of nature's ferocity—with a grim thoroughness that suggests the authors of *Candide* or *Rasselas* or *Moby Dick* much more vividly than the author of "The Over-Soul." Here is all the familiar imagery of naturalistic pessimism—the imagery of earthquakes and volcanic eruptions, of plagues and famine, of tooth and claw. "The habit of the snake and spider, the snap of the tiger and other leapers and bloody jumpers, the crackle of the bones of his prey in the coil of the anaconda"—these are all in nature, he insists, and so are "the forms of the shark . . . the jaw of the sea-wolf paved with crushing teeth, the weapons of the grampus, and other warriors hidden in the sea." Could Voltaire or Melville or Zola say more?

Yet the savagery of nature—nature's Darwinism, to call it so—furnishes less of the stuff of the essay on "Fate" than what I spoke of a moment ago, the restrictiveness of nature; the tight limits set about the human will, human aspiration, human effort, by all the forces of heredity and circumstance that Emerson dramatizes by the old word Fate. "The Circumstance is Nature," says he. "Nature is what you may do. There is much you may not. . . . The book of Nature is the book of Fate." Within these merely natural and material boundaries men are the creatures of their conditioning. "How shall a man," asks Emerson, "escape from his ancestors, or draw off from his veins the black drop which he drew from his father's or his mother's life?" A demonstration of these painful truths that fascinated Emerson for a time, a few years earlier, had been the new science of statistics—the science that seemed to settle it that human behavior can be reduced to mathematical terms and predicted as confidently as the precession of the equinoxes. Perhaps it can, says Emerson, with a quiet smile, in the essay on Swedenborg: "If one man in twenty thousand, or in thirty thousand," he says, "eats shoes or marries his grandmother, then in every twenty thousand or thirty thousand is found one man who eats shoes or marries his grandmother." At any rate, viewed from the outside, as objects, as mere creatures of nature and society, men live and work within lines that are for the most part drawn not by them but for them. We must learn what not to expect.

In short it is not true that Emerson's optimism is quite so unmodulated as it has often been represented as being, or that he was so incapable as Yeats thought him to be of the Vision of Evil. I have been speaking of Evil just now in the sense of suffering and frustration, but even if it is a question of moral evil, of human malignancy, depravity, and vice, it is not true that Emerson averted his gaze from it quite so steadily as his detractors have said. Neither suffering nor wickedness is his primary theme; they are not even secondary; in his work as a whole they are tiny patches of grayness or blackness in a composition that is flooded with light and high color. But, even if we ignore the sermons of his youth, in which the New England sense of guilt and sinfulness sometimes throbs and shoots as painfully as it ever does in Hawthorne—even if we ignore these early writings, it is not true that Emerson's view of human nature was a merely smiling and sanguine one. To be sure, it was the feebleness of men, their incompetence, their imbecility, that he castigated, when he was in this vein, more often than their depravity. But, when he chose, he could express himself as unsentimentally as any moral realist on the brutishness of which men are capable. It was no mere idealist who said, with some humor indeed, in speaking of the Norman Conquest: "Twenty thousand thieves landed at Hastings."

This bluntness is very characteristic of him, and when he was really deeply stirred by the spectacle of systematic cruelty and injustice, as he was during the long anguish of the anti-slavery struggle, he could wrench off certain specious masks and disguises as unsparingly, as realistically, as any of his Calvinist ancestors could have done. Read the "Address" he delivered at Concord on the anniversary of the emancipation of slaves in the West Indies if you wish to have a glimpse of Emerson the moral realist. They tell us, he says in his speech, that the slave-holder does not wish to own slaves for the love of owning them, but only because of the material advantages his ownership brings. Experience, however, he goes on to say, does not bear out this comfortable evasion, but shows "the existence, beside the covetousness, of a bitterer element, the love of power, the voluptuousness of holding a human being in his absolute control." Men are capable, says Emerson, of liking to inflict pain, and the slave-holder "has contracted in his indolent and luxurious climate the need of excitement by irritating and tormenting his slave."

It is hard to see how the Vision of Evil, at least for a moment, could be much keener or more terrible than this; and in the whole slavery connection Emerson said a good many things almost equally piercing. But it remains true that his animadversions on human wickedness, like his allusions to human suffering, are closer to the circumference than to the center of Emerson's thought; they give his writings their moral chiaroscuro, but they are not dominant, and I have perhaps dwelt too long on them. His controlling mode of thought, even in his later and more skeptical years, is a certain form of Optimism and *not* a form of the Tragic Sense, and what I should like to say now is that, however we may ourselves feel about this philosophy, it was one that rested not only on a deep personal experience but on a considered theory of Evil, and moreover that this was a theory by no means peculiar to Emerson, or original with him: on the contrary, it had a long and august tradition behind it in Western thought and analogies with the thought not only of Europe but of the East. To put it very briefly, it is the theory that identifies Evil with non-existence, with negation, with the absence of positive Being. In his own writings Emerson expressed this doctrine first in the famous "Address" at the Divinity School at Harvard in 1838, the manifesto of his heterodoxy. "Good is positive," he said to the graduating class that day. "Evil is merely privative, not absolute: it is like cold, which is the privation of heat. All evil is so much death or nonentity. Benevolence is absolute and real."

Such language as this has become terribly unfamiliar to us, and Heaven knows for what good reasons, in our own guilt-ridden and anxious time; some of us may find it hard to believe that reasonable men ever entertained such a view. The truth is, however, that it is not only a philosophical but an essentially religious view, and that its sources, to speak only of the West, are in the Platonic and Neo-Platonic tradition and in Christian theology on the side on which it derives from that tradition. It was from these sources, indeed, that Emerson drew his theoretical Optimism. When Plato identified the Good with absolute reality, and Evil with the imperfectly real or the unreal, he was speaking a language beyond Tragedy; and let us not forget that he proposed to banish tragic poetry from his ideal Republic—to banish it on the ground that the wise and virtuous man will wish to control the emotions of grief and sorrow rather than to stimulate them. As for Plotinus, the greatest of the Neo-Platonists, whom Emerson read with such excitement in the few years before the "Address" at the Divinity School, he too denied that Evil can have a part in real existence, since this—real existence—is by definition good. "If then evil exists," says Plotinus, "there remains for it the sphere of not-being, and it is, as it were, a certain form of not-being." The sentence reads very much like Emerson's own.

At any rate it was this Neo-Platonic denial of any absolute or ultimate reality to Evil that seems to have found its way into Christian orthodoxy in the writings of St. Augustine—"a man," as Emerson says, "of as clear a sight as almost any other." The Manicheans had attributed to Evil a positive and independent existence, and Augustine as a young man had fallen under their spell; but he had broken away from them at the time of his conversion, and steeped as he was in the thought of the Neo-Platonists, he arrived at a theory of Evil that, on one level, seems indistinguishable from theirs. "Evil has no positive nature," he says in *The City of God*; "but the loss of good has received the name 'evil.'" In itself it is purely negative, a diminishment or corruption of the good, for, as he says, "no nature at all is evil, and this is a name for nothing but the want of good." Of course, as one need not say, Augustine does not deny that *sin* has a kind of reality, but he conceives of it as an essentially negative reality—as a rejection or refusal of the Good, not as an ultimate and independent essence in itself.

No sane man, of course, whatever his metaphysics, can refuse to recognize that wrong-doing is in some sense a *fact;* and Emerson was much too clear-sighted a moralist not to find a place in his thought, as Augustine

of such intensity, yet of such calm, that neither of the words, "active" or "passive," quite does justice to it. In recording such moments he expresses most perfectly that joy which, according to Kierkegaard, demands religious courage. One of the most eloquent of these passages occurs in the great address on "The Method of Nature" which he read at Waterville College, now Colby, in 1841:

> We ought to celebrate this hour by expressions of manly joy. Not thanks, not prayer seem quite the highest or truest name for our communication with the infinite,—but glad and conspiring reception,—reception that becomes giving in its turn, as the receiver is only the All-Giver in part and in infancy. I cannot,—nor can any man,—speak precisely of things so sublime, but it seems to me the wit of man, his strength, his grace, his tendency, his art, is the grace and the presence of God. It is beyond explanation. When all is said and done, the rapt saint is found the only logician. Not exhortation, not argument becomes our lips, but paeans of joy and praise.

If I had to say where we are most likely to find the quintessential Emerson, I should point to passages like this. Certainly there are other Emersons, and they are not to be made light of; there is the trumpeter of nonconformity; there is the attorney for the American intellectual; there is the New England humorist. But none of these, it seems to me, speaks in quite so special and incomparable tones as the Emerson whom one would like to call, not after all a moralist, nor a prophet, nor even a teacher, but a hymnist or psalmist—one who, at his most characteristic, utters psalms of thanksgiving, or, as he says, "paeans of joy and praise"; whose most intimate mode of expression is always a *Te Deum*. This is the Emerson who is bound to disappoint us if we look in his work for a steady confrontation of Tragedy or a sustained and unswerving gaze at the face of Evil. They are not there, and we shall lose our labor if we look for them. But there is no writer in the world, however comprehensive, in whose work we are not conscious of missing *something* that belongs to experience; and now that critical justice has been done to what is wanting in Emerson, we can surely afford very well to avail ourselves of all that is positively there. What is there, as we have to recognize when we have cleared our minds of the cant of pessimism, is perhaps the fullest and most authentic expression in modern literature of the more-than-tragic emotion of thankfulness. A member of his family tells us that almost his last word was "praise." Unless we have deafened ourselves to any other tones than those of anguish and despair, we should still know how to be inspirited by everything in his writings that this word symbolizes.

# Emerson's Problem of Vocation

*by Henry Nash Smith*

## I

Among the many fine perceptions of Henry James's essay on Emerson in the *Partial Portraits* is his allusion to the period of "movement, experiment and selection . . . of effort too and painful probation" through which Emerson had to pass before he could discover his true vocation as artist and thinker.[1] James, with his instinct for subjective values, saw clearly enough that Emerson's withdrawal from the ministry was less significant than the years of inner quest and adventure which followed. The plot was given: the hero was destined in the end to attain a luminous poise, "the equanimity of a result," [2] with great power to nourish his disciples. Yet the heart of the drama was not its beginning or its end, but the perplexed motives of the rising action. Sympathizing with a fellow craftsman, James offered a technical statement of the problem: "Emerson had his message, but he was a good while looking for his form." [3] Yet this seems at once too purely aesthetic and too simple a way of explaining what happened; it suggests that the message was fully developed at the outset, and fails to allow for the all-important interaction between half-formed intuition and increasingly adequate expression. If Emerson's message was eventually (to use a telegraphic abbreviation) self-reliance, it gained clarity and force only by virtue of the inner struggle preceding its utterance. The problem was very much more than stylistic; it was so nearly central in his early development that it calls for fuller exploration.

Emerson's effort to work out a satisfactory relation to society had two principal phases centering in two problems posed for him successively by

"Emerson's Problem of Vocation—A Note on 'The American Scholar.'" from *The New England Quarterly,* Vol. XII (March-December, 1939), 52-67. 

[1] *Partial Portraits* (London and New York, 1888), 6.

[2] *Partial Portraits,* 5.

[3] *Partial Portraits,* 6.

the declining Puritan tradition in which he had been reared and by the new industrial society which was rapidly taking shape about him during his young manhood. As an undergraduate he had accepted the conventional assumption that young men of unusual gifts should be dedicated to the ministry. This choice, made for him (as he later, perhaps unjustly, implied) "against his inclination," or, to speak more accurately, made by him "before he was acquainted with the character of his own mind," [4] was the first serious obstacle he encountered in his effort to find his true vocation. But after he had abandoned the ministry he still had to come to terms with that astonishing Massachusetts of the 1830's whose Calvinistic soil had nourished Romantic and humanitarian seed to yield such an unprecedented harvest of reformers and improvers and plain cranks. Militant humanitarianism, closely related to the rapid urbanization and industrialization of eastern Massachusetts, replaced the clerical tradition as the most alarming threat of the outer world to impose restraint upon Emerson's career of self-realization. His earlier struggle had been against the established order; now, ironically, his most formidable adversaries were men even more hostile to the established order than he.[5] They, or the ethical ideal they represented, gave him little peace until he could make it plain to everyone, including himself, that even in dissent he could belong to no man's party but his own. A further complication was the difficulty of justifying an artist's apparent idleness in a strenuous society unaccustomed to behold Man Thinking outside the pulpit or the college classroom.[6]

As was always his practice, Emerson set down his meditations concerning both phases of his inner struggle. His effort to throw off the clerical convention, for instance, underlies an early sermon, recently published, which his editor calls "Find Your Calling." [7] The later struggle with the humanitarian ideal finds expression in the *Journals* and in several of the

[4] Arthur Cushman McGiffert, Jr., editor, *Young Emerson Speaks: Unpublished Discourses on Many Subjects by Ralph Waldo Emerson* (Boston, 1938), 251. The passage containing these words has been scratched out in the manuscript of a sermon delivered February 5, 1832—some four months before Emerson decided to resign his pastorate.

[5] An illustration is the meeting with George and Sophia Ripley, Margaret Fuller, and Bronson Alcott in October of 1840 to discuss the "Social Plans" for Brook Farm, described in *Journals,* edited by E. W. Emerson and W. E. Forbes (Boston, 1909-1914), v, 473-474. This entry contains the famous passage about the hen-coop and the siege of Babylon. On September 26, Emerson had written a passage later incorporated in "Man the Reformer" (*ibid.,* v, 466), and two days after the meeting occurs another entry used in the same essay (*ibid.,* v, 480). The meeting also yielded reflections for "Self-Reliance" (*ibid.,* v, 477). John T. Flanagan has documented Emerson's coolness toward various schemes of reform in "Emerson and Communism." *The New England Quarterly,* x (1937), 243-261.

[6] Cooper, in *Notions of the Americans . . .* (1828), had pointed out that the people of the United States had been too fully absorbed in securing the necessaries of everyday life to support a class of "learned idlers" (II, 124-125).

[7] McGiffert, 250.

public discourses and essays. But the clearest single statement of all the issues as Emerson saw them is contained in the "Lecture on the Times," delivered in December of 1841.[8] Here, in dramatic form, appear the two phases of the problem of vocation as he had faced it during the previous decade. The first phase, related to the crisis of ten years before, when he had decided to withdraw from the ministry, appears in the address as a tension between the Party of the Past and that of the Future. It is the eternal conflict between "the dissenter, the theorist, the aspirant" and the established order of things: the ground-pattern of Transcendentalism, springing as the movement did from the whole Puritan past of New England, yet violently protesting against the society in which it grew. But the conflict between the Past and the Future, the World and the Newness, yields place almost at once to a debate between two groups within the party of the Future: the Actors, easily recognizable as the humanitarians of Emerson's day, who favor direct, tangible reforms in the structure of society; and the Students, who are likewise hostile to the Past, but who are withheld from action by a Romantic perplexity and ennui, a perception that their faculties are superior to any concrete task lying before them. In spite of Emerson's ironic realization that neither attitude represents the whole truth, he is obviously on the side of the Future against the Past, and of the Student against the Actor.

It does not take much reading between the lines to find in this address a condensed chapter of Emerson's autobiography, an imaginative statement of dominant issues in his ethical development. Expanded by reference to his other early writings, the symbolic shorthand can be interpreted as a gloss on Emerson's complex attitude toward humanitarianism, and even —if one reads quite closely—on that ultimate idiosyncrasy which the doctrine of self-reliance so cryptically expresses.

## II

The decision to withdraw from the ministry in 1832 has been recognized as a significant event in the history of Transcendentalism. "The mind of the young preacher," says Emerson's most recent editor, "was the stage on which struggled for supremacy two theories of the universe. . . . His decision to abandon the profession of the ministry was his vote in favor of the new age."[9] Certainly a profound change in outlook was necessary before the descendant of generations of ministers could deliberately reject a vocation representing the noblest aspirations of the past in order to embark upon a quest for a new and higher calling that could not even be said to exist. But it would be unwise to conclude that Emerson's action was made inevitable by the logic of Transcendentalism.

[8] *Nature, Addresses, and Lectures* (revised edition, Boston, 1883), 245-276.
[9] McGiffert, 240.

The doctrinal issue concerning the Lord's Supper was not fundamental, for he later declined a call from the congregation at New Bedford which, influenced by Hicksite Quakers, had accepted a view of the rite similar to his.[10] And Theodore Parker was to demonstrate even ten years later that an apostle of the Newness in its fully developed form might throw off the mild yoke of Unitarianism, yet continue pastoral functions at full blast. In fact, two contrasting theories of vocation could be derived from the Unitarian assertion of man's divinity. The most obvious development of the new faith led to an energetic humanitarianism and thus into the many vital or quaint proposals for reform characteristic of the thirties and forties. This was the vocation of the Transcendentalist as Actor, admirably illustrated by Parker. But on the other hand the exploration of the infinity within might lead far away from society to the highly individualistic and passive cult of self-reliance. This was the vocation of the Transcendentalist as Student, represented by Emerson and, with an even more uncompromising rigor, by Thoreau.

The intellectual forces impelling Emerson toward contemplation instead of action were quite various. Very early he expressed a Deistic confidence that "the everlasting progress of the universe" needs no tinkering from human hands, and certainly does not "hang upon the bye-laws of a Missionary Society or a Sunday School." [11] Later he developed the Neoplatonic argument that "facts and persons are grown unreal and phantastic by reason of the vice in them," so that the philosopher sacrifices his dignity in confronting evil on the phenomenal level.[12] Even more important was the belief, confirmed by the major voices of the Christian tradition, that no changes of outward circumstances can bring about "mental and moral improvement." [13] One must also take into account Emerson's temperamental dislike of association in any form. As R. M. Gay has pointed out, what Emerson objected to in Brook Farm was not communism but organization.[14] "At the name of a society," he wrote in 1840—significantly, to Margaret Fuller—"all my repulsions play, all my quills rise and sharpen." [15] Yet action, in the specific environment of time and place, almost inevitably meant for Emerson "movements," participation in the work of what would now be called "pressure groups," while contemplation seemed possible only through a complete withdrawal from the busy life of the community. Reform, like religion, was inherently institutional. Emerson was committed to the aims of both,

[10] McGiffert, 255.

[11] *Journals,* II (1828), 240-241.

[12] *Ibid.,* V (1840), 405. See also *ibid.,* III (1834), 355; *Nature, Addresses, and Lectures* (1841), 219.

[13] *Nature, Addresses, and Lectures* (1841), 267.

[14] *Emerson: A Study of the Poet as Seer* (New York, 1928), 142.

[15] Quoted by Gay from James Eliot Cabot, *A Memoir of Ralph Waldo Emerson* (Boston, 1887), II, 434.

but the same lack of the talent for coöperation and social living which unfitted him for the pastorate[16] made him chary of joining the new secular church of the philanthropists. One wonders, too, whether the precarious state of his health was not an important influence leading him to avoid the strenuous career of a reformer.

But the most interesting influence upon Emerson's cult of solitude and contemplation, and thus upon the doctrine of self-reliance, was English Romanticism. The Romantic cult of nature tended to ignore society altogether by placing the intuitive genius alone in the cosmos as Nature's Priest; and the Wordsworthian anti-urban primitivism, touching Emerson just when Boston was growing in population from 43,000 in 1820 to 100,000 in 1842, neatly coincided with the other forces that were leading him to the bucolic setting of Concord.

All these conflicting impulses, and many others, were involved in Emerson's problem of Action versus Contemplation. The issue was thoroughly real for him. "Elusive, irreducible, merely gustatory," [17] and in a paradoxical sense even irresponsible, he was very reluctant to take up his trumpet and his pitcher with the other warriors of New England. Yet he could not easily escape from the sense of social responsibility that was important in his Puritan heritage, and he was hampered in his desire to reject both the clerical and the humanitarian conventions by the lack of a clearly defined ethical ideal to which he could turn. He had indeed abandoned a material profession, despairing no doubt of finding his true and unique vocation in a society which was not "fertile in variations";[18] but if the society was simple it was highly responsible, and Emerson could hardly avoid meeting the moral issue involved in the problem of vocation. If he found no profession already formed for him, he must create one for himself, even if only as an ideal; and the ideal must not only be defensible before the world, but also represent adequately all the forces of tradition, temperament, and literary contagion that were at work in him. Given such varied and conflicting stimuli, the task was to devise a response that would sacrifice as few as possible of the valid impulses. The test of any proposed response as an acceptable ideal of vocation was the extent to which, in Emerson's words, it could bring every power of his mind into freedom and action.[19]

This was the situation which gave rise, in the decade following Emerson's withdrawal from the ministry, to the various hero types which appear in the *Journals* and the published addresses. The best-known of these is of course the Scholar. But during the thirties Emerson created, tested, and abandoned a whole company of these somewhat ghostly

[16] McGiffert, xii.
[17] *Partial Portraits,* 25.
[18] *Partial Portraits,* 7.
[19] McGiffert, 166.

characters, such as the Man of Genius, the Seer, the Contemplative Man, the Student, the Transcendentalist.[20] The terms are to some extent interchangeable; they fix points on the circumference of a circle at whose center is an undefined conception, the final cause of the others. All the characters are in some sense Emerson, and all of them are what Emerson strove toward as an ethical ideal; they resemble the hypotheses of a scientist which are continually being subjected to experimental verification and revision in the laboratory. Some of the fictions, in addition, seem intended as generic representations of recurrent types in the fermenting New England that Emerson knew; and occasionally the terms seem to become ironic designations for eccentricities which he wishes to avoid.[21] In fact, since the possible degrees of dramatic disengagement (or "plasticity" in the Aristotelean sense) are almost infinite, each occurrence of these terms presents a fresh problem. One seems to be studying a collection of embryos that might have developed eventually into characters of fiction, save for the fact that Emerson did not have a truly dramatic imagination. The phenomenon resembles that quality in Wordsworth which Coleridge called "ventriloquism." [22] The Scholar is the hero of Emerson's unwritten *Prelude,* and belongs with all the Werthers and the Childe Harolds and the Teufelsdröckhs of the period. It will be readily understood that essays and addresses in which characters of this sort appear should be regarded as rudimentary narratives rather than as structures of discursive reasoning. Their form is that of the plot, not the syllogism, their force not demonstrative but dramatic.

[20] Some of the more important terms in this class are: the contemplative man (*Journals,* III (1834), 349); the man of genius (*ibid.,* IV (1836), 131; V (1840), 443); the scholar (*ibid.,* IV (1836), 6); the torch-bearer (*ibid.,* V (1838), 82); the seer (*Nature, Addresses, and Lectures* (1841), 230); the saint (*ibid.,* 223); the dissenter (*ibid.,* 255); the aspirant (*idem*); the radical (*ibid.,* 301); the spiritualist (*ibid.,* 271); the idealist (*Journals,* VI (1841), 65); the Transcendentalist (*Nature, Addresses, and Lectures* (1842), 317); and the hero (*ibid.,* 337). Henry James says, somewhat hastily, that Emerson means by the Scholar "simply the cultivated man, the man who has had a liberal education" (*Partial Portraits,* 20). But the real complexity of the term's denotation is well indicated by James's very discerning statement that Thoreau "took upon himself to be, in the concrete, the sort of person that Emerson's 'scholar' was in the abstract" (p. 24). This endeavor involved, among other things, non-payment of taxes, refusal to wear a necktie, and the preparation of one's own food: items in a program which, while one may agree with James that it is "not of the essence," requires more explanation than the mere endeavor to act like a man with a liberal education. The term Scholar, with its charming connotation of rustic awe before a man with a tincture of books which James so deftly fixes upon, is in Emerson's use sometimes made to serve other and quite surprising purposes.

[21] James points out that when Emerson was bored by the literalness and eccentricity of people like Thoreau and Alcott, he could declare himself "guiltless" of the transcendental doctrine (*Partial Portraits,* 25).

[22] *Biographia Literaria,* J. Shawcross, editor (Oxford, 1907), II, 109.

## III

The corpus of Emerson's work that shows his concern with the problem of vocation is extensive. In addition to one or two early sermons and many entries in the *Journals* during the thirties, it includes "The American Scholar" and the four important lectures on "The Times" delivered in the winter of 1841-1842, as well as two later addresses on "The Man of Letters" and "The Scholar." As a rule, one can detect in Emerson's writing on the subject an original tension or conflict of impulses arising from his inability to satisfy simultaneously the conventions of his youth, the demands of the humanitarians, his own temperamental inclination, and the ethical ideals of English Romanticism. Emerson the artist repeatedly responds to these mingled stimuli by projecting various imaginative forms of the contemplative ideal. As a result, the symbols have a curiously mixed character. The Scholar is the Genius, but is also a lineal descendant of the New England clergyman.[23] For a decade Emerson was unable either to merge the two ideals successfully, or to abandon one in favor of the other.

On occasion he tried to resolve the tension by the desperate procedure of equating the opposites—in "Man the Reformer" (1841), for instance, redefining reform as love with the declaration that "one day all men will be lovers; and every calamity will be dissolved in the universal sunshine." [24] But such an evasive solution could not satisfy him for long, and as a rule he recognized that a choice was necessary, that the alternatives before him were not identical, that something must be given up. It is this inner debate which explains the peculiar vehemence with which Emerson insisted upon poise and proclaimed the doctrine of self-reliance. Only by envisaging the Actor can one understand the strongly apologetic basis of Emerson's conception of the Scholar.

One of the earliest phases of Emerson's concern with vocation may be observed in the notion of "character" which appears in the *Journals* in 1828. Character stands at first for a confident acquiescence in God's perfect governance of the universe.[25] From another point of view character is interpreted as global integrity, self-sufficiency, self-reliance resulting from the soul's "absolute command of its desires," with a corresponding loss of solicitude concerning what other men do.[26] The idea lends itself, again, to a Neoplatonic declaration of the unreality of all action, concerned as it necessarily is with the realm of mere phenomena and of

[23] Emerson makes the clerical lineage of the Scholar quite explicit in *Journals,* v (1839), 337; and *Nature, Addresses, and Lectures,* 95.

[24] *Nature, Addresses, and Lectures,* 242.

[25] *Journals,* II (1828), 240-241.

[26] *Journals,* II (1832), 527-528.

evil.[27] Yet character can also become—very significantly—the equivalent of lawless, irrational genius, a synonym of the German's *Daimonisches*;[28] and so desperate is Emerson's concern to defend his ideal of passivity against "carpenters, masons, and merchants" who "pounce on him" for his supposed idleness[29] that he can resort to an almost physiological determinism, maintaining that God "has given to each his calling in his ruling love, . . . has adapted the brain and the body of men to the work that is to be done in the world." If some men "have a contemplative turn, and voluntarily seek solitude and converse with themselves," in God's name, he exclaims with surprising heat, let them alone! [30]

The famous address on "The American Scholar" is in large part but a summary of these and other ideas that had been recurring in the *Journals* for a decade.[31] Character is recognized here as the special attribute of the Contemplative Man; and it is noteworthy that the address contains a long and confused discussion of the issue of Action versus Contemplation.[32] Emerson is still troubled by the popular conception of the Scholar as a recluse, realizing that such an interpretation makes contemplative inaction a species of valetudinarianism, and he seeks to redeem the Scholar from the implied charge of weakness and cowardice. Yet the passage on the value of manual labor in enriching a writer's vocabulary merely confuses the issue by using "action" in a new sense; and the praise of action because it is "pearls and rubies to [the Scholar's] dis-

[27] *Journals,* v (1840), 405. This idea is associated with both the Scholar and the problem of reform in "Man the Reformer" (*Nature, Addresses, and Lectures,* 219).

[28] *Journals,* IV (1837), 224.

[29] *Journals,* IV (1836), 6-7.

[30] *Journals,* III (1834), 407.

[31] Some of the more important ideas of "The American Scholar" concerning vocation which appear earlier in the *Journals* are the following: (1) The Scholar's task is to classify the facts, to discover the spiritual laws which determine them (*Nature, Addresses, and Lectures,* 87; see *Journals,* IV, 7-8); (2) The Scholar is closely related to the man of genius (*Nature, Addresses, and Lectures,* 91-92; see *Journals,* IV, 198, where Shelley's skylark-poet is mentioned, although the identity of the Scholar and the man of genius is not made explicit); (3) The Scholar is scorned by practical men because he is not active (*Nature, Addresses, and Lectures,* 95; see *Journals,* IV, 6-7); (4) The Scholar operates through the unconscious radiation of virtue upon his associates, and this power is associated with "character" (*Nature, Addresses, and Lectures,* 99-100; see *Journals,* III, 403; IV, 105-106; and IV, 183); (5) The Scholar is in a state of "virtual hostility" to society (*Nature, Addresses, and Lectures,* 102; see *Journals,* IV, 6-7); (6) The Scholar must resist vulgar prosperity and avarice (*Nature, Addresses, and Lectures,* 102 and 113; see *Journals,* IV, 89-90, where it is stated that the two most important handicaps upon American intellectual performances are "our devotion to property" and the "influence of Europe"); (7) The Scholar realizes the world is mere appearance and beholds absolute truth through contemplation (*Nature, Addresses, and Lectures,* 91 and 102; see *Journals,* III, 355); (8) The Scholar will leave government to clerks (*Nature, Addresses, and Lectures,* 107; see *Journals,* II, 527-528).

[32] *Nature, Addresses, and Lectures,* 95-100.

course" seems almost *fin de siècle* in its subordination of life to art. Only by an extreme irony or a thoroughly artistic failure to distinguish the actual from the imagined can Emerson go on to exclaim, "I run eagerly into this resounding tumult [of the world]. I grasp the hands of those next to me, and take my place in the ring to suffer and to work. . . ." And the proposed end is still merely literary: the Scholar enters the world not in order to reform it, but in order that the dumb abyss of his inarticulate thought may become "vocal with speech." A deeper level of Emerson's meaning appears in the warning that the Scholar, in committing himself to action (here in its usual sense of humanitarian reform), runs the danger of forfeiting his self-reliance to the tyranny of "the popular judgments and modes of action." And at the end of the address the Contemplative Man's scrutiny is directed to "the perspective of [his] own infinite life"—that is, integrity, character—to be explored and developed by introspection. It hardly settles the issue to add to the Scholar's "study and . . . communication of principles" the further task of "making those instincts prevalent, the conversion of the world." [33] For the original problem was the choice of a means—active reform or passive mediation—for converting the world. Emerson's refusal to choose between these alternatives is highly significant. On the one hand it reveals again the essentially contemplative nature of his Scholar-ideal; on the other it shows his curious reluctance to surrender the Scholar's claim to the contradictory virtues of the active reformer.

It has become customary to interpret "The American Scholar" as a statement of literary nationalism. But in the light of Emerson's prolonged struggle with the problem of vocation, the nationalistic phase of the address seems of diminished importance. Emerson was struggling to affirm a creed of self-reliance, and the fiction of the Scholar was a phase of the struggle. To the extent that the intellectual domination of Europe interferes with the Scholar's integrity, he must of course throw it off. But Europe is by no means the Scholar's worst enemy. His hardest struggles are civil and American: with vulgar prosperity; with the tyranny of the past; with "the popular cry," even though this be momentarily for some good thing—in short, with all the forces against which Emerson was striving to protect the inarticulate secrets of his own mind, the intuitive belief in his personal mission.

Impressive as the fiction of the Scholar was for Emerson's contemporaries, it did not bring about at this time a permanent equilibrium of conflicting impulses within the author himself. The address contains no coherent statement of the Scholar's positive functions. In many respects Emerson's situation in 1837 was the same as it had been five years before, when he withdrew from the pulpit: he had made concrete discoveries concerning what he must deny, but had not found a tangible

[33] *Nature, Addresses, and Lectures,* 114.

alternative to the program of the reformers. He was still disturbed by his inability to renounce the ethical ideal of overt action.

It is not surprising, therefore, that the theme of apology for not fulfilling a supposed obligation to assist in "the philanthropic enterprises of Universal Temperance, Peace, Abolition of Slavery" soon reappears in the *Journals*.[34] The conflict which persisted is clearly illustrated by an incident in the spring of 1838—the famous letter, "hated of me"—which he consented to write to President Van Buren about "this tragic Cherokee business."[35] There had been a public meeting, and Emerson agreed that the persecution of the Indians by land-hungry Georgians was "like dead cats around one's neck," even for a peaceable resident of Massachusetts. He yielded to popular pressure and wrote his letter of protest, but afterwards experienced a revulsion from such "stirring in the philanthropic mud." The violence of Emerson's language concerning this relatively trivial act reveals how tense was his inner debate with regard to humanitarianism. The solicitation of his friends, the reformers, in alliance with his own impulse to make active war upon the evils of society, had momentarily overcome his intuition concerning his true vocation. He had failed in perfect self-reliance, for although he sympathized with the sentiments he had set down, the letter itself was not his own, not prompted from within. His resentment over outside interference leads him into an almost savage renunciation of philanthropic meetings and "holy hurrahs."[36] The whole response, in its morbid disproportion to the importance of the occurrence, shows how deep in Emerson originated both the impulse to accept and the stronger impulse to reject the humanitarian program.

During the following years the conception of the Scholar takes on an increasingly Romantic cast. In 1840, asserting that he has been working at his essays as "a sort of apology to my country for my apparent idleness," Emerson threatens to abandon even this form of the deed.[37] A later congener of the Scholar, the Youth, appearing in the lecture on "The Conservative" also as the Reformer and the Hero,[38] represents an almost fantastic extreme of Emerson's effort to explain how the Scholar-Sage can fulfill his supposed obligation to eradicate evil from the uni-

[34] *Journals*, IV (1837), 301.

[35] *Journals*, IV (1838), 426.

[36] *Journals*, IV (1838), 430-431.

[37] *Journals*, V (1840), 469. The order of ideas in this entry is revealing. Emerson begins with an allusion to critics who accuse him of sloth and invite him to participate in active reforms. The threat to abandon the act of composition is developed from a Neoplatonic theory of the Scholar's indifference not only to philanthropies but to all "mere circumstances."

[38] *Nature, Addresses, and Lectures*, 298 and 305. In the introductory lecture the idea of reform had appeared as a function of the Students because they are in contact with "the spiritual principle"—another attempt to redefine reform so as to remove its actively humanitarian connotations (*ibid.*, 269-271).

verse. The Hero's desire to descend as "a Redeemer into Nature" is, in its theological implications, even more startling than the Divinity School Address, for here the Transcendental merging of a divine *logos* with an apotheosized humanity is not so much affirmed as casually taken for granted: the idea seems to come straight from the subconscious. It is not easy to tell how seriously Emerson means this suggestion, which lends itself to almost every nuance of interpretation known to Christian theology. But some sort of magical version can hardly be avoided when one places beside the remark Emerson's later statement that "the path which the hero travels alone is the highway of health and benefit to mankind." [39] Here the extension to all mankind of the divinity reserved for Jesus in the Calvinistic scheme seems to have had its natural consequence in the rehabilitation of the whole myth of the man-god in a pre-Christian form, and we are led unexpectedly into the sphere of *The Golden Bough.* The Scholar makes the most impressive of all his appearances as the Priest-King, the uniquely endowed representative of the tribe, doomed endlessly to die and to live again that he may redeem humanity and nourish his people upon the life-force in nature. If such an interpretation reads too much anthropology into Emerson, it may at least serve as a reminder of the magical presuppositions underlying Romantic theories of communion between man and nature.

Whatever the final form of the Scholar-ideal may have been, the fiction apparently served its purpose, and Emerson's problem of vocation was solved in terms of self-reliance and contemplation. At the end of the lecture on "The Transcendentalist," the dialogues between opposed characters give way to a description of two opposed "states of thought." Although Emerson must still lead two lives, "of the understanding and of the soul," at any rate the conflict between opposed ideals is gone.[40] In its stead appears a simpler tension between the actual Emerson and an ideal which, to be sure, he sometimes betrays, but which is itself accepted without question. The passive life of the soul has been legislated into a norm; the fiction of the Transcendentalist is a relatively adequate and stable synthesis of the conflicting impulses; and the issue of Action versus Contemplation has disappeared along with the opposed fiction of the Actor.

After 1842 the ideal of the Scholar seems not to have undergone any significant evolution; the two later addresses on similar topics[41] are

[39] *Nature, Addresses, and Lectures,* 337. The earlier proposal that the Scholar should "replenish nature" from "that most real world of Ideas within him" (*Journals,* v (1840), 405) is probably another version of the same idea, leading through Plotinus to a hint of the regeneration of sinful physical nature by the incarnation of the *logos* (as in the Hymn in "On the Morning of Christ's Nativity").

[40] *Nature, Addresses, and Lectures,* 332-334.

[41] "The Man of Letters" (1863) and "The Scholar" (1876), in *Lectures and Biographical Sketches* (Boston, 1884), 229-246 and 247-274.

little more than repetitions of Emerson's earlier utterances. Possibly his growing realization of his influence as a writer and lecturer, and his countrymen's disposition to accept him as a man of letters exempt from the obligation to follow some obviously useful occupation, provided the support he needed in his inner debate.

The most discerning general comment that could be made regarding Emerson's attitude toward the problem of vocation is his own reminder that the Transcendentalists were the heirs of Puritanism.[42] But they no longer had a church to furnish a profession for them; they were "scholars out of the church." [43] By 1832 Emerson had in effect seceded from the state as well.[44] Having gone out from the shelter of the conventional cadres of society, he had to perform the intellectual and imaginative labor of conceiving a new vocation for himself, and almost a new society in which this vocation might have meaning.[45] He was fully aware that in place of the "ease and pleasure of treading the old road, accepting the fashions, the education, the religion of society," the Scholar had to take up "the cross of making his own, and, of course, the self-accusation, the faint heart, the frequent uncertainty and loss of time, which are the nettles and tangling vines in the way of the self-relying and self-directed. . . ." [46] In the face of this task, it is small wonder that Emerson found his "strength and spirits . . . wasted in rejection." [47] But like so many other artists before him, he discovered that the very tensions which drained his strength provided him with important themes for his art.

[42] *Journals,* VI (1841), 53. See also *Nature, Addresses, and Lectures,* 258.

[43] *Journals,* V (1840), 337.

[44] One recalls Emerson's statement that the Scholar stands in a state of "virtual hostility" to society (*Nature, Addresses, and Lectures,* 102), his terming the Transcendentalists "unsocial" (*ibid.,* 323), and his insistence that they were "not good citizens, not good members of society" (*ibid.,* 328). The entry of similar import for 1827 is in *Journals,* II, 527-528. See also *Journals,* V, 302.

[45] Thoreau put the matter quite pointedly: "The society which I was made for is not here" (*The Writings of Henry David Thoreau: Journal,* Bradford Torrey, editor (Boston, 1906), II (1851), 317).

[46] *Nature, Addresses, and Lectures,* 101-102.

[47] *Nature, Addresses, and Lectures,* 336.

# Emersonian Genius and the American Democracy

*by Perry Miller*

Ralph Waldo Emerson was a poor boy, but in his community his kind of poverty mattered little. Few of his classmates at Harvard had more money than he did, and they made no such splurge as would cause him to feel inferior or outcast. His name was as good as, if not better than, anybody else's. At reunions of the class of 1821, Emerson and his fellows, without embarrassment, quietly took up a collection for their one insolvent member. In the logic of the situation, Emerson should have received the stamp and have embraced the opinions of this group—self-consciously aristocratic, not because of their wealth but because of their names and heritage, at that moment moving easily from the Federalist to the Whig party. In 1821 there could hardly be found a group of young Americans more numb to the notion that there were any stirring implications in the word "democracy."

Actually, Emerson did take their stamp and did imbibe their opinion. We know, or ought to know, that to the end of his days he remained the child of Boston; he might well have lived out his time like Dr. Holmes (whom he admired), secure in his provincial superiority, voting Whig and Republican, associating the idea of the Democratic party with vulgarity, with General Jackson and tobacco-chewing. In great part he did exactly that; for this reason he poses difficult problems for those who would see in him America's classic sage.

For reasons which only a sociological investigation might uncover, youths at Harvard College after the War of 1812 began to exhibit a weariness with life such as they fancied might become a Rochefoucauld, which, assuredly, was nothing like what the college in its Puritan days had expected of sons of the prophets. Perhaps this was their way of declaring their independence of Puritan tradition. At any rate it is exactly here that the pose of indifference commenced to be a Harvard

"Emersonian Genius and the American Democracy." From *The New England Quarterly,* Vol. XXVI, No. 1 (March, 1953), 27-44. 

tradition and to take its toll. But in the first days it was difficult to maintain; only a few resolute spirits really carried it off, and Emerson, of course, lost much of his Prufrock-ism in the enthusiasm of Transcendentalism. Yet not all of it—he never got rid of the fascination he early felt for this first, faint glimmer of an American sophistication; unless we remember it, we shall not understand his essays on "Culture," "Manners," "Aristocracy," or the bitterness of those who, like Parker and Ripley, had to look upon him as their leader even while hating just these aspects of him.

At the age of eighteen, in July, 1822, Emerson was bored with the prospect of another Independence Day. (At this time he also found Wordsworth crude, and what he heard of German philosophy absurd.) We Americans, he wrote his friend Hill, have marched since the Revolution "to strength, to honour, & at last to ennui." There is something immensely comic—and sad—in this spectacle of a young American of intelligence and good family, in 1822, already overcome with lassitude. Suppose the event should prove—the disdainful youth continued—that the American experiment has rashly assumed that men can govern themselves, that it demonstrates instead "that too much knowledge, & too much liberty makes them mad?" He was already determined to flee from the oratory of the Fourth of July to the serenity of cherry trees: "I shall expend my patriotism in banqueting upon Mother Nature."

However, events and ideas in Europe were already indicating that nature was a dangerous refuge for a nice young Bostonian. In America they were soon to demonstrate just how dangerous: the crisis in Emerson's intellectual life, which he endured for the next several years, coincided with those in which the natural politician—General Andrew Jackson—rose by nature's means, certainly not those of culture, to the Democratic Presidency.

With part of his brain—a good part—Emerson reacted to the triumph of Jackson as did any Bostonian or Harvard man. He informed his new friend, Carlyle, on May 14, 1834, that government in America was becoming a "job"—he could think of no more contemptuous word—because "a most unfit person in the Presidency has been doing the worst things; and the worse he grew, the more popular." Nothing would be easier than to collect from the *Journals* enough passages about the Democratic party to form a manual of Boston snobbery. In 1868, for instance, meditating upon the already stale Transcendental thesis that beauty consists largely in expression, he thus annotated it: "I noticed, the other day, that when a man whom I had always remarked as a handsome person was venting Democratic politics, his whole expression changed, and became mean and paltry."

This was the Emerson who, in his last years, escaped as often as he could from Concord to the Saturday Club. I believe that students of Emerson get nowhere unless they realize how often Emerson wished that the cup of Transcendentalism had not been pressed to his lips. Had he been spared that, he might comfortably have regarded the Democratic party as a rabble of Irish and other unwashed immigrants, and could have refused, as for long he did refuse, to find any special virtue in democracy as a slogan.

But he could not thus protect himself; other ideas forced themselves upon him, and he was doomed to respond. He lacked the imperviousness that armored State Street and Beacon Street; intellectually he was too thin-skinned. To the friends about him, and I dare say also to himself, the reason was obvious: he was a genius. This was his burden, his fate, and the measure of his disseverance from the ethos of his clan.

He emerged into literature as the castigator of the genteel, the proper, the self-satisfied; he aligned himself with forces as disruptive of the Whig world as Jacksonianism was of the world of John Quincy Adams. He called for a stinging oath in the mouth of the teamster instead of the mincing rhetoric of Harvard and Yale graduates, who stumbled and halted and began every sentence over again. He called the scholar decent, indolent, complacent. When he cried that the spirit of the American freeman was timid, imitative, tame, he did not aim at Democrats but at the fastidious spirits who made up Boston society. He meant the corpse-cold Unitarianism of Harvard College and Brattle Street. Or at least he said that is what he meant (whether he really did or not may be argued), wherefore he seemed to uphold standards as uncouth as those of that Democrat in the White House.

The first of these, notoriously, was the standard of self-reliance, but behind it and sustaining it was the even more disturbing one of genius. Emerson had to have a flail for beating those who stammered and stuttered, and he found it in the conception of genius; he pounced upon it, and spent the rest of his life vainly struggling with its political consequences.

It is a commonplace of literary history that the cult of genius came to a special flowering in the early nineteenth century. (We cannot possibly employ the word today with a like solemnity; half the time we use it as an insult.) Wherever it prospered—whether with the Schlegels and Tieck in Germany, with Hugo and George Sand in France, with Byron and Coleridge in England—it meant revolt against convention, especially the kind of social convention that made up Harvard and Boston. "If there is any period one would desire to be born in," Emerson asked the Harvard Phi Beta Kappa, "is it not the age of Revolution?" This was precisely the sort of period many of his listeners did not want to be born in, for revolution meant Old Hickory. But to some Emerson opened alluring prospects which, he appeared to say and they wanted to hope, would have nothing to do with politics; leaving the political revolution aside, they responded to his exhortation and became, overnight if necessary, geniuses. The works of Emerson served them as a handbook; with him in one hand they learned to practice with the other the requisite gestures, much as a bride holds the cookbook while stirring the broth. But his own *Journals* show him as never quite so certain as he appeared from the outside, never entirely sure as to just what constituted genius or just how politically healthy it actually was.

Genius, he would write, consists in a trueness of sight, in such a use of words "as shows that the man was eye-witness, and not a reporter of what was told." (The early lectures are full of this idea.) Still, he had to admit at the beginning—and even more as he thought about it—that genius has methods of its own which to others may seem shocking or incoherent or pernicious. "Genius is a character of illimitable freedom." It can make greatness out of trivial material: well, Jacksonian America was trivial enough; would genius make it great? Genius unsettles routine: "Make a new rule, my dear, can you not? and tomorrow Genius shall stamp on it with starry sandal." Year after year, Emerson would tell himself—coming as near to stridency as he was capable—"To Genius everything is permitted, and not only that, but it enters into all other men's labors." Or again, he would reassure himself: "I pardon everything to it; everything is trifling before it; I will wait for it for years, and sit in contempt before the doors of that inexhaustible blessing." He was always on the lookout for genius; wherefore he sweetly greeted Whitman at the dawn of a great career, and was dismayed when this genius—who assumed that to him everything was permitted, including the attempt to make greatness out of a trivial democracy—used Emerson's endorsement in letters of gold on the back cover of the second edition of *Leaves of Grass*.

There the problem lay: it was pleasant to appeal to nature against formality, to identify religion with the blowing clover, the meteor, and the falling rain—to challenge the spectral convention in the name of the genius who lives spontaneously from nature, who has been commended, cheated, and chagrined. But who was this genius—if he wasn't Andrew Jackson, was he then Walt Whitman? Was he, whichever he was, to be permitted *everything?* An inability to spell or parse might, as in the case of genius Jones Very, be amusing; but suppose genius should find permissible or actually congenial sexual aberration or political domination? If before it all convention is trifling, must genius flout both monogamy and the social hierarchy? Suppose the youth did learn to affirm that a popgun is a popgun, in defiance of the ancient and honorable of the earth—and then chose as his guide to genius not the reserved sage of Concord but the indisputably greatest literary genius of the age, Goethe, or the outstanding genius in politics, Napoleon?

There were other dangerous geniuses, of course—above all, Lord Byron. He, said Andrews Norton (who clearly thought Emerson no better), was a corrupter of youth, a violator of "the unalterable principles of taste, founded in the nature of man, and the eternal truths of mortality and religion." But Emerson and the New England geniuses were not too perturbed by Byron; he did indeed exhibit that love of the vast which they thought the primary discovery of their times, but, as Emerson said, in him "it is blind, it sees not its true end—an infinite good, alive and beautiful, a life nourished on absolute beatitudes, descending into nature to behold itself reflected there." The moral imperfections of geniuses—including the obscenities of Shakespeare—could likewise be exculpated. But the early nineteenth century, more acutely conscious of its peculiar identity than any age yet recorded in history, could not permit itself to tame the two greatest geniuses it had produced, the two who above all others, in the power of nature and of instinct, shattered the "over-civilized" palace of artifice. An ethic of self-reliance could not pretend that such reliers upon self as Goethe and Napoleon were blind. They were the twin "representatives of the impatience and reaction of nature against the *morgue* of conventions,—two stern realists, who, with the scholars, have severally set the axe at the root of the tree of cant and seeming, for this time, and for all time." But the point Emerson had to make, obstinately, was that if Napoleon incarnated "the popular external life and aims of the nineteenth century," then by the same token Goethe was its other half, "a man quite domesticated in the century,"—in fact, "the soul of his century."

The story of Emerson's lifelong struggle with Goethe has been often recounted. He could not give over the contest, for if Goethe had to be pronounced wicked, Emerson would become what Norton called him, an infidel. "All conventions, all tradition he rejected," says Emerson, in order to add that thus Goethe uttered "the best things about Nature that ever were said." The ancient and honorable of the earth—well, of Boston's earth—sneered that the man was immoral, but the New England geniuses dug in their heels and insisted with Margaret Fuller that Goethe was "the highest form of Nature, and conscious of the meaning she has been striving successively to unfold through those below him." Those below were demonstrably (like Andrews Norton) non-geniuses.

Life for geniuses would have been simpler could Goethe have been separated from Napoleon. But the two giants met at Erfurt—and recognized each other. (Emerson punctiliously copied into his *Journals* what Goethe said about Napoleon: it was as though he kept hitting himself with a hammer.) Emerson came back from Europe to start his brave adventure as a free-lance lecturer with a series entitled "Biography." To judge from the notes for the first lecture, he spent much time explaining that Napoleon was beneath contempt: he was "the very bully of the common, & knocked down most indubitably his antagonists; he was as heavy as any six of them." Measure him against any of the tests young Emerson proposed, and Napoleon failed on every count. One test was whether a man has a good aim: "Well, Napoleon had an Aim & a Bad one." Another was whether he be in earnest: "Napoleon was no more a believer than a grocer who disposes his shop-window invitingly." The lectures held up to American admiration Luther, Washington, Lafayette, Michelangelo, Burke, Milton, Fox, but the constant moral was this (Emerson came back to it from every angle): "Of Napoleon, the strength consisted in his renunciation of all conscience. The Devil helps him." Emerson delivered this statement on January 29, 1835—eleven months after he had assured Carlyle that "a most unfit person" was President of the United States, when that person was still in office.

There is no better gauge of Emerson's progress into sophistication than the contrast between this moralistic lecture and the chapter published in 1850 in *Representative Men*—although that too has its ambiguities. No one would call it a paean of praise to Bonaparte, but still, the conscienceless devil of 1835 has become one who "respected the power of nature and fortune, and ascribed to it his superiority, instead of valuing himself, like inferior men, on his opinionativeness, and waging war with nature." But if Napoleon was now on the side of the meteor, against the timidity of scholars, what of the democracy in America? What of our own Napoleons—Jackson and Van Buren? Neither Napoleon nor they could be consigned to the Devil, for in that case there would exist in the universe of the Over-Soul a foreign, an extraneous, element, something uncontrollable; in that case, for children of the Devil to live from the Devil would be really demonic, really unnatural—as it often did seem to cultured New Englanders that Democrats lived.

There was a great temptation to identify this upsurging of democracy with nature. (Brownson was willing to risk it, but not for long; except Bancroft, hardly an American before Whitman dared—that is, after Jefferson's nature became "romantic" nature.) If the stinging clarity of a teamster's oath was worth paragraphs of Harvard prose, was not Jackson a rod of nature reproving the timid, the imitative and tame? Emerson sometimes made this identification, or almost made it; but he was still the Bostonian, ninth in a line of ministers, and by no stretching of his conception of nature could he learn to look upon the naturals who composed the Jacksonian rabble with anything but loathing. The soliloquy—the endless debate with himself—runs throughout the *Journals*; it turns upon a triangle of counterstatement: democracy raises the problem of genius; genius the problem of Napoleon and the American politician; they in turn raise the problem of democracy and of America. The pattern is not always quite so explicit, but over and over again any mention of genius is sure to be followed, within an entry or two, by a passage on democracy, the Democratic party, Napoleon. The inconclusiveness of the inner meditations makes a striking contrast to the seeming serenity of the published oracles. The art—or should we call it the artfulness?—of Emerson is nowhere more charmingly revealed than in the fashion in which he managed to separate in the *Essays* the three themes that in the *Journals* were constantly intertwined. Yet even his great ingenuity could not keep genius, Napoleon, and democracy from coming together and forming knotty passages in the *Essays,* and especially in *Representative Men.*

Surely he ought, did he respect logic, to have been like Whitman a democrat, and therefore a Democrat. Returning from Europe in 1834, having seen how monarchy and aristocracy degrade mankind, he could write:

> The root and seed of democracy is the doctrine, Judge for yourself. Reverence thyself. It is the inevitable effect of that doctrine, where it has any effect (which is rare), to insulate the partisan, to make each man a state. At the same time it replaces the dead with a living check in a true, delicate reverence for superior, congenial minds. "How is the king greater than I, if he is not more just."

But the fact remained that, in the America of Jackson or of Polk, democracy in the abstract could not be dissociated from the gang of hoodlums who showed nothing more, to Emerson's view, than withering selfishness and impudent vulgarity. The boy had fled from the ranting of orators to the cherry trees; the man of 1834 sought the same comfort: "In the hush of these woods I find no Jackson placards affixed to the trees."

Yet, the literature of the new age, the revolt against "upholstery," gave a hollow sound to the names of king and lord because it voiced the forces "which have unfolded every day, with a rapidity sometimes terrific, the democratic element." Today "the Universal Man is now as real an existence as the Devil was then." At the mention of the Devil, if not of the king, Emerson must recollect himself: "I do not mean that ill thing, vain and loud, which writes lying newspapers, spouts at caucuses, and sells its lies for gold." He meant only "that spirit of love for the general good whose name this assumes." A man need not be a Transcendentalist to find this ill thing disgusting: he need only to have gone to Harvard. Viewed from this angle, there was nothing to be preferred in Abraham Lincoln over General Jackson. After the assassination, Emerson tried to atone; but in 1863 the President caused him to reflect that people of culture should not expect anything better out of the operations of universal suffrage:

> You cannot refine Mr. Lincoln's taste, extend his horizon, or clear his judgment; he will not walk dignifiedly through the traditional part of the President of America, but will pop out his head at each railroad station and make a little speech, and get into an argument with Squire A. and Judge B. He will write letters to Horace Greeley, and any editor or reporter or saucy party committee that writes to him, and cheapen himself.

In the clutch of such reflections, Emerson was frequently on the point of making democratic naturalism signify an open, irreconcilable war between genius and democracy. Genius, he said in 1847, is anthropomorphist and makes human form out of material, but America—"eager, solicitous, hungry, rabid, busy-bodied"—is without form, "has no terrible and no beautiful condensation." Had he let himself go in that direction, we could summarize him in a sentence: America's philosopher condemned America's democracy as something unnatural.

He came perilously close to this way out: he dallied with the solution that was always available for romantic theorists, that some great and natural genius, out of contempt for the herd, might master them. A man of strong will "may suddenly become the center of the movement, and compel the system to gyrate round it." Cromwell was never out of Emerson's mind. Such an actor would settle the problem, would redeem both nature and the ideal, the stability and the security of the commonwealth:

> We believe that there may be a man who is a match for events,—one who never found his match—against whom other men being dashed are broken, —one of inexhaustible personal resources, who can give you odds, and beat you.

The rest of us could even tell ourselves that we did not abdicate self-reliance should we follow such a genius: "We feed on genius."

Still, Emerson had to add, we "have a half-belief." There was always the danger that a resolution of the political question into the personality of the great man would be like trying to resolve the poetic problem into the personality of Byron. Genius has laws of its own, but in the workings of a commonwealth neither whim nor demonism should be permitted. "Politics rest on necessary foundations, and cannot be treated with levity."

Levity! There was indeed the devil. It would be levity to give way to looking down one's nose at Jackson and Lincoln, to turn from them to the great man who promised to bring mediocrity to heel. For suppose this genius should prove a demon of the only plausible devil, of levity?

Here Emerson was back again with Napoleon. Upon his mind, upon the mind of his generation, was indelibly impressed the spectacle of that meeting in Erfurt. The Goethean genius met with and subscribed to the Napoleonic. Henceforth it was impossible to lift the standard of the epicurean, civilized Goethe against the leveling thrust of Napoleon, or to rally around him against Jackson. Assuredly Napoleon was unscrupulous, selfish, perfidious, a prodigious gossip: "his manners were coarse." So was Jackson, so was Lincoln. But Napoleon fought against the enemies of Goethe: timidity, complacence, etc., etc. If Goethe had sided with Bonaparte, how then ought an American intellectual act toward the Democratic party? After all, as Emerson in "Politics" was obliged to say, "Democracy is better for us, because the religious sentiment of the present time accords better with it."

He hoped that the rhetorical balance of his famous sentence would remove his anxiety, that while the Whigs had the best men, the Democrats had the best cause. The scholar, philosopher, the man of religion, will want to vote with the Democrats, "but he can rarely accept the persons whom the so-called popular party propose to him as representatives of these liberalities." On the other hand, the conservative party was indeed timid, "merely defensive of property." No wonder that men came to think meanly of government and to object to paying their taxes: "Everywhere they think they get their money's worth, except for these."

This was a miserable prospect, an intolerable dilemma, for the author of *Nature*. Yet Emerson was never more the spokesman for nature, and never more the American, than when he added, "I do not for these defects despair of our republic." He might have mourned with Henry Adams and every disillusioned liberal, with every disgruntled businessman, that the country was going to the dogs, that there was no hope left (there being no longer hope in a compensatory Christian heaven) except in the great man, the political genius, the dictator. There was everything in Emerson's philosophy to turn him like Carlyle into a prophet of reaction and the leader-principle.

But he did not go with Carlyle; and he meant what he said, that he did not despair of the republic. Why not? Was it merely that he was stupid, or mild-mannered, or temperamentally sanguine? Was it dogmatic optimism for the sake of optimism? Perhaps it was partly for these reasons, but the play of his mind kept hope alive and vigorous by circling round and round, by drawing sustenance from, the inexhaustible power of genius. However odd, fantastic, or brutal might be the conduct of genius, it does submit to laws. Levity gets ironed out. So in society: "No forms can have any dangerous importance whilst we are befriended by the laws of things." Emerson's historical perspective was deeper, richer than that of a Cooper—great historical novelist though he was. Cooper had Natty Bumppo to give grandeur to the sordid scene of *The Pioneers,* but no philosophy of genius to sustain him once he entered into conflict with *Home as Found*. Cooper let himself dream of violent catastrophe, a devasting judgment not of Jehovah but of nature, as an ultimate solution to the ills of democracy, and prophesied it in *The Crater*. But Emerson could comprehend democracy in a larger frame of reference, as a phase of western society, and see its connection, where the *rentier* could not, with the new kind of property. Emerson could point out that it was not something a gentleman could afford to despise and then expect still to have the refuge of being a gentleman. In other words, Emerson understood the portent not alone of Goethe but of Napoleon.

For this reason, Napoleon figures in the carefully planned structure of *Representative Men* as a prologue to Goethe, as the next-to-the-last. There is some perversity—one might say almost levity—in the other choices (Swedenborg most obviously) or in the arrangement, but Emerson was pushing his way through the book to the two problems which, his genius informed him, constituted one problem: that of genius in modern society, where the bad manners of democrats would not be sufficient reason for consigning them, on that ground alone, to the limbo of levity.

*Representative Men* had its origins in a few simple ideas which took hold of Emerson in the 1830's, of which he was the prisoner but which, for as long as possible, he held off from publishing. The secret record of his life with these ideas is the *Journals,* but there was a public record before his fellow countrymen: the lectures, those discourses he gave for audiences and for money, out of which he mined paragraphs for what became *Essays* but which, guided by some obscure impulse, he never translated directly from the platform to the page. From the beginning of his career as a lecturer down to his last series at Harvard in 1871, there was always a discourse on "Genius"; materials from one or another recasting of this draft found their way into "Self-Reliance," "Art," "Intellect,"—but never into a full-dress essay on genius. With the lecture of January, 1837 (entitled "Society"), Emerson had already gone so far beyond 1835 that he could define the genius as one who has access to the universal mind and who receives its influx in wise passivity. He could employ terms he was to use throughout many subsequent lectures, but which, at least in this same and revealing language, he would never print:

> Genius is never anomalous. The greatest genius is he in whom other men own the presence of a larger portion of their common nature than is in them. And this I believe is the secret of the joy which genius gives us. Whatever men of genius say, becomes forthwith the common property of all. Why? Because the man of genius apprises us not so much of his wealth as of the commonwealth. Are his illustrations happy? So feel we [that] not *his* mind but *the* mind illustrate[s] its thoughts. A sort of higher patriotism warms us, as if one should say, "That's the way they do things in my country."

Thus early the problem took shape in his mind—never to leave it—of genius and "my country." All men share in "*the* mind," and all men are the democracy; genius must be, in some sense, a patriotic triumph. But Napoleon was a threat to the conception of a "good" genius; his American aliases, Jackson and the Democrats, were a threat to State Street. Writers are often obliged to ask themselves exactly who they are, and fear to find out that they may be the most evil of their creations. Was Emerson, in his heart of hearts, a Napoleon? If not, were the Over-Soul and all its spokesmen, all the geniuses, to be counted in the Whig column? Obviously Whiggery was no home for genius. Maybe one would have to admit that Jackson was a genius? Maybe one would have to confess—as the easiest way out—that Lincoln was a genius? Lincoln was, nominally, a Republican, but before 1865 Emerson saw him only as the creature of universal suffrage; the assassination and the rapid canonization undoubtedly helped, but Emerson was still feeling his own way and not merely moving with the times when in 1871 he told his Harvard audience, "John Brown and Abraham Lincoln were both men of genius, and have obtained this simple grandeur of utterance."

Years before he was thus able to reconcile himself to Lincoln, Emerson tried to reconcile himself to the whole panoply of genius, and the result was *Representative Men*. The value of the book is not that it invents a way out of the quandary which we now confront as terribly as did Emerson. It is not a guide for the preserving of personality against mass pressures. Too many of his terms are altered; few of us can accept his metaphysics, and many of the geniuses we admire do not seem so clearly to contribute wealth to any commonwealth. But the exhilaration of the book consists in the fact that Emerson here got his many-sided perplexity in hand, sacrificed no one aspect to any other, and wrote a book not about heroes and how to worship them, but about how an intelligent and sensitive man lives, or must learn to live, in a democratic society and era.

By calling great men not heroes but representatives, Emerson, in the most American of fashions, put them to work; the first chapter is slyly entitled "Uses of Great Men." He divides genius as a genus into subordinate species, whereupon for each type a specific set of laws can be worked out. Thus the individual genius, even when seemingly lawless, adheres to a pattern of coherence in relation to the sum total of the parts. If it be necessary—as we are compelled to recognize—that all sides of life be expressed, then each genius has a function, be he good or evil; what each incarnates we recognize as an accentuated part of ourselves—because all men are one, and any one man is all men.

Likewise, genius is fragmentary, and so deficient on several sides. Sometimes the moralizing Emerson appears to line up his great men like naughty children and tell them wherein they all fall lamentably short of what teacher expects of them. But you forgive him some (although not all) of this didacticism not so much because he was a New Englander but because behind it lay the intense moments recorded in the *Journals*, such as that in which he had taken the very existence of such a person as the Democrat Hawthorne to signify "that in democratic America, she [nature] will not be democratized." Therefore in this book Emerson can go far—as far as clear sight can see—toward making genius democratic. The genius is great not because he surpasses but because he represents his constituency. His crimes and foibles are as much a part of the record as his triumphs and nobilities; Napoleon belongs to genius not as a child of the historical Devil whom Emerson foolishly invoked in 1835, and not even as a creation of the metaphorical devil, levity, but as a serious, real, and terrifying power in modern western civilization.

Wherefore something more should be required of the scholar, the poet, the man of religion, than timid antipathy to a blatant democracy. Napoleon was "the agent or attorney of the middle class of modern society"—of those in shops, banks, and factories who want to get rich. He represents "the Democrat, or the party of men of business, against the stationary or conservative party." And—Emerson here plunges to the bottom of his insight—"as long as our civilization is essentially one of property, of fences, of exclusiveness, it will be mocked by delusions"—against which some Bonaparte is bound to raise the cry of revolt, for which men again will die.

What Emerson most gained, I believe, by this analysis was an ability to comprehend, even while never quite reconciling himself to, the vices of democracy—whether with a small "d" or a capital "D." He did not need to blind himself by patriotic fanaticism; by the same token he did not need to despair. He could confess his mistake about Lincoln without retracting his contempt for Franklin Pierce. He could criticize his country without committing treason, without having to demand, as did an irate Cooper, that they become like himself or else go to hell. The example and the laws of genius might work, would work, even in the ranks of the Democratic party.

Of course, Emerson trusted the self-operating force of moral law more than do most of us today. Napoleon (for him read Jackson, Lincoln, the boss, the district leader) did everything a man could do to thrive by intellect without conscience. "It was the nature of things, the eternal law of the man and the world, which balked and ruined him; and the result, in a million experiments, would be the same." Emerson was fully aware of what the lesson cost: "immense armies, burned cities, squandered treasures, immolated millions of men, . . . this demoralized Europe." He did, we must confess, look upon the desolation with what seems to us smugness, we who have seen Europe infinitely more burned and demoralized; but these things are relative, and he was happy to note that out of the destruction arose a universal cry, "assez de Bonaparte."

Emerson was too often chilly. But had he been only that, *Representative Men* would have been for him the end of a theme, would have put a period to a chapter in his *Journals*. It was nothing of the sort. No sooner was it published than the debate was resumed, and many of the most fascinating combinations of the triple meditation on genius, Napoleon, and democracy occur in later entries. The Civil War was for him as for others an excruciating ordeal, the more so as during the worst years he believed Lincoln the example of democratic incompetence. But in the darkest moments he never quite lost his bearings. The sanity (the chilly sanity, if you will) that sustains the essay on "Politics" and informs *Representative Men* never deserted him—the levelheadedness which is his most precious bequest to a posterity that is understandably exasperated by his unction. In 1862, although not yet respecting the President, he was able to keep the personality from obscuring the issue:

> A movement in an aristocratic state does not argue a deep cause. A dozen good fellows may have had a supper and warmed each other's blood to some act of spite or arrogance, which they talk up and carry out the next month; or one man, Calhoun or Rhett, may have grown bilious, and his grumble and fury are making themselves felt at the legislature. But in a Democracy, every movement has a deep-seated cause.

This was written by no flag-waving, tub-thumping patriot shouting, "My country right or wrong." This is no campaign orator mouthing the word "democracy" even while desecrating it by his deeds. It was written by a great American, a serious man who could finally run down the devil of politics and declare that his name is levity, who understood as well as any in what the difficult ordeal consists, the magnificent but agonizing experience of what it is to be, or to try to be, an American.

# Emerson and the Progressive Tradition

*by Daniel Aaron*

## I

In the early days of the Republic, men wrote of the "national, moral, and political advantages of the United States" with the confidence of believers; they did not need to place their faith in distant utopias, in "spiritual frontiers." Before them lay the gigantic outlines of a continent ripe for exploitation and capable of supplying the wants of its restless and ambitious population. Momentary crises might ruin particular sections and classes; injured parties might thunder at the politicians for hindering the march of progress; but behind the extravagances of the boosters and the complaints of the unsuccessful lay what most Americans conceived to be the solid gains of an expanding nation.

Contrasted with the gloomy summations of 1950, some of the national advantages listed by an anonymous writer in 1823 are revealing:

> . . . Our territory affords every variety of soil and climate, so as to render us independent of foreign nations as any country whatever.
>
> Our stores of all the important articles of coal, iron, lead, copper, and timber are inexhaustible . . .
>
> Our population is active, industrious, energetic, enterprising, and ingenious.
>
> Our government is the most free and liberal that ever existed. . . .
>
> Our debt is insignificant, not equal to the annual interest paid by some other nations.
>
> Taxes are so light as not to be felt . . .
>
> We have no nobility or gentry, with the enormous annual incomes, derived from the labors of the mass of the community.
>
> Our farmers and planters are, in general, lords of the soil they cultivate. . . .
>
> Our citizens are unrestrained in the choice of occupation.
>
> We have abundant room for all the valuable superfluous population of Europe.

"Emerson and the Progressive Tradition." From *Men of Good Hope* (New York: Oxford University Press, 1951). 

During this golden age, American orators quite understandably saw their country as an area set aside by God for heavenly experiments. They rejoiced in its progress and contemplated a deteriorating Europe with mingled pity and contempt. The American's faith in progress, his utilitarianism, his scorn for precedent were justified by economics, even if he liked to attribute his country's triumphant march to the magic of democratic institutions. If all the sections were not equally satisfied and if certain classes enriched themselves at the expense of others, most Americans shared the elation of the times, the sense of movement and progress.

Visitors from abroad who came to look at the Americans during the early decades of the nineteenth century were struck by the general well-being of the country and impressed by the vast fermentation taking place in the United States. But the more philosophical and discerning of the foreign observers, while appreciating the immense significance of the democratic experiment and rarely stooping to petty recriminations, probed for weaknesses and discovered them. There was not only the fact of slavery to reckon with. Even more portentous in some ways was the future of a society frankly and avidly materialistic, a society adhering to a series of public truths determined by a sometimes ruthless and mindless majority, a society agitated by a perpetual restlessness and an insatiable appetite, a virtuous society yet one that revealed on occasion what Emerson called an "invincible depravity."

Alexis de Tocqueville, the most intelligent critic America has ever had, was on the whole a sympathetic and flattering interpreter, but his *Democracy in America* more than hinted of corruption in the American Eden. The advantages of democracy were perfectly evident to him, and yet he detected certain symptoms in the American behavior that mocked the national aspiration to greatness. Tocqueville did not draw up any systematic indictment, but the following series of observations, selected at random from his book, indicate the nature of his criticism:

> What chiefly diverts the men of democracies from lofty ambition is not the scantiness of their fortunes, but the vehemence of the exertions they daily make to improve them. They strain their faculties to the utmost to achieve paltry results, and this cannot fail speedily to limit their range of view, and to circumscribe their powers. They might be much poorer, and still be greater.

(This was also to be the complaint of Emerson, Thoreau, and Whitman: "the mediocrity of desires," the inordinate attention to getting and having, so that the true meaning of life is lost. As Thoreau said, Americans have appetites but no passions.)

> A native of the United States clings to this world's goods as if he were certain never to die; and he is so hasty at grasping at all within his reach, that one would suppose he was constantly afraid of not living long enough to enjoy them.

(Tocqueville comments frequently upon the American's restlessness, his chronic dissatisfaction with what he has. He attributes this prevailing feeling to the openness of American society, where no limits are imposed and no holds barred, where the prospects are boundless but where the equalitarian conditions make any discrepancies in individual fortunes all the more glaring.)

> To say the truth, though there are rich men, the class of rich men does not exist; for those rich individuals have no feelings or purposes in common, no mutual traditions or mutual hopes; there are individuals, therefore, but no definite class.

The American rich are simply a group who willy-nilly and independently have broken through democratic anonymity in the approved way—by making money. Tocqueville did not see this group as constituting any danger to democracy, but the rising industrial aristocracy, which "first impoverishes and debases the men who serve it, and then abandons them to be supported by the charity of the public," he regarded as a more serious threat to the country.)

> Selfishness is a passionate and exaggerated love of self, which leads a man to connect everything with himself, and to prefer himself to everything in the world. Individualism is a mature and calm feeling, which disposes each member of the community to sever himself from the mass of his fellows, and to draw apart with his family and friends; so that, after he has thus formed a little circle of his own, he willingly leaves society at large to itself. Selfishness originates in blind instinct; individualism proceeds from erroneous judgment more than from depraved feelings; it originates as much in deficiencies of mind as in perversity of heart.

(This quotation, taken from Book II, Chapter II of the second volume, makes certainly one of the most important distinctions in *Democracy in America* and expresses the democratic dilemma more succinctly, if less eloquently, than anyone before or after Tocqueville has done. Individualism, Tocqueville goes on to say, although not consciously and impulsively antisocial, begins by sapping public virtue and ends in unmitigated selfishness. What is more important, it is "of democratic origin" and springs up at a time when class obligations have been removed. Theoretically, from a democratic point of view, "the duties of the individual to the race" should rightfully supercede the limited allegiances of class, but Tocqueville asserts that in America, "the bond of human affection is extended, but it is relaxed." Something has been gained, and something has been lost. At best, "Aristocracy had made a chain of all the members of the community, from the peasant to the king: democracy breaks that chain, and severs every link of it.")

The great American writers of the nineteenth century recognized these divisive tendencies in their society and were deeply concerned about them. For Hawthorne the unforgivable sin was spiritual isolation, the breaking of the "magnetic chain of being," and Melville and Whitman celebrated democratic sociality. And yet these writers and others who preached a similar belief were Americans and children of their times, consciously reflecting the preconceptions of their generation. Hawthorne, despite his ancestral longings, would have found no melancholy implications in Tocqueville's remark that in America, "the woof of time is every instant broken, and the track of generations effaced." On the contrary, Hawthorne took a sardonic pleasure in recording the vicissitudes of families and the crumbling away of aristocratic distinctions. Would he have agreed with Tocqueville that democracy breaks the "magnetic chain"? One wonders how deliberately he made his beloved and innocent country, unshrouded as yet by European gloom, the background for his parables of wickedness. Hawthorne's and Melville's powerful egotists, Ethan Brand and Captain Ahab, damned and destroyed for their pride, are still heroes who carry their creators' benedictions with them into the flaming lime kiln and the ocean grave. Are they not the perfect exemplars of Tocqueville's American individualists?

> They owe nothing to any man, they expect nothing from any man; they acquire the habit of always considering themselves as standing alone, and they are apt to imagine that their whole destiny is in their own hands.

Thus, as Tocqueville says, democracy makes "every man forget his ancestors" (a desirable end from Hawthorne's and Melville's point of view, although both are fascinated by the past) and democracy "separates his contemporaries from him; it throws him back forever upon himself alone, and threatens in the end to confine him entirely within the solitude of his own heart." Here, if you will, is the Unpardonable Sin, or, to put it still another way, the great Transcendental fallacy, which emerges most clearly in the writings of Emerson.

Emerson's simultaneous acceptance and rejection of American civilization illustrates the condition of the divided intelligence even more strikingly than the ambivalent positions of Hawthorne and Melville. He was both the critic and the celebrator of his and subsequent generations, the Yea-sayer and the Nay-sayer. By Tocqueville's standards he was the most articulate exponent of democratic individualism, whose philosophy of self-reliance, or self-sufficiency, harmonized with the disintegrative tendencies of American life, and yet at the same time he quite characteristically attacked the social consequences of his own philosophy.

This contradiction also appears, although to a lesser extent, in the ideas of the reformers who regarded themselves as his disciples or who unconsciously reflected his influence; and since Emerson was the real prophet of the progressive tradition—the Scholar without plan or system, who impressed men of all radical creeds—his polarized attitude toward the individual has a direct bearing on the history of progressivism in America. For the progressives who followed him felt his impatience with men in the mass—this "maudlin agglutination," as Emerson put it. Like him, they held forth the possibility of human development while noting the appalling evidences of human mediocrity. Like him again, they fervently condemned the shortsightedness and selfishness of the middle class at the same time that they cherished its virtues and faith. Emerson was their perfect representative, and his ambivalent attitude toward man in the aggregate was shared by the progressives who followed him.

## II

Consider first his lesser role as the seer of *laissez-faire* capitalism and the rampant individual.

To anyone who has habitually imagined Emerson as the sedentary philosopher invariably upholding with transcendental logic the Ideal-Real against the evanescent Material, his delight in the harmonies of the market-place might appear somewhat paradoxical. A closer survey of his writings, however, show that his communications with the Over-Soul did not always preclude a secular interest in vulgar appearances. His transcendentalism, in fact, provided an ideal explanation for the conduct and activities of the business classes and offered the necessary criteria by which he was able to justify or to criticize them. This leisure-loving beneficiary of a commercial economy, whose antecedents were ministerial rather than mercantile, outlined a rationale for the entrepreneur of an industrial age.

Emerson's fastidious tastes found little that was congenial in the vulgarity and crassness of workaday business. It is all the more remarkable that he was able to sublimate his instinctive distaste for the hucksters in counting-houses and see them finally as exemplifying divine principles. His journals and essays are filled with disparaging references to the business classes; their sordidness, their undeviating pursuit of wealth, their narrow self-interests, and their timidity are bluntly and scornfully arraigned. But he seems to have cherished a particular dislike only for the meaner of the species. Businessmen of larger appetites and bolder ambitions, notwithstanding their faults, often called forth his admiration, and he consistently identified business intrepidity with the exploits of warriors and heroes.

The portrait of Napoleon in *Representative Men* is perhaps the best illustration of Emerson's ambivalent attitude toward aggressiveness and self-seeking; it is not by accident that he saw "this deputy of the nineteenth century" as the "agent or attorney of the middle class of modern society; of the throng who fill the markets, shops, counting-houses, manufactories, ships, of the modern world, aiming to be rich." The essay falls roughly into two parts. In the first section Emerson exalts Napoleon into a superman; in the concluding three or four paragraphs, he dwells fiercely upon his uglier defects—his coarseness and lack of ideality. "In short," Emerson concludes, "when you have penetrated through all the circles of power and splendor, you were not dealing with a gentleman, at last; but with an imposter and a rogue." But the deflation of the great man undertaken at the close of the essay cannot entirely obliterate the earlier impression of Emerson's enthusiastic admiration, which he shared with thousands of his American contemporaries. In praising Napoleon's practicality, prudence, and directness, his powers of synthesis and cool audacity, Emerson is underscoring precisely those attributes that made up the American success code; his emphasis helps to explain the peculiar fascination Napoleon held for the warriors of American business. Emerson's strictures against the blowhard, the strutting egotist, the low vulgarian are devastating, but the following encomium also represents his settled convictions:

> We cannot, in the universal imbecility, indecision and indolence of men, sufficiently congratulate ourselves on this strong and ready actor, who took occasion by the beard, and showed us how much may be accomplished by the mere force of such virtues as all men possess in less degrees; namely, by punctuality, by personal attention, by courage, and thoroughness.

Emerson's respect for power and its achievements is even more glowingly expressed in two other essays, "Power" and "Wealth." Here he reiterates his preference for the "bruisers" and "pirates," the "men of the right Caesarian pattern" who transcend the pettiness of "talkers" and "clerks" and dominate the world by sheer force of character. "Life is a search after power," he announces, and the successful men who understand the laws of Nature and respond to the Godhead within themselves, who convert "the sap and juices of the planet to the incarnation and nutriment of their design," are unconsciously fulfilling the plan of a benevolent Providence.

In these essays and elsewhere, Emerson was not only synchronizing the predatory practices of the entrepreneur with the harmony of the universe and permitting merchants (as Bronson Alcott shrewdly said) to "find a refuge from their own duplicity under his broad shield"; he was also outlining a code of behavior that the superior man must follow, and sketching the ideal political economy under which the superman might best exercise his uncommon talents. Specialize, he advised, "elect your work" and "drop all the rest." Do not dissipate your efforts. Concentrate! "Concentration is the secret of strength in politics, in war, in trade, in short all management of human affairs." Make up your mind and stick to your decisions. Practice again and again; it is constant drilling that distinguishes the professional from the amateur and enables the "indifferent hacks and mediocrities" to win out over men of superior abilities. He quoted the business slogans of Poor Richard with warm approval and identified "counting-room maxims" with the "laws of the universe."

Emerson's optimistic faith, his belief that all apparent evil ultimately cancels out into good, allowed him to view the depredations of business more tranquilly than, let us say, a Theodore Parker, less given to transcendentalizing business enterprise. A little wickedness, Emerson believed, served as a kind of energizing principle. "Men of this surcharge of arterial blood cannot live on nuts, herb-tea, and elegies," he characteristically remarked. The hot speculators exploiting the country, the "monomaniacs" of trade who clash in the market-place, build up the country as they enrich themselves. Unworldly moralists who rant against the violence of competition are in reality working against the laws of the world. Were they successful in their efforts to subdue the spirit of competitive enterprise, they would be forced to rekindle the fires of avarice if civilization were to continue. Thus it inevitably followed that any attempt to check the capitalistic incentives was a futile and unjustifiable interference with the iron laws of circumstance:

> Wealth brings with it its own checks and balances. The basis of political economy is non-interference. The only safe role is found in the self-adjusting meter of demand and supply. Do not legislate. Meddle, and you snap the sinews with your sumptuary laws. Give no bounties, make equal laws, secure life and property, and you need not give alms. Open the doors of opportunity to talent and virtue and they will do themselves justice, and property will not be in bad hands. In a free and just commonwealth, property rushes from the idle and imbecile to the industrious, brave and persevering.

Quotations like this represent only a single strain in Emerson's thought. Equally eloquent passages might be included in which he affirms his strong democratic attachments and humanitarian sympathies, but the Nietzschean side of Emerson is unmistakable. As a transcendentalist he had to recognize the divine potentialities of all men and to reconcile all social manifestations with the general will of God. Hence his interest in and sympathy with all causes and movements, however absurd, and his tolerance of creeds and men not instinctively congenial to him. His conservative and autocratic biases, however, reasserted themselves from time to time, just as the materiality he philosophically denied anchored his rhapsodic speculations to brute fact. Emerson enjoyed almost sensuously the plump and solid tangibles, and he admired the "inventive or creative class" that made them possible.

Running through his writings is a constant disparagement of men in the mass, the "imbeciles," as he calls them on several occasions, the "uninventive or accepting class" held down by "gravity, custom, and fear" and tyrannized by convention. What quickened his faith in the latent capacities of man was the "grand" talent rising like a huge wave over the placid ocean of humanity. Although Emerson lived in rural Concord during periods of economic and political upheaval, he sanctioned unconsciously the forces of exploitation that were at work in the United States and the powerful men, impelled by what he called a "keener avarice," who were directing this exploitation. Rarely does he credit the collective energies of the common man as the great transforming power. Man in the mass is inert until galvanized by the great captains of enterprise. Wealth is created by ability, and it is the rich man "who can avail himself of all man's faculties. . . . The world is his toolchest, and he is successful, or his education is carried on just so far, as is the marriage of his faculties with nature, or the degree in which he takes up things into himself."

It would not be too extreme to say that Emerson envisaged the scholar as employing these "business principles" in exploiting the frontiers of the mind, drawing "a benefit from the labors of the greatest number of men, of men in distant countries and in past times." The function of Emerson's scholar was to mold the plastic world and shake the "cowed" and the "trustless" out of their lethargy. The scholar was to create an intellectual revolution by gradually "domesticating" the idea of culture (the metaphor is Emerson's) and to illustrate the proved maxim that "he who has put forth his total strength in fit actions has the richest return of wisdom." After a period of worry and doubts, the Emerson who agonized over the choice of his vocation was able to reconcile the divergent appeals of practical action and reflection in the vocation of the scholar, which became for him a symbol of dynamic passivity.

Whether or not there is any truth in the contention expressed above, it can be plausibly argued that Emerson's "transcendentalizing" of business conduct testified to his awareness of the growing significance of commerce and industry in American life. When an age is dominated by the economic mind, Henry Adams once observed, "the imaginative mind tends to adopt its form and its faults." By temperament, inclination, and circumstance, Emerson belonged to a class out of sympathy with the rising industrial *bourgeoisie,* but he was extremely sensitive to the currents of his age and deeply infected by its omnipresent materialism. Ostensibly preoccupied with nonutilitarian ends, he nevertheless showed an almost inordinate interest in the practical performances of men and their mundane accomplishments.

Emerson helps us to see the motive forces that drove American individualists to absorb themselves in money-making; he makes clear their ambition and self-reliance, their inspired faith in limitless opportunities. His emphasis on the value of natural exploitation, of opening the world like an oyster, was only a more articulate and rhetorical expression of what millions already dimly felt, and his celebration of the practical doers was a kind of transcendental concession to those who scorned the useless visionary. He had been impressed by the magnificence of American commercial and industrial enterprise, by the dramatic implications of a continent unsubdued. To a romantic and poetic nature, such a phenomenon helped to compensate for the drabness and sameness of American life, to reduce the tedium of democratic anonymity. It allowed him to celebrate audacious individual accomplishment, and it gave a martial air to a nation of civilian traders. "Whatever appeals to the imagination, by transcending the ordinary limits of human nobility," Emerson said in speaking of Napoleon, "wonderfully encourages and liberates us." Emerson encouraged his countrymen to cultivate their inward greatness, and one of the ways he did so was to glorify the characters and deeds of the world's heroes who followed transcendental impulses.

## III

Neither Emerson nor his disciples, oddly enough, saw any connection between the cult of self-trust and the mercenary paradise about to be revealed after 1865, although a closer perusal of Tocqueville might have hinted as much. Emerson was simply acknowledging, perhaps unduly, a side of the national character that was aggressive and rapacious, that hated physical impediments, whether things or people. The significance of the frontier has been exaggerated, but the fact that for two centuries it represented a challenge and an obstacle as well as an opportunity to generations of "go-getters" is of crucial importance in understanding the American experience. If the frontier did not make the American character, it whetted the appetites and aggravated the assertive compulsions of the men who camped along its fringes.

Another kind of individualism, however, that took root and flourished in America did not express itself in a compulsion to dominate, to impose by force. Rather it emphasized the need for individual fulfillment and enlargement, for self-containment and passive growth. Individualism, taken in this sense, did not manifest itself in gouging the outer world, in fighting and scrambling in order to keep one's identity. It encouraged inner cultivation, and in so far as it was concerned with external realities—the problems of government and economics and culture—it conceived of them in terms of individual welfare. This kind of individualism or Personalism regarded the "self" as a rare and tender thing. Thoreau caught its spirit when he wrote: "The finest qualities of our nature, like the bloom on fruits, can be preserved only by the most delicate handling." And Emerson reflected this passive and humane conception of individualism even more unmistakably than he did its aggressive antitype. If as a Yankee he sympathized with the latter and vicariously enjoyed the coups of the unshrinking entrepreneurs, as a Poet and Seer he repudiated them and their philosophy.

Emerson, a radical wedded to principle, never intended his exhortations to justify the practices of "robber barons." In fact Emerson came to have a supreme contempt for the commercial mentality. He made fun of State Street timidity. He charged the bankers with fearing transcendentalism, because it would unsettle property and impair the obligation of contract. The businessman, he said, preferred slavery to illegality. Emerson addressed himself, finally, to democrats and humanitarians, not to property-worshippers, and for every conservative who hailed him there were a dozen reformers who constructed their systems upon his radical assumptions.

Emerson's political philosophy—it might be called transcendental democracy—had marked Jeffersonian and Jacksonian overtones. Strongly individualistic, it also spoke for equality of opportunity in economic and political affairs, and it lent support to the belief in *laissez-faire* and the necessity of the minimized state. But it was more spiritual and intellectual than the organized movements for political democracy and less concerned with political and economic considerations, less a matter of economic rationalization. Its chief proponents tended to be professional and literary people; ministers, writers, teachers, and reformers made up its ranks rather than businessmen, office-holders, or lawyers. This is not to say that the Transcendentalists played down political and economic questions—far from it—but they were not defenders of an "interest" or a "faction." If they had no desire to capture and operate a government, they stubbornly protested when government overstepped its limited confines and by its acts trespassed on their spiritual domain.

The men and women who made up this transcendental corps were mostly of New England origin, although a handful were born outside New England. As children of the professional or commercial classes or of the sturdy farming yeomanry, they received educational advantages above the average of their day, and for the most part they came from families distinguished neither by great wealth nor by poverty. Almost all of them seemed to have been reared in homes where the business of life was taken seriously and idealistically. It was this group that, disgusted by the prevailing materialism of the day, turned to culture and to reform.

Although the reformers shared their contemporaries' faith in progress, they could not accept the corollary that America was the best of all possible worlds or that the American experiment could be called a complete success. Shocked by the materialism and the inhumanity they saw everywhere about them, they found themselves in the position of condemning the social practices and behavior of a class with whom they were closely connected by birth and education and of speaking for an underprivileged group with whom they had little in common. Like the intelligentsia in societies before and after, they deliberately alienated themselves from the moneyed interests who had nurtured and sustained them. Because they still took seriously the Puritan tradition of stewardship, of class obligations, at a time when community responsibilities were being increasingly ignored, they could not be oblivious to the ruinous consequences of "enlightened self-interest." Many of them, moreover, believed quite literally in natural rights and other eighteenth-century humanitarian doctrines that proclaimed the necessity of the mutual concern of every man for another. Since the Transcendentalists respected the sacredness of the human individuality, the crassness and the insensitivity of the employing classes, indeed most of the values of the rising business elite, were personally distasteful to them.

Although Emerson was the most famous exponent of the transcendentalized democratic philosophy, his was neither the most original nor the most incisive mind among the New England reformers. William Ellery Channing had prepared the way for him; Thoreau and Whitman developed certain strains of his thought more acutely and profoundly; and Theodore Parker, as we shall see, surpassed him as a political and economic analyst. But Emerson, the master transcendentalist, somehow subsumed them all and most successfully comprehended his age. In him, as Howells wrote, "conscience and intellect were angelically one."

Emerson's political ideas emerged quite logically from transcendental principles. He believed in a divine power sometimes referred to as the Over-Soul, and he taught that all men shared in that divinity or at least were capable of establishing a rapport with it. Men's joint participation in this Spirit, their common share of the divine inheritance, made them brothers and gave the lie to artificial distinctions. In the great democracy of spirit that Emerson conjured up as a kind of Platonic archetype of the imperfect American model, all men were potentially great. Men were not great in fact (Emerson had no such leveling ideas, as we have seen), but every man could be great if he harkened to the admonition of the Over-Soul in himself.

Like John Adams and Thomas Jefferson, Emerson believed in a natural aristocracy, although his *aristoi* bore little resemblance to Jefferson's. Society divided itself into the men of understanding and the men of Reason. The former, the most numerous and the most ordinary, lived in "a world of pig-lead" and acted as if "rooted and grounded in adamant." Sunk in this profound materialism, they lacked the imaginative penetration of the true aristocrats, the men of Reason, who plumbed the spiritual reality behind the world of fact. The men of Reason—poets, seers, philosophers, scholars—the passive doers, served humanity as the geographers of the "supersensible regions" and inspired "an audacious mental outlook." They formed no inflexible caste, but they wonderfully "liberated" the cramped average afraid to trust itself.

Emerson did not intend his political theories to provide a sanction for social lawlessness, even though his celebration of the individual intuition, abstracted from the body of his thinking, seemed to justify an aggressive individualism. If it encouraged the predatory entrepreneur, it also invalidated contracts. It dissolved the power of tyrannical authority; it undermined tradition. If carried to its logical conclusion, the Emersonian theory that every person should act as a majority of one would result in anarchism, but he never pushed this idea to its end. Although his writings are filled with disparaging remarks about the state as the "principal obstruction and nuisance with which we have to contend," he opposed it only when it sought to supervene the higher laws, when it prevented men from living naturally and wisely and justly.

His views on the function of government were by no means entirely negative. Government, he said, "was set up for the protection and comfort of all good citizens." If the withered state represented his ultimate ideal, he could subscribe to Thoreau's remark: "To speak practically . . . I ask for, not at once no government, but *at once* a better government." He explained the community experiment at Brook Farm as proceeding

> in great part from a feeling that the true offices of the state, the state has let fall to the ground; that in the scramble of parties for the public purse, the main duties of government were omitted,—the duty to instruct the ignorant, to supply the poor with work, and . . . the mediation between want and supply.

Emerson reached this mature and liberal view of government and its purpose after a considerable amount of candid self-examination and after a long look at his own country. But Emerson came to believe that the Democrats had the best principles if not the best men, and the more he dirtied himself with politics (for he regarded the demands of the social world with resentment and anger) the more disgusted he became with the "thin and watery blood of Whiggism."

> Instead of having its own aims passionately in view, it cants about the policy of a Washington and a Jefferson. It speaks to expectation and not the torrent of its wishes and needs, waits for its antagonist to speak that it may have something to oppose, and, failing that, having nothing to say, is happy to hurrah.

Emerson's contempt for timid conservatism is best conveyed in his sarcastic description of its doctrine: "Better endure tyranny according to law a thousand years than irregular unconstitutional happiness for a day."

## IV

That he could feel this way about a conservatism continuously on the defensive and still retain his affection and respect for the "active, intelligent, well-meaning and wealthy part of the people" who made up its party is characteristic not only of Emerson but also of the middle-class reformers who succeeded him. Like Emerson, they belonged to that corps of sensitive intellectuals who placed spiritual values above material ones and human considerations above the rights of property. Like him, they made the flowering of the individual personality their ultimate goal and estimated all political and social ideologies, whether conservative or radical, by this single test. They had no quarrel with the machine nor did they advocate a return to a smokeless, factoryless America. They repudiated Thoreau's remedy by isolation, for they agreed completely with Mazzini's repeated injunction that the only way an individual man could fuse with his fellows was through social institutions. Although desiring a more equitable distribution of the wealth produced by the new technology, they did not stop with material consideration. To preserve the integrity of "souls" suffocating in the impersonal fog of the market system, to eliminate the evils so inextricably bound up with industrialism, these seemed to them the most pressing responsibilities of the reformer.

Their sensitiveness to the blights caused by the industrial revolution and to capitalistic methods is the trait that distinguishes them most sharply from their thicker-skinned contemporaries. The shabby and sordid slums, creeping like an infection across the face of their cities, repelled them. So did the intemperance and pauperism and vice that inevitably accompanied the overcrowding of towns and deadened human sympathies. This revulsion, aesthetic as much as ethical, turned them toward reform at a time when community obligations were increasingly ignored and successful go-getters justified themselves by drawing false analogies from Darwin. In a sense these men were artists appalled by a disorderly world and driven by some kind of creative compulsion to reshape it and give it meaning. As Lester Ward observed with his usual acuteness,

> if the social artist is moved more by pain to be relieved than by pleasure to be enjoyed in his ideal society, this is only a difference of degree, since there can be no doubt that one of the strongest motives to creative art is the pain caused by the defects, maladjustments, discords, jars, and eyesores that the real world constantly inflicts upon the hypersensitive organization of the artist.

It was this aesthetic aspect of the reformist impulse that William Morris felt in himself, but which he failed to detect in American reformers like Edward Bellamy. "The only ideal of life which such a man can see," Morris concluded in a review of *Looking Backward,* "is that of the industrious *professional* middle-class men of today purified from their crimes of complicity with the monopolist class, and become independent instead of being, as they are now, parasitical." There is a good deal of justice in such a statement, as anyone familiar with the character and personality of George or Bellamy or Howells or Lloyd can attest; capitalism and its fruits made them morally uneasy. And yet who would attribute their zeal and unselfishness, their association with unpopular causes merely to a queasy conscience?

Most of the progressives, of course, were not extremists and malcontents camped outside the bastions of respectable society. Their programs must in no way be construed as incendiary attacks against private property or the family or the state. Society, they felt, needed to be reformed, to be brought into closer correspondence with American democratic precepts; it did not need to be uprooted. To conserve the best and eradicate the wrong, to redirect the social energies without disturbing fundamental social laws, to maintain an open society and to oppose the tendencies in national life that made for rigid class stratifications, these were the real aims of most of the reformers. If their proposals sounded revolutionary (as, in certain respects, they certainly were), their objectives were conservative in the sense that they were intended to provide stability in an insecure social order.

The progressives conceived of themselves as mediators reconciling the interests of the exploited and the exploiters and seeing to it that the America so enthusiastically pictured by the intoxicated booster should more closely approximate his roseate description. With a few exceptions they shared the general optimism of the day, not because they felt the laws were perfect, as Andrew Carnegie did, but because they had faith in the resources of human nature and a profound belief in the limitless power of the unfettered individual. This optimism, if excessive, was not unreflective. It rested on a conviction that something could be done with the stuff of the world and with man who molded it. Their vision of the good society made them angry and impatient with the men and forces who they felt prevented its emergence. But they never ceased their agitation nor doubted the final victory. Their affirmations grew out of knowledge and experience, out of defeat and humiliation.

Although the progressives carried on their programs with an untroubled assurance that their values were sound and their goals attainable, they rarely sentimentalized human nature or failed to consider the inertia of prejudice, ignorance, and viciousness that had to be overcome. For the most part they looked to their own class to provide the shock troops for the battle of reform, since they distrusted both the plutocratic few who had been corrupted by success and the masses of the propertyless who had never been given the opportunity to cultivate their latent virtues. The latter were to be the trusted citizens of the future, but until they demonstrated their God-given capacities, the reformers refused to celebrate them uncritically. Yet the reformers never deserted the leaderless majority to whose cause they had consecrated themselves, and they concurred with the spirit of Emerson's fervid condemnation of the apostate-scholar who abandoned his trust:

> Meantime shame to the fop of learning and philosophy who suffers a vulgarity of speech and habit to blind him to the grosser vulgarity of pitiless selfishness, and to hide him from the current of Tendency; who abandons his right position of being priest and poet of these impious and unpoetic doers of God's work. You must, for wisdom, for sanity, have some access to the mind and heart of common humanity. The exclusive excludes himself. No great man has existed who did not rely on the sense and heart of mankind as represented by the good sense of the people, as correcting the modes and over-refinements and class prejudices of the lettered men of the world.

# "A Few Herbs and Apples"

### *by F. O. Matthiessen*

> Heaven walks among us ordinarily muffled in such triple or tenfold disguises that the wisest are deceived and no one suspects the days to be gods.
>
> —Emerson to Margaret Fuller, October 2, 1840.

With Emerson's worst lines in our ears, it might seem hardly profitable to consider him as a poet any further. Yet he himself persisted in that view, and, nearly thirty years after that letter to his wife, still wrote in almost the same terms of his vocation, with no pretension but with quiet certainty: "I am a bard least of bards. I cannot, like them, make lofty arguments in stately, continuous verse, constraining the rocks, trees, animals, and the periodic stars to say my thoughts,—for that is the gift of great poets; but I am a bard because I stand near them, and apprehend all they utter, and with pure joy hear that which I also would say, and, moreover, I speak interruptedly words and half stanzas which have the like scope and aim:—What I cannot declare, yet cannot all withhold."

Emerson, Thoreau, and Whitman all conceived of themselves primarily as poets, though, judged strictly by form, none of them was. All of them would have agreed with Emerson's decree that "it is not metres, but a metre-making argument that makes a poem"; for, with the release of energy in which they shared, they were sure that their content outran the boundaries of earlier conventions of expression. But the writing of poetry becomes inordinately difficult without a living tradition to draw upon and modify. Thoreau and Melville both evolved richly modulated harmonies in their prose rhythms but were able to command far less music when they tried to borrow the more exacting medium of verse, which had hardly yet become acclimated in America.

The want of continuity in Emerson's form was a natural product of what we have seen, the confusing alternation in his experience. The reasons for the cleavage between his "two lives, of the understanding and of the soul," would require a book to establish, a book that could start with the breakdown after Edwards of the Puritan synthesis. Edwards had managed to reunite the two chief strains from the seventeenth century, its logic and its emotion, its hard grasp of fact and its deep capacity for mysticism, but after his death they split apart. The mysticism was caught up into Methodism and the evangelical movement, and was proportionately discredited in the cool eyes of the rationalists, who were Emerson's forerunners in the Unitarianism which he grew to find so inadequate. But with his fresh insistence on idealism, he no longer shared, or wanted to share, in the older dogma. He was a symptom of his age's expansiveness—but here would have to come another chapter, which would deal with the increasingly violent divergence between the world of transcendentalism and that of the industrial revolution. Emerson understood some of the consequences of this latter split, and dwelt on the acute difficulties of the thinker in making vital contact with a rapidly changing society.[1] He declared, "Our relations to each other are oblique and casual," a condition that Hawthorne regarded far more seriously as he examined the tragic effects of isolation. Emerson went on to say, in the same essay on "Experience": "Well, souls never touch their objects . . . There is an optical illusion about every person we meet . . . The individual is always mistaken. It turns out somewhat new and very unlike what he promised himself." Even here he was still serene in his confidence in ultimate truth; but Melville saw in those very facts the sources of ambiguity that so goaded and tormented him in *Pierre*.

Emerson concluded that a frontal attack could not overcome the discrepancy between the world of fact and the world that man thinks. For that reason in particular the symbol came to possess supreme value for him, since it enabled him to transcend the gap between these worlds. The quality that he continually ascribed to its power was that of "indirection." As he expressed it in a favorite figure, "The gods like indirect names and dislike to be named directly." [2] A similar feeling is frequent in Whitman. Contemplating the overwhelming variety of the continent, he said in his first preface: "For such the expression of the American poet is to be transcendent and new. It is to be indirect and not direct or descriptive or epic." [3] This feeling was due in part to the realization by both poets that the word was finally inadequate to cover the thing, that there always remained a revelation beyond. Their exaltation of content over form,

[1] See his comment on the problem of the artist in an age of Property, *American Renaissance,* p. 143.

[2] He found one of his chief texts for indirection in Zoroaster: "It is not proper to understand the Intelligible with vehemence, but if you incline your mind, you will apprehend it: not too earnestly, but bringing a pure and inquiring eye. You will not understand it as when understanding some particular thing, but with the flower of the mind." Emerson pronounced this a statement of fact "which every lover and seeker of truth will recognize."

[3] See for the fuller discussion of Whitman's indirection, *American Renaissance,* pp. 519, 575.

their belief that expression was, to use Shelley's phrase, but "a fading coal" in comparison with the moment of inspiration, inevitably led them to affirm that reality could be caught only tangentially, and conveyed obliquely.[4]

In Emerson's case the value of indirection was more heavily weighted still, since he secured by means of it the one kind of continuity that he knew. When he said, "Everything in the universe goes by indirection," he proceeded to develop his conviction that the only way in which his mind could gain knowledge from experience was not by worrying it with analysis, but by unquestioning immersion in the flow of every day, thus penetrating the mystery by living it. This process was what he meant in saying that "we learn nothing rightly until we learn the symbolical character of life." [5] Only by such knowledge could he bring the two separated halves of his consciousness into unity. He tried again and again to recount his actual steps. The first movement was to lie open and fallow, responding to the belief that man "is great only by being passive to the superincumbent spirit." He described this state under many guises, for instance in these sentences in a letter, the relaxed rhythm of which suggests what the sensation gave him:

> Gray clouds, short days, moonless nights, a drowsy sense of being dragged easily somewhere by that locomotive Destiny, which, never seen, we yet know must be hitched on to the cars wherein we sit,—that is all that appears in these November weeks. Let us hope that, as often as we have defamed days which turned out to be benefactors, and were whispering oracles . . . so this may prove a profitable time.

Only through thus yielding himself to a trust in the hours as they pass could a man then "put his ear close by himself and hold his breath and listen." [6] And in that way only could he come finally to share in the active element, to escape the limitations of his private self and feel that he was swept by a force beyond his will, that he obeyed "that redundancy or

[4] The excesses of vagueness and obscurity into which this transcendental doctrine can run are only too apparent. They are mocked thus by Poe: "Above all, study innuendo. Hint everything—assert nothing. If you feel inclined to say 'bread and butter,' do not by any means say it outright. You may say any and every thing *approaching* to 'bread and butter.' You may hint at buckwheat cake, or you may even go so far as to insinuate oatmeal porridge, but if bread and butter be your real meaning, be cautious, my *dear* Miss Psyche, not on any account to say 'bread and butter.' "

[5] The passage continues: "Day creeps after day, each full of facts, dull, strange, despised things, that we cannot enough despise,—call heavy, prosaic and desert. The time we seek to kill: the attention it is elegant to divert from things around us. And presently the aroused intellect finds gold and gems in one of these scorned facts,—then finds that the day of facts is a rock of diamonds; that a fact is an Epiphany of God."

[6] This aim of Montaigne's was quoted admiringly by Emerson in his first letter to Carlyle.

excess of life which in conscious beings we call *ecstasy*." Such ecstasy in its flood-tide of abandonment was, as we have seen, Emerson's conception of genius. His process of entering into possession of its power has been regarded by many as an incomplete pseudo-mysticism, and the conception itself may be judged a specially innocent kind of romantic spontaneity. It may cause some readers to take at its face value his observation to Margaret Fuller that he could discern no essential difference between the experience of his boyhood and that of his maturity, that he

> had never been otherwise than indolent, never strained a muscle, and only saw a difference in the circumstance, not in the man; at first a circle of boys—my brothers at home, with aunt and cousins, or the schoolroom; all agreed that my verses were obscure nonsense; and now a larger public say the same thing, "obscure nonsense," and yet both conceded that the boy had wit. A little more excitement now, but the fact identical, both in my consciousness and in my relations.

Yet that unchanging identity beneath all seeming contradictions and inconsistencies is also Emerson's peculiar integrity, and gives the chief value to the life recorded in his journals. Its essential quality came to indirect expression in "Days" (1851), which, as he himself thought, is the best of his poems:

> Daughters of Time, the hypocritic Days,
> Muffled and dumb like barefoot dervishes,
> And marching single in an endless file,
> Bring diadems and fagots in their hands.
> To each they offer gifts after his will,
> Bread, kingdoms, stars, and sky that holds them all.
> I, in my pleached garden, watched the pomp,
> Forgot my morning wishes, hastily
> Took a few herbs and apples, and the Day
> Turned and departed silent. I, too late,
> Under her solemn fillet saw the scorn.

This vision of an Oriental procession through his Concord garden rose into words with such singular completeness that he commented upon it:

> I find one state of mind does not remember or conceive of another state. Thus I have written within a twelvemonth verses ("Days") which I do not remember the composition or correction of, and could not write the like to-day, and have only, for proof of their being mine, various external evidences, as the MS. in which I find them. . . .

To be thus caught up and possessed was what he believed the sign of the real poet. He repeated often, and, indeed, wrote in his own copy of his *Poems,* as a motto to "Bacchus," Plato's saying that "the man who is his own master knocks in vain at the doors of poetry." He went so far in his belief in the selfless release of creation as to say, "The muse may be defined, *Supervoluntary ends effected by supervoluntary means*"—a theory to be developed, in ways unforseen by Emerson, by modern poets of the unconscious.

Supervoluntary or not, what he said here in a single sustained paragraph of blank verse corresponds to what he tried to say on literally dozens of other occasions. He had even made an approach to the central image of the poem more than a decade earlier, in the sentence to Margaret Fuller quoted as the epigraph to this section.[7] Four years before he composed the poem, he wrote on the eve of his birthday: "The days come and go like muffled and veiled figures sent from a distant friendly party, but they say nothing, and if we do not use the gifts they bring, they carry them as silently away." Six years after the poem he not only used its metaphor in "Works and Days," but actually developed it into the theme of that entire essay. Looser variations of the image appear in verse in the final lines of "Saadi" (1842), as well as in "May-Day" (1865), and can be traced to an earliest version in a quatrain in the journal for 1831.[8]

What distinguishes "Days" from all these and other partial efforts is that Emerson's gift for swift and fragile images has for once been reinforced by the extension and enlargement of his metaphor into a parable. The poem possesses more concentrated clarity than the essay, though exactly what it enunciates, and the importance of that content for Emerson, can be seen most adequately against the long background of its preparation. In one sense that may be held a limitation, since the best poetry speaks most fully for itself, without need of support from biography. But the point is not that "Days" is obscure, but simply that it will shine more luminously in its proper setting. One reason why Emerson managed here to create a rounded and abiding form is that the thought and feeling of the parable rose from the central dilemma in his way of life. You could arrange under the rubric of its theme a thick anthology from his work, for it expresses the rhythm of his existence from at least his twen-

[7] A letter to his wife in 1846 contained this variant: "But though days go smoothly enough they do not bring me in their fine timely wallets the alms I incessantly beg of them. Where are the melodies, where the unattainable words . . . ?" This suggests a partial source for Emerson's procession in Shakespeare's *Troilus and Cressida,* in the magnificent personification of Time with

a wallet at his back,
Wherein he puts alms for oblivion.

[8] The days pass over me
And I am still the same;
The aroma of my life is gone
Like the flower with which it came.

tieth year, when he tried to voice it: "The worst is, that the ebb is certain, long and frequent, while the flow comes transiently and seldom." This mood could impinge with much greater intensity. In his hunger for abundance he could feel, as Thoreau was also to do, that life wastes itself while we are preparing to live, that "on the brink of the waters of life and truth, we are miserably dying."

He cast this conviction into several different images. At times he felt that he and his contemporaries were re-enacting the myth of Tantalus, again that they were like millers on the lower levels of a stream where the factories above had diverted the water. His only solution was to accept wholeheartedly the potentiality of what each day might bring. Shortly after his year in Europe and with the future still uncertain before him, he wrote to Carlyle that he rejoiced in his example, in the fact that "one living scholar is self-centered, and will be true to himself." He also said, "Possessing my liberty, I am determined to keep it, at the risk of uselessness (which God can very well abide)." Such a course was sufficiently rare in America with its press of competition and its demand for conformity to some practical occupation. As Cooper had pointed out with irony, his countrymen found no room for a class of "learned idlers." Carlyle knew the hazards involved for his friend, and was struck by his quiet tenacity: "It is not one of your smallest qualities in my mind, that you *can* wait so quietly and let the years do their hest . . . Sit still at Concord." [9]

From the time of his very earliest passages of self-analysis we can see him feeling his way to the realization that his kind of truth was to come through inaction and hope, through waiting for moments of illumination. But he sometimes regarded this tendency with misgiving: "There is a dreaminess about my mode of life (which may be a depravity) which loosens the tenacity of what should be most tenacious—this my grasp on heaven and earth. I am the servant more than the master of my fates."

[9] The view taken of Emerson by the respectable was summed up by John Quincy Adams in 1840: "The sentiment of religion is at this time, perhaps, more potent and prevailing in New England than in any other portion of the Christian world. For many years since the establishment of the theological school at Andover, the Calvinists and Unitarians have been battling with each other upon the atonement, the divinity of Jesus Christ and the Trinity. This has now very much subsided; but other wandering of mind takes the place of that, and equally lets the wolf into the fold. A young man, named Ralph Waldo Emerson, and a classmate of my lamented son George, after failing in the everyday avocations of a Unitarian preacher and schoolmaster, starts a new doctrine of transcendentalism, declares all the old revelations superannuated and worn out, and announces the approach of new revelations and prophecies. Garrison and the non-resistant abolitionists, Brownson and the Marat democrats, phrenology and animal magnetism, all come in, furnishing each some plausible rascality as an ingredient for the bubbling cauldron of religion and politics." After the scandal of the Divinity School Address, Emerson was not invited to lecture in Harvard's halls again for thirty years. Following the Civil War, when transcendentalism could no longer be thought dangerous, he was chosen one of the Harvard Board of Overseers.

Ten years later than this entry he was writing to his brother Edward (1834): "Here we sit, always learning, and never coming to the knowledge of." Yet the "apathy" and "indolence" which he so often bewailed may well have been his unconscious protection against the terrible stimulus of nervous Yankee life. And even in the midst of his moods of regret that the days were slipping past without fulfilment, he did not doubt that his course was right. Out of the depth of his consent to his lot welled up the opposite mood, his dilation in response to the flux. His enunciation of this mood is very like some of Melville's passages about standing the mast-head. Particularly in a letter that Emerson wrote from Nantasket in the summer of 1841 do his rhythms seem affected by the soothing monotonous movement of the waves as well as by his having just been re-reading Plato: "But is it the picture of the unbounded sea, or is it the lassitude of the Syrian summer, that more and more draws the cords of Will out of my thought and leaves me nothing but perpetual observation, perpetual acquiescence and perpetual thankfulness. Shall I not be Turk and fatalist before to-day's sun shall set? and in this thriving New England too, full of din and snappish activity and invention and wilfulness."

His positive doctrine could thus be reduced to the single command, "Hear what the morning says and believe that." But he was always alternating back to the other mood. He declared that a man has not learned anything until he knows that "every day is Doomsday"—but what of the judgment upon him if it has dragged by with nothing done? He was ever being distracted by the disproportion between the means and the end, by the feeling that "we are always getting ready to live, but never living." There were so many years of education and earning a livelihood, of routine and sickness and travel, but "very little life in a lifetime . . . a few, few hours in the longest." In that state of mind all of existence seemed a disguise that he could not penetrate. Moreover, even when he was flooded with power, he had to confess to an inability to handle it. He continued in his letter from Nantasket: "Can you not save me, dip me into ice water, find me some girding belt, that I glide not away into a stream or a gas, and decease in infinite diffusion?" For no less than Melville did he recognize the peril of being drowned in the "honey-head of Plato," as he went on to say: "Noah's flood and the striae which the good geologist finds on every mountain and rock seem to me the records of a calamity less universal than this metaphysical flux which threatens every enterprise, every thought and every thinker. How high will this Nile, this Mississippi, this Ocean, rise, and will ever the waters be stayed?"

Thus he could alternate his metaphor that "we are always on the brink of an ocean of thought into which we do not yet swim," with this other metaphor, which expresses his realization that, even on the rare occasions when he was immersed, he was swept by currents beyond his control. Inundated by a new revelation, he felt that he lacked the ability to articulate it. His escape from the practical restrictions of his age had been so complete, the freedom of his consciousness was so absolute, that he sensed the need of some strict challenge to bring him back into manageable dimensions. Put in terms of artistic expression, the want of coherence between his understanding and his reason, his feeling that he was either parched or drowned, meant that he lacked the tension between form and liberation, between abandon and restraint. Coleridge knew that the power of art lay in reconciliation of these very opposites. Margaret Fuller was commenting on the absence of this dynamic struggle in Emerson when she said: "It is a fine day for composition, were it not in Concord. But I trow the fates which gave this place Concord, took away the animating influences of Discord. Life here slumbers and steals on like the river. A very good place for a sage, but not for the lyrist or the orator."

Emerson's belief in the ballast of experience and his belief that experience is illusory; his trust in the fullness of the moment and his sense that the moment eluded him, and his Puritanic scruple at the waste; his sense of being on the verge of a great discovery and of being inadequate to grasp it—all lie behind "Days." One weakness of his poems that he deplored was that they did not contain sufficient evidence of the "polarity" of existence, of how its inevitable law is action and reaction, of how every statement contains the seed of its opposite. He said: "I am always insincere, as always knowing there are other moods." But in this poem there is for once set up the implication of counterstatement, which adds the density of real experience. These lines express his misgiving at his failure to rise to his opportunity, to enter into possession of the transcendent kingdom of stars and sky that has been stretched out before him. This feeling deepens into guilt as hieratic scorn confronts him for penetrating too late the disguise of appearance, for blindly neglecting to abandon himself at once to the mysteries of the Reason. But if this was his conscious intention in the poem, its undertone conveys something else. The symbol that he uses for the choice he made does not share in the ugliness of wrong. His instinctive taking of the few herbs and apples is the fitting expression for his spontaneous trust in the amplitude to man's needs of his immediate surroundings. The beauty that he sees is again in the commonest forms of nature. His clinging to this frail harvest, even though he regrets it, is what empowers him here to suggest the poignant complexity of his existence. By means of his parable he has been true to both halves of his consciousness and has set going a dynamic tension between them. In recompense he has received a gift: not of asserting the final Unity through dozens of monotonous lines, but of creating a variegated, if delicate, poetic whole.

# Emerson on the Organic Principle in Art

*by Norman Foerster*

## I

One could not desire a better instance of the need of defining critical terms than is afforded by a comparison of Poe's and of Emerson's definition of art. Since Poe defined poetry as "the rhythmical creation of beauty," he would necessarily have defined art in general as "the creation of beauty." Now, although Emerson's view of art is in striking contrast with Poe's, he begins with these very words. In his first book, *Nature,* he says, "The creation of beauty is Art." What does he mean?

In the Introduction to *Nature* Emerson inaugurates his career as a writer with the Aristotelian distinction between art and nature and between useful and fine art. Expanding these distinctions, he discusses Nature in section I, useful art in section II (Commodity), and fine art in section III (Beauty). The love of beauty, or Taste, exists in various degrees in all men; the creation of beauty, or Art, is the capacity of the few. These few, not content with admiring beauty, "seek to embody it in new forms"—to combine the innumerable forms of nature in such wise as to show that they are fundamentally the same. For "nature is a sea of forms radically alike," and "gliding through the sea of form" is that which makes the forms alike. Beauty.[1] Beauty is an ultimate end, "eternal beauty,"—"God is the all-fair." It cannot, therefore, as Emerson says elsewhere, be defined, lying, like Truth, beyond the limits of the "understanding."

But if we cannot define eternal beauty, we can indicate with some definiteness what we mean by "the creation of beauty." Much as the artist loves the manifold things of nature, he intuitively perceives that their differences are of small account, that, penetrated with his thought, they are all alike. "A leaf, a sunbeam, a landscape, the ocean, make an analogous impression on the mind." It is this intuition, this spiritual activity within the artist's mind, that is fundamental. Thought is supreme, and

"Emerson on the Organic Principle in Art." From *PMLA,* XLI (1926), 193-208. Reprinted by permission of the author and *PMLA.*

[1] The imagery is from the Neo-Platonist Proclus, "Beauty swims on the light of forms," quoted in *Journals,* 1843, page 436.

nature is only its vehicle, as Emerson asserts at length in the fourth section of *Nature* (Language). The objects of nature are symbols of our thought; "the whole of nature is a metaphor of the human mind." It is the office of the artist, not to know unity in unity, but to show unity in variety. He must relate the two worlds, connect his thought with an appropriate symbol or mass of symbols. If he dwells at the heart of reality, indeed, he finds all symbols expressive of all meanings. "In the transmission of the heavenly waters," Emerson writes in *Representative Men,* "every hose fits every hydrant"; or, to return to *Nature,* we may see in Shakespeare a sovereign mastery of the world of symbols: "His imperial muse tosses the creation like a bauble from hand to hand, and uses it to embody any caprice of thought that is uppermost in his mind. The remotest spaces of nature are visited, and the farthest sundered things are brought together, by a subtile spiritual connection." His symbols, literally "far-fetched," fit the thought perfectly, like print and seal. It is the lesser poets, whose symbols and thought are ill related, that give us figures far-fetched in the usual sense. The great poet shows the equivalence of symbolical value; he can reveal spiritual meaning, or beauty, in all of nature. To him there is no ugly, for what we call the ugly is merely that which is viewed alone—the "Each" seen out of relation with the "All." He takes the objects of nature, any objects of nature, unfixes them, "makes them revolve around the axis of his primary thought, and disposes them anew." That is "the creation of beauty."

Again and again, in the series of volumes that follows *Nature,* Emerson returns to these ideas, fully elaborating if not quite defining them. His favorite approach may be indicated by saying that he regarded all great art as organic expression.

This fruitful biological analogy, which had its origin in Plato and Aristotle but was submerged or ignored in the centuries that followed, was revived early in the romantic movement, and has been prominent ever since, markedly in the aesthetic of Benedetto Croce. Emerson doubtless encountered it in various places—in Coleridge at the least. In Coleridge, too, Poe probably encountered it, without being impressed; for although Poe asserts that Shelley contained his own law, in the main he thought of artistic laws as being consciously evolved by the critic and consciously applied—almost mechanically applied—by the artist. To Emerson, on the other hand, it was a fundamental conception capable of answering all our questions about the nature and practice of art. It is true that in his own writing, his own practice of art, Emerson was notoriously deficient in the organic law in its formal aspect; his essays and poems are badly organized, the parts having no definite relation to each other and the wholes wanting that unity which we find in the organisms of nature. Rarely does he give us even a beginning, middle, and end, which is the very least that we expect of an organism, which, indeed, we expect of a mechanism. Yet if he could not observe the law of organic form, he could interpret it; in this matter his practice and his theory are not equivalent—happily, he could see more than he could do. Moreover, he could both see and exemplify the workings of the organic law in its qualitative aspect. He is the friend and aider of those who would live in the spirit, because of his insight—rare in these times of inner disharmony—into the life of the spirit, and because of his power to speak as one having authority. Whatever the lapses into caprice and wilfulness of which he was guilty, in the main he makes us feel that his utterance proceeds from a transcendent reality.

Like Schlegel and Coleridge, Emerson distinguishes between the organic and the mechanic. The conception of beauty to which the preceding century tended, that it is "outside embellishment," he decisively rejects. Seeking analogies in nature, he reminds us that grace of outline and movement, as in the cat and the deer, are produced by a happily proportioned skeleton, and that "the tint of the flower proceeds from its root, and the lustres of the sea-shell begin with its existence." The difference between mechanical construction and organic form, he writes in the *Journals,*

> . . . is the difference between the carpenter who makes a box, and the mother who bears a child. The box was all in the carpenter; but the child was not all in the parents. They knew no more of the child's formation than they did of their own. They were merely channels through which the child's nature flowed from quite another and eternal power, and the child is as much a wonder to them as to any; and, like the child Jesus, shall, as he matures, convert and guide them as if he were the parent.

The doctrine of the organic, though it does not appear in the earliest writing of Emerson, was readily assimilated into the idealism with which he began. Thus in *Nature* the way is already prepared in such a Neo-Platonic passage as this:

> There seems to be a necessity in spirit to manifest itself in material forms; and day and night, river and storm, beast and bird, acid and alkali, pre-exist in necessary Ideas in the mind of God, and are what they are by virtue of preceding affections in the world of spirit. A Fact is the end or last issue of spirit.

The emanation which here explains the concrete facts of nature is paralleled by the inspiration which, in Emerson's philosophy of art, explains the concrete work of art. Fact and poem alike spring from the creative spirit, and the poet, as the romantic critics liked to say, repeats in the finite the creative process of the Infinite Creator, and is the agent of that Creator. So long as he is a faithful agent and reports truly his high message, his verse is necessary and universal. Intuition and expression alike are dictated by that supreme Life or Spirit, and so are organic in the profoundest sense. Spirit expresses itself in the poet's intuition, and the poet's intuition expresses itself in the words and music of the poem. Spirit gives the divine hint to the poet, and the poet passes it on to all men, using a form that is excellent in proportion as it is determined by the hint itself, not arbitrarily devised by the poet. "For it is not metres, but a metre-making argument that makes a poem,—a thought so passionate and alive that like the spirit of a plant or an animal it has an architecture of its own, and adorns nature with a new thing." Thus the poem, we may say—though Emerson does not use the terms—has organic beauty in a twofold sense, qualitatively and quantitatively. That is, it derives a qualitative beauty from the relative depth of the intuition or hint which the poet possessed, and a quantitative beauty from the degree of success with which he externalized, or expressed concretely, this intuition. If Emerson nowhere states his meaning quite so definitely, it is nevertheless plain that this distinction exists implicitly in his text. We are clarifying his sense, not distorting it.

Which of the two, quality or quantity, interested him the more needs no shrewd guess—he was engrossed in organic quality, as Poe was in mechanical quantity. Yet if he does not say much about the explication of the intuition, what he does say is well worth dwelling upon.

## II

The law of the organic or necessary regarded quantitatively requires above all that there be a fitness of means to end. It holds not only of physical nature—the cell of the bee, the bone of the bird, having this perfect adaptation—but equally of spiritual nature—of the architect's building, of the poem. Emerson quotes Michelangelo's definition of art as "the purgation of superfluities" and holds that in artistic structures as in natural structures not a particle may be spared. The simplest expression, the severest economy, is the test of beauty of means. "We ascribe beauty to that . . . which exactly answers its end." There must be no fumbling with words, no acceptance of the nearly fit, no satisfaction in the rhythm that may be sung but does not sing itself, no embellishment, no laying on of colors, but the work of art must perfectly represent its thought. "Fitness is so inseparable an accompaniment of beauty that it has been taken for it"—beauty is more than fitness, but must include fitness. Wanting that, the poem, the picture, the sculpture, however high it may aim, will be frustrate, of negligible effect on the reader or beholder. Having fitness, it will stir men forever. All the great works of art, whatever the intuition they embody, have this perfect adaptation of means to end.

So intimate, indeed, is this adaptation in the work of the supreme artists that we shall try in vain to separate intuition and expression: here Emerson in large measure anticipates the expressionist criticism of Signor Croce. What form should the poet give to his intuition? Let him "ask the fact for the form. For a verse is not a vehicle to carry a sentence as a jewel is carried in a case: the verse must be alive, and inseparable from its contents, as the soul of man inspires and directs the body." The superior poem is unanalyzable; word and thought cannot be severed. But in the inferior poem they fall apart, and we can distinguish between the vaguely held thought and the awkward or conventional expression. In any poem, we can measure the degree of inspiration by the degree of necessity in the expression. In the ideal poem, this necessity is absolute, down to the single word. "There is always a right word, and every other than that is wrong," Emerson inscribed in his journal when he was but twenty-eight years old, long before Flaubert announced this austere doctrine. Not by calculation, by conscious selection, does the master find the right word: "There is no choice of words for him who clearly sees the truth. That provides him with the best word." "The master rushes to deliver his thought, and the words and images fly to him to express it; whilst colder moods are forced to respect the ways of saying it, and insinuate, or, as it were, muffle the fact to suit the poverty or caprice of their expression, so that they only hint the matter, or allude to it, being unable to fuse and mould their words and images to fluid obedience." The poet seeks to marry music to thought, "believing, as we believe of all marriage, that matches are made in heaven, and that for every thought its proper melody exists, though the odds are immense against our finding it, and only genius can rightly say the banns." "The poet works to an end above his will, and by means, too, which are out of his will. . . . The muse may be defined, Supervoluntary ends effected by supervoluntary means." In such passages as these Emerson anticipates the profoundest reaches of recent æsthetics.

Yet on one point he is curiously inconsistent. While holding this conception of the inseparableness of content and vehicle, Emerson was well pleased with translations, which are virtually a denial of this conception. One need not speak very strictly to say that the precious life-blood of a master-spirit cannot be successfully transfused; obviously, those who would really commune with the master must partake of his body and blood directly. The intuition that has been expressed we can experience only through its expression; for the translation is the equivalent, not of the original intuition, but of the translator's intuition, and between the two there is commonly a wide difference. Accordingly, Thoreau, for example, says that he does not read the classics in translations, for there are none; and he knows his Homer in Greek, long after college days. His friend Emerson, on the contrary, virtually loses his Greek, and although eager to do justice to Goethe, learns German reluctantly—as when Margaret Fuller administers five or six private lessons in that robust language, "rather against my will." Some years later he writes in his journal that to him the command is loud to read foreign books in translation, since not to do so would be as foolish as to forego the use of railroad and telegraph, or, as he says in *Society and Solitude,* to swim across the Charles River to Boston instead of using the bridge. To tell the truth, Emerson was never the scholar, in our rather than his sense of the term; he shrank from the labor of mastering a language, a mere instrument, and his view of translation is perhaps not so much the statement of conviction as the expression of temperament.

With this abatement, which subtracts little, Emerson set forth clearly the inalienable unity of thought and word, thought and music, thought and color, and the consequent law that the degree of inspiration may be measured by the work's approximation to this unity. Given a certain intuition, how completely has it been realized?—This must be our first question in the criticism of art, though not, as romantic critics have often assumed, the only question. The answer to this question will determine the quantitative beauty of the work of art; but there remains the question of qualitative beauty.

## III

When Emerson says that the beauty of a work of art is "ever in proportion to the depth of thought"; when he says that "the Poet should not only be able to use nature as his hieroglyphic, but he should have a still higher power, namely, an adequate message to communicate; a vision fit for such a faculty," he avails himself of a standard of criticism that has to do with the kind, rather than the degree, of inspiration and expression. It is not enough that the poet should receive impressions and express them; he should question the authority of his impressions, whether inferior or superior, as his reader will likewise do. For, as Emerson declares when speaking of the impressionable, myriad-minded Goethe, "It is not more the office of man to receive all impressions, than it is to distinguish sharply between them." In the criticism of art we are to consider, then, not only exterior excellence, the virtue of explication, but also, and even more, interior excellence, the virtue of reality. The beauty of a work of art resides in both, and is supreme when there is a synthesis of perfect quality and quantity. This synthesis we find, for example, in Michelangelo, of whom Emerson writes that "Beauty in the largest sense, beauty inward and outward, comprehending grandeur as a part, and reaching to goodness as its soul—this to receive and this to import, was his genius."

The vital source of this fusion is ideal Nature. It is by taking a central position in the universe, by submitting to the guidance of Nature, and helping her, so to speak, to make herself known, that the poet attains his triumphs. Art imitates Nature—ἡ τέχνη μιμεῖται τὴν φύσιν—this doctrine, substantially in Aristotle's sense, Emerson teaches, most fully in the essay on Art in *Society and Solitude,* at the beginning of which his topic is art in its wide meaning, as embracing both fine art and useful art. "The universal soul," he writes, "is the alone creator of the useful and the beautiful; therefore to make anything useful or beautiful, the individual must be submitted to the universal mind. . . . Art must be a complement to Nature." That this is true of the useful arts may be seen at a glance; the airplane, to take an example that would have delighted Emerson, is useful, practicable, if it embodies a sort of continuation of nature's law, and fatally useless if it contradicts that law. Likewise "in art that aims at beauty must the parts be subordinated to Ideal Nature, and everything individual subtracted, so that it shall be the production of the universal soul." Hence the doctrine of necessity, which affirms that in the great poem what was written must be written; when you first hear it you feel that it was "copied out of some invisible tablet in the Eternal mind." To Shakespeare writing his plays, Emerson remarks finely, his thought must have come to him with the authority of familiar truth, "as if it were already a proverb and not hereafter to become one."

Art is therefore not idle play, nor a pleasurable expressive activity, but an arrestment and fixation of reality. For Poe, Wordsworth was far too solemn in his view of poetry as aiming at truth; for Emerson, he was not serious enough. In his enthusiasm for poetry's lovely revelation of truth, he tells himself in his *Journals* that poetry is "the only verity," adding, "Wordsworth said of his Ode it was poetry, but he did not know it was the only truth." The term "realism" or "realism in literature" recurs in the *Journals*; Emerson desires, as ardently as any modern realistic novelist, that literature shall give us that of which we can say with the fullest conviction that it *is*. But he will by no means deny reality to the ideal. Even while in college, writing a Bowdoin dissertation, he approvingly quoted Burke's assertion that "Nature is never more truly herself than in her grandest forms; the Apollo of Belvedere is as much in nature as any figure from the pencil of Rembrandt, or any clown in the rustic revels of Teniers." He might have substituted, "*more* in nature"; for he adopted, then or later, the classical conception of the ideal in art. For example, though never a lover of Aristotle, he reproduces in his *Journals* the dictum that poetry is more philosophical and higher than history (more *true* is Emerson's word), attributing it, however, to Plato.[2] He is apparently repeating Aristotle again when he adjudges tragedy higher than the epic; and once more when he praises such statesmen as Pitt, Burke, and Webster, because [italics Emerson's] "They do not act as unto *men as they are,* but *to men as they ought to be,* and as some are." His view of art was remote from the equalitarian tendencies of modern realism, which inclines to find its reality in that which is most obviously widespread; it was selective, aristocratic, holding the best to be the realest of realities—men as they ought to be, and as some are.

[2] This is corrected in another journal passage a quarter of a century later. Cf. *Journals,* 1834, 255, and 1861, 296.

## IV

His debt was far greater, however, to Plato and the Platonists. Of the many doctrines that he owed mainly to them, perhaps the most important is the doctrine of inspiration, which winds its golden course in and out of nearly every poem and essay that Emerson wrote. Aristotle, even when interpreted generously, must have seemed to him too external in his conception of poetry; for ideal imitation is yet imitation, and therefore inferior in inwardness to the Platonic conception of inspiration. He suffered no delusion as to the light in which Plato himself viewed the poet's inspiration, but like many another Platonist chose to disregard the philosopher's disparagement of the poet's unconscious activity. He was content that the poet should be philosophic without being a philosopher:

> The universal nature, too strong for the petty nature of the bard, sits on his neck and writes through his hand; so that when he seems to vent a mere caprice and wild romance, the issue is an exact allegory. Hence Plato said that "poets utter great and wise things which they do not themselves understand."

Nor does he hesitate to quote Oliver Cromwell as saying that "A man never rises so high as when he knows not whither he is going." Mystical in his idea of truth, Emerson set small store by "knowing" and "understanding," as these are usually regarded. "I am gently mad myself," he confides to Carlyle after referring to the Transcendental reformers, no doubt secretly persuaded that his was a divine madness. It is true that five years later he felt that mysticism had been rather overdone, and that it ought to go out of style for a long time "after this generation"—a reservation that fortunately left him free to be inspired and to follow his genius as of old. And perhaps he was right; perhaps we ought occasionally to indulge a whole generation of mystics, in order to see, as Whitman might put it, what can be done "in that line."

From universal nature sitting on his neck, the poet derives his power. "Beyond the energy of his possessed and conscious intellect he is capable of a new energy (as of an intellect doubled on itself), by abandonment to the nature of things." He must speak somewhat wildly—"wildly well" says Poe—and with his mind used not as an organ or instrument but "released from all service and suffered to take its direction from its celestial life." Using a symbol significantly different from Plato's charioteer and horses, Emerson pictures the poet as a lost traveler who throws up the reins and trusts to the horse's instinct to guide him aright. The Platonic charioteer has abdicated, and there is but one horse, half black and half white, half celestial and half earthy, and there is no saying which half is leading the way, or whither it is carrying him! This apparent preference of abandon to control may be found in conceptual language at the end of the essay on Inspiration, where Emerson says that a chief necessity in life is "the right government" (the phrase is Greek), "or, shall I not say? the right obedience to the powers of the human soul" (which is rather Christian and Transcendental). Consequently Emerson is prepared to praise Michelangelo, for instance, on the ground that he has more abandon than the classical Milton.

Yet while it is true that Emerson leads the casual reader to think of him as urging enthusiasm, obedience to one's genius, without providing for the caprices of romantic emotionalism, it is also true that he does indicate the necessary safeguards. The poet's problem, he writes in his treatise on Poetry and Imagination, is "to unite freedom with precision"; thus, for example, "Dante was free imagination,—all wings,—yet he wrote like Euclid." The inexorable poetic rule is *either inspiration or silence.* "It teaches the enormous force of a few words, and in proportion to the inspiration checks loquacity." Here we have abandon with a difference; here we have a test of inspiration that regards it as valid according to its measure of restraint, a criterion that would make short work of the poets who offer us vaporous expansiveness instead of a truly inspired utterance. Again, there is the passage in the essay on Swedenborg, which most readers fail to connect with the ardors of the popular essay on Self-Reliance:

> The Spirit which is holy, is reserved, taciturn, and deals in laws. . . . The teachings of the high Spirit are abstemious, and, in regard to particulars, negative. Socrates' Genius did not advise him to act or to find, but if he purposed to do somewhat not advantageous, it dissuaded him. "What God is," he said, "I know not: what he is not, I know." The Hindoos have denominated the Supreme Being the "Internal Check." The illuminated Quakers explained their Light, not as somewhat which leads to any action, but it appears as an obstruction to anything unfit. But the right examples are private experiences, which are absolutely at one on this point.

This is Emerson's criticism of the bizarre revelations reported by the Swedish mystic; along with other passages[3] it indicates conclusively that he recognized the need of a principle of restraint in inspiration as the credential of its quality. When he did not expressly insist upon that need, it is plain enough that he assumed it.

Nor does he fail to point out certain spurious intoxications that must be differentiated from the raptures of inspiration—the intoxications of alcohol and opium, and of wild passions, such as those of gaming and war, which "ape" the flames of the gods and are attractive to men who are unwilling to seek genuine inspiration through discipline. He reminds us that the experience of meditative men indicates agreement respecting "the conditions of perception," citing Plato again, to the effect that the

[3] The most explicit is in *The Natural History of Intellect,* pp. 36-37.

perception demands "long familiarity with the objects of intellect, and a life according to the things themselves." Wine, coffee, narcotics, conversation, music, travel, mobs, politics, love, and the like are, he affirms, more or less mechanical substitutes for "the true nectar, which is the ravishment of the intellect by coming nearer to the fact." They do, indeed, release the centrifugal powers of a man, help him out into "free space"; but it is not the heavens that he attains, but "the freedom of baser places," for nature refuses to be tricked. "The sublime vision comes to the pure and simple soul in a clean and chaste body," he writes with the Puritan accent, and draws support from the noblest of all the Puritans, who would allow the lyric poet to drink wine but requires of the epic poet that he live sparely and drink water from a wooden cup. To this page on false intoxications in The Poet, writes Emerson in his journal, is to be appended the confession that "European history is the Age of Wine," an age that is at last waning as the new Age of Water begins. "We shall not have a sincere literature, we shall not have anything sound and grand as Nature itself, until the bread-eaters and water-drinkers come." What Emerson has in mind, of course, is simply the ancient virtues of simplicity and self-control, though he conceives them, it must be acknowledged, rather ascetically.

## V

Closely related with the doctrine of inspiration is the distinction between genius and talent that plays such a large part in the history of romanticism. Although Emerson's distinction between the two terms differs widely from the orthodox romantic distinction, it nevertheless has its romantic aspect, or accent. To his teaching of self-reliance, of obedience to the genius or immanent universal, Emerson frequently gives a twist that all but reverses his actual meaning, inviting a wilfulness and irresponsibility quite alien to his intention. "I would write on the lintels of the door-post, *Whim*," he tells us; and many of his disciples not only would but did and do write it there. "No law can be sacred to me but that of my nature"; this may mean almost anything, and has consequently been interpreted in the sophistical sense dominant throughout the past century and a half. "Insist on yourself; never imitate." Here the diction is such that one naturally infers Emerson's approval of the eccentric man of genius, living from within with no concern for outer consequences. "Is it not the chief disgrace in the world . . . not to yield that peculiar fruit which each man was created to bear . . . ?" Surely we are to be pardoned if we are here reminded of Rousseau's declaration that he was made unlike anybody he had ever seen, and of the monotonous cult of idiosyncrasy that followed that temperamental declaration of independence. "Our moral nature is vitiated by any interference of our will" and people mistakenly "represent virtue as a struggle," writes the genuine "beautiful soul" of Concord; and again we cannot but remember the unbroken succession of dubious beautiful souls from Rousseau down to our own times. In such utterances as these more is involved than mere "accent"; for, after all, accent involves meaning, connotation, and Emerson's man of genius is not without relation to the typical man of genius in the rampant days of the *Geniezeit.*

Having given this modification all the force that it deserves, we are free to say that the stock antithesis between genius and talent is transformed by Emerson into one that is much nearer the truth. "Genius is but a large infusion of Deity." It is inspiration working through the intellect, rather than through will or affection. When, on the other hand, the intellect "would be something of itself" instead of being the agent of the divine, that is talent. Genius looks toward the cause, proceeding from within outward, while talent proceeds from without inward. Genius is organic (here we have the qualitative organic)—it is "the organic motion of the soul" and assumes a union of the man and the high fact; whereas talent is at best in the position of spectator, and at worst is merely "acquainted with the fact on the evidence of third persons." Genius is growth; talent is carpentry. Genius instructs; talent amuses. Genius beholds ideas and utters the necessary and causal; talent derives only power—not light—from above, and finds its models, methods, and ends in society, exhibiting itself instead of revealing what is above itself. Genius is not anomalous, but more like and not less like other men; content with truth, it may seem cold to readers "who have been spiced with the frantic passion and violent coloring of inferior but popular writers" —these latter are the men of talent. Genius is broadly representative, "a larger imbibing of the common heart"; the talent of most writers is, on the other hand, "some exaggerated faculty, some overgrown member, so that their strength is a disease." "Genius is always ascetic. . . . Appetite shows to the finer souls as a disease, and they find beauty in rites and bounds that resist it." Talent, on the other hand, is self-indulgent.

Here are distinctions *ad nauseam;* and indeed it must be confessed that Emerson devoted an excess of attention to these quarreling twins within his mind, recording in his journal that he and Alcott "talked of the men of talent and men of genius and spared nobody" and expressing himself in Transcendental jargon, as when he concludes that "Miss Edgeworth has not *genius,* nor Miss Fuller; but the one has genius-in-narrative, and the other has genius-in-conversation." Nevertheless, however much of "talent" Emerson may display in making these antitheses, the fact remains that he displays "genius" also in his intimate sense of a spiritual activity expressing itself through the happily endowed man when he has prepared for its reception by rising above the low plane of egotism and passion. Moreover, allowance must be made for the time and place in which Emerson sang the praises of genius,—a time of unblushing materialism on the one hand, and of self-indulgent emotionalism on the other, and a country characterized by "a juvenile love of smartness." As Emerson points out in the essay on Goethe, we Americans set great store by mere talent, as the English do, and the French even more. While Poe finds himself sympathetic with the brilliant and logical French mind, Emerson extols the very Germans that Poe ridiculed, on the ground that they have "a habitual reference to interior truth."

> The German intellect wants the French sprightliness, the fine practical understanding of the English, and the American adventure; but it has a certain probity, which never rests in a superficial performance, but asks steadily, *To what end?* A German public asks for a controlling sincerity. Here is activity of thought; but what is it for? What does the man mean? Whence, whence all these thoughts?

In another essay he speaks of the Germans as "those semi-Greeks, who love analogy, and, by means of their height of view, preserve their enthusiasm, and think for Europe." He has in mind their philosophers; but when he considers their poets, he is obliged to say that the chief of them, Goethe, though deserving of ungrudging praise in such an age, is defective because of his worldly gospel of self-culture. "The idea of absolute, eternal truth, without reference to my own enlargement by it, is higher." And for his type of the inspired poetic genius he turns, after all, to the English Shakespeare.

There is an early journal passage in which Shakespeare is compared with a high mountain seen in the morning by the traveler, who deems he may quickly reach it, pass it, and leave it behind, but who, after journeying till nightfall, finds it apparently as far from attainment as in the morning light. The comparison recalls that of Poe, at the opening of his "Letter to B——," where a succession of critics, from the fool onwards, are conceived as occupying ever higher steps on the Andes of the mind, "and so, ascendingly, to a few gifted individuals who kneel around the summit, beholding, face to face, the master spirit who stands upon the pinnacle." But although the comparisons are similar, Poe and Emerson themselves differ widely in their attitude toward the poet. Poe begins his career as a critic with a passage of pseudo-romantic veneration, and then an end—never again does he kneel before the master spirit on the pinnacle. Emerson, beholding the mountain in the morning of his life, studying its lineaments with a rapture akin to that of Keats on first reading Homer, strove toward it all his years. To Shakespeare, Emerson regularly yields supremacy over all other poets and intellects, and it is noteworthy that among his "authorities," in O. W. Holmes's table, Shakespeare easily stands first.

He is superior to all other poets in quantitative beauty; "for executive faculty, for creation, Shakespeare is unique." Before all other poets, he had an intellect responsive to Spirit, so that his expression was organically necessary. Whatever came into his mind, that he could express in the fit terms. His writings everywhere bear the stamp of a divine inevitability. And he is equally superior in qualitative beauty; while able to express anything that he could think, he was also able to think more justly than any other man. His mind ever touched reality, and an almost limitless range of reality. He was always wise, equal to the heights and depths of his argument and all that lay between. He was not Shakespeare but universal man; "an omnipresent humanity co-ordinates all his faculties." He shows no trace of egotism, commits no ostentation, does not harp on one string, like the man of talent. Talent is the severalty of man, genius the universality, and if ever poet had universality it was this modern Proteus. He spoke truth from the inner depths—unconsciously, like Plato's inspired bard. "I value Shakespeare, yes, as a Metaphysician," writes Emerson in a Coleridgean passage, "and admire the unspoken logic which upholds the structure of Iago, Macbeth, Antony, and the rest." And yet, supreme as he is, we can imagine a still loftier poet. Although he gave us a larger subject than had ever existed and pushed human order forward into Chaos; although he was no less than an agent of nature, endowed with an unique power of insight, he was nevertheless wanting in such a high seriousness as befits his capacities, content to serve as the master of revels to mankind instead of employing his powers for the spiritual realization of himself and of humanity, so that he remains, after all, like the grim priests and prophets, a half-man, and we must still await the whole man, the reconciler, the poet-priest, who alone can satisfy the human spirit.

# Emerson

*by Henry B. Parkes*

Throughout the nineteenth century there was a steady deterioration in the tone of American life and character. A study of Emerson may illuminate some of the causes for that deterioration. Emerson himself was a person of great moral strength and integrity; but the whole tendency of his philosophy was to destroy the tradition in which virtues such as his own could be cultivated.

"I unsettle all things," was his own boast. "No facts are to me sacred; none are profane; I simply experiment, an endless seeker with no Past at my back." [1] It is true—more true than he realized—that his preaching unsettled all things; but his claim to represent homo Americanus—that mythical man-in-himself without teachers or ancestors—cannot be accepted. His own character owed everything to the past; and it was from the past—ultimately the European past—that he borrowed the weapons with which he cut his connections with it.

Emerson's virtues were of a kind that only develop in a long-established and well-ordered society. His self-assurance, his public spirit, his sensitiveness to moral values were the fruit of a social organism more stable and more compact than any that now exists in either Europe or America.

The New Englanders of that epoch had long memories. Their roots were back in medieval Europe; the original colonists had made in the new world a replica of their birthplace and many customs which appear characteristically Yankee can be duplicated in the annals of medieval England. Immigrants had not become so numerous that they could not be absorbed. Concord, already two centuries old, had an air of permanence. There was little to indicate that another hundred years would not find Massachusetts still Puritan and its citizens still governing the Republic. When every particular seems to have its established place in the cosmic scheme, it is possible to find the universal in it; it was part of Emerson's strength that he could see universal laws in terms of his Concord neighbors.



[1] *Essays* (Riverside Library edition, 1929), I, 297.

Society was still rural. There were factories at Lowell; but Emerson saw little of industrialism and never understood it. The men among whom he lived had the strength and the wholeness of a life in direct contact with nature. Puritanism, though it tended always to produce bluntness of speech and eccentricity of behavior, had confirmed this healthy independence; and it had not wholly destroyed instinctive good taste and feeling for craftsmanship.

The whole of New England was permeated by a system of moral values; the function of all social organization was to cultivate them, and those persons who realized them most completely were honored by their neighbors. For two centuries piety, self-control, devotion to learning and the public interest had been ideals; ministers, scholars, and statesmen had been an aristocracy. The Puritan values, compared with those of any community in Europe or the East, were cripplingly narrow; but when they were inherited by someone who was not temperamentally disposed to fight against them, their narrowness was partly compensated for by their strength. Emerson was such a person. Sprung from seven generations of ministers, abstemious by temperament, he accepted the New England morality without hesitation; it became so nearly nature in him that it never occurred to him to doubt it. He enjoyed, therefore, the advantage of harmony with the world in which he lived; if he fought with his contemporaries it was not about values but about their application, because they paid only lip-service to virtues which both he and they acknowledged. He was not isolated from his environment, or compelled by its hostility to doubt himself.

The New England values rested on supernatural and traditional buttresses. Emerson's lifework was to remove those buttresses. He accepted the values so unquestioningly that he believed that they would remain, suspended in midair, so to speak, without any buttress whatsoever.

## II

Emerson's mistake seems to have been due to the very perfection of his own character. He was an optimist because he was himself innocent of evil. A study of the chief defect in the New England religion will explain how this happened.

The medieval Catholic was never innocent of evil. Human nature was sinful; but the whole of that nature had once been good, and by grace it could be restored to its original perfection. The inordinate desire for worldly goods was a perversion of the love of supernatural good. The Catholic, therefore, studied his evil desires and, instead of suppressing them, endeavored to divert them to good ends. Catholic dogma provided a scheme of values by which desires could be evaluated and progressively reformed.

Puritanism, on the other hand, declared that the depravity of nature was hopeless. Any virtue which man might achieve was the work not of nature purified by grace but of grace alone; grace and nature, instead of cooperating, were eternally at war. Grace showed itself, for Luther and Calvin, in certain feelings, and, for the New England orthodoxy, in obedience to a code of moral laws summarized in the Decalogue. Nature, therefore, must be stifled; if possible, it must be driven below the level of consciousness, so that grace might be universal. The result was that many Puritans obviously suffered from serious pathological aberrations; on the other hand, those in whom immoral impulses were naturally weak were serene and innocent in the enjoyment of grace.

It seems evident that Emerson was never seriously troubled by the demands of the flesh; he had little physical vitality, and his Spartan life carried him safely through the disturbances of youth. He was educated into the strict Calvinist code, which persisted long after Calvinist theology had been abandoned. It is probable that most of the illegal impulses to which his nature may have been subject were suppressed before they became conscious. It is certain that he never felt any serious moral struggle within himself; his writings contain no trace of it. He once complained that novels which depicted sensual temptation were untrue to life.[2]

A few indications of something pathological in his adjustment to life can be noticed. No Puritan, probably, was wholly free from it. He was, for example, naïvely shocked when, during his second visit to England, Carlyle and Dickens discussed the rarity of premarital chastity among Englishmen.[3] And he was very unwilling to know the physical constituents of any dish set before him at dinner, checking such statements with the remark that it was "a perfect crystallization" or "made of roses." It is obvious, however, that in the main he was healthy.

A more robust contemporary said of him that he was "utterly unconscious of himself as either good or evil. He had no conscience, in fact, and lived by perception."[4] This was also his own opinion. He proposed to inscribe the word "whim" over his doorpost; and he declared that "No law can be sacred to me but that of my nature. Good and bad are but names very readily transferable to that or this; the only right is what is after my constitution; the only wrong is what is against it."[5] Yet in practice no man was ever freer from unworthy desires or stricter in obedience to what he considered to be duty. If he had no conscience, it was because his constitution performed the same functions. The result was a philosophy valuable only for those who have suppressed the baser side

[2] *Journals,* III, 472.
[3] *Journals,* VII, 441.
[4] Henry James, Senior; quoted by Bliss Perry, *Emerson Today,* 130.
[5] *Essays,* I, 52.

of their nature with the same completeness. Not knowing what it was to be an erring human being, he was unable to prescribe for such.

## III

Emerson's philosophy was a reaction against Unitarianism. Unitarianism had had too low an opinion of human nature; Emerson sinned in the opposite direction. Since other transcendentalists, notably Bronson Alcott and Theodore Parker, arrived more or less independently at identical conclusions, the movement was probably inevitable; it could have been saved from error only by the appearance of a genius who knew other parts of the world besides New England.

Unitarianism had rejected every dogma of traditional Christianity except supernatural revelation. It was based on the philosophy of John Locke. Man was not a sinner—it was impossible to *sin* against a God whose sole characteristic was His benevolence; but he was ignorant of how best to make himself happy (or virtuous, which meant the same thing, virtue being merely enlightened self-love) until Jesus was commissioned by God to instruct him. Religion, therefore, meant obedience to the commands of Jesus. Since there were no innate ideas and all knowledge was deduced from sensuous perception, any kind of mysticism was impossible. This dreary moralism, which virtually denied the existence of the soul, was preached by such men as Henry Ware and Andrews Norton, and was hailed as a release from superstition.

The transcendentalists reaffirmed the existence of the soul. Man, they declared, had an innate knowledge of religious truth, and religion meant a direct relationship between man and God.

To these ideas Emerson was predisposed by both character and education. His innocence convinced him that no external instruction was necessary in order to be good. Calvinist tradition, which reached him through his aunt, Mary Moody Emerson, taught him that man in a state of grace could approach God without intermediaries. At the age of seventeen he noted, while reading Price, that conceptions of good and evil were innate.[6] From that time on he selected, in his reading, whatever harmonized with his new religious attitude; he neglected or condemned whatever was opposed to it. For the beliefs of Unitarianism he substituted a new set of beliefs. These beliefs were derived from books, and only the principles of their combination and certain deductions from them were in any way original. He adopted them because they explained his experience more adequately than those which he had rejected; but the same experience might, in a different intellectual environment, have been explained by wholly different beliefs. In other words his philosophy is to be judged on its merits as an intellectual structure, not accepted as the word of a man who had any unusually deep insight into reality.

[6] *Journals,* I, 78.

Emerson's masters all belonged to the mystical tradition of religious thought. Mysticism is not incompatible with Christianity, and some of the greatest Christian philosophers have also been mystics. The mystical tradition has, however, been more often heretical than orthodox. At its origin it was definitely hostile to Christianity. Emerson becomes most intelligible when he is considered as a Christian heretic.

The core of heretical mysticism is the belief that the soul of man, not merely *like* God, as orthodox Christianity declares, is *of the same substance* as God; it is, therefore, untouched by original sin, has an innate knowledge of religious truth, and may attain to absolute union with the Godhead. Christian mystics modify these beliefs by admitting that the union of the soul with God is not so complete that it is absorbed in God, and that even if the soul is good the will is still perverted and needs to be instructed by external authority. Mysticism also teaches a monism verging on pantheism.

The founder of European mysticism was Plotinus. The doctrines of Plotinus were given a Christian coloring by Dionysus the Areopagite. Dionysus was translated into Latin by John Scotus Erigena, through whom the mystical tradition was handed down to the medieval heretics and to a Catholic on the verge of heresy, Eckhart. The Germans who followed Eckhart influenced Luther, from whom Protestantism, and indirectly New England Puritanism, acquired mystical tendencies. More directly the tradition was inherited by various Protestant sects, notably the Quakers, by Jacob Boehme, and by Swedenborg. In the eighteenth century it influenced the German philosophers, especially Schelling, and by them it was passed on to their English interpreters, Coleridge and Carlyle. Emerson touched this chain of thought at various places. His especial masters were Plotinus and his immediate disciples, and the contemporary English and Germans. He was influenced also by Boehme, Swedenborg, the Quakers, and the English Christian Platonists; and he was predisposed to these ideas by his Calvinist background, in which, after the definitely Christian beliefs had been eliminated, only the mysticism remained.

Mystical philosophy was an attempt to explain a very specific experience. All genuine mystics agree remarkably in their descriptions of it. The mystic begins by withdrawing completely from the external world; he goes, said Tauler, into "the quiet solitude where no word is spoken, where is neither creature nor image nor fancy." He does not think of God; his God can be defined only by negatives; he must deny to God, said Albert of Cologne, "first of all, bodily and sensible attributes, then intelligible qualities, and lastly, that being which would keep him among created things." And when he has thus shut out every memory of the material world, he arrives at what Tauler called "the quiet Desert of the Godhead, the Divine Darkness," and Eckhart "the end of all things" where is "the hidden Darkness of the eternal Godhead, unknown and never to be known." It follows that there can be no relationship between the mystical experience and conduct ("If I say God is good, it is not true," said Eckhart); when the mystic returns to the world he must obey the laws as before. Pseudo-mysticism, on the other hand, the mysticism of those who have not themselves had any genuine mystical experience, regards the divinity which man finds within himself as positive, giving positive commands—not as something so completely removed from sensible things that it can be described only in negatives. The medieval heresies were caused by pseudo-mysticism of this kind.[7]

Emerson was a pseudo-mystic. He had mystical feelings, but no true mystical experience. His mysticism was founded on those moments of exhilaration, caused by a feeling of harmony between oneself and the external world, which everyone occasionally experiences. "Crossing a bare common," he said, "in snow puddles, at twilight, under a clouded sky, without having in my thoughts any occurrence of special good fortune, I have enjoyed a perfect exhilaration." "Standing on the bare ground—my head bathed by the blithe air and uplifted into infinite space,—all mean egotism vanishes. I become a transparent eyeball; I am nothing; I see all; the currents of the Universal Being circulate through me; I am part or parcel of God."[8]

The resultant philosophy was very similar to that preached by the heretical mystics of the middle ages.

## IV

With the exception of "English Traits" nearly everything that Emerson wrote was an embroidering of a few very simple ideas. These ideas were as follows: God as moral law; the world as an emanation from God; man as having divinity within himself; "self-reliance"; and a religion not of authority but of the spirit.

Emerson's conception of God was the result of his New England ancestry. Puritanism, forbidding the use of images or concrete symbols and insisting that man could know God directly, had seen Him chiefly as a law-giver; He had delivered the Ten Commandments on Sinai, and the purpose first of His Covenant with the Jews and afterwards of the Christian revelation was to induce men to obey those commandments. In each generation the Massachusetts churches had affirmed this moralism more emphatically, until with Unitarianism it had become the whole of religion. Emerson admitted that God might have other attributes besides morality, but, since he accepted the New England prohibition of images, man could not know those attributes. "We have faculties to perceive his laws," he said, "but himself how obscurely." For practical pur-

[7] R. M. Jones, *Studies in Mystical Religion* (1936), 278, 219, 225.
[8] *Works* (Centenary Edition, 1903), 1, 9, 10.

poses God meant nothing except moral law. "My point is," he declared, "that the movement of the whole machine, the motive force of life, and of every particular life, is moral. . . . The iron of iron, the fire of fire, the ether and source of all the elements, is moral forces." This was Emerson's most important addition to the mystical tradition. By thus combining mysticism and Puritanism he manufactured a compound more anarchical than either of its elements had been alone.[9]

That the world was an emanation from God was a doctrine which Emerson derived from Plotinus, and found confirmation of in the Indian mystics. He became not only a moralist but a pantheist. "I believe," he said, "in the omnipresence; that is, that the All is in each particle; that entire nature reappears in every leaf and moss." [10]

Why, then, did the world appear to be partly evil? For this Emerson had two answers. The earlier in time was that evil should be considered not in itself but as a part of the cosmos. We should "observe how finely in nature all these disagreeable individuals integrate themselves into a cleanly and pleasing whole." "God is promoted by the worst. . . . They perform a beneficence they know not of." "Scarce an infant or idiot exists who cannot somehow or other contribute to the well-being of the universe." This had been the answer given by Augustine and by Jonathan Edwards, and in Emerson's youth it was accepted by most of the Calvinist churches. Since Emerson had formulated it before he was eighteen it seems evident that he derived it from the intellectual atmosphere of his time. But whereas Edwards had seen this contrast between good and evil as aesthetic, to Emerson it was primarily moral. It became his law of compensation, which he explained, while still at Harvard, as due to "the intentions of Providence to limit human perfectibility and to bind together good and evil, like life and death, by indissoluble connections." [11]

Emerson later added a second explanation, which he probably took from Plotinus, though he could have found it also in such Christian mystics as Augustine and St. Thomas or in Jonathan Edwards. This was that evil was a negation; it had no real existence. "Essence, or God," said Emerson, "is not a relation or a part, but the whole. . . . Nature, truth, virtue, are the influx from thence. Vice is the absence or departure of the same. Nothing, Falsehood, may indeed stand as the great Night or shade on which as a background the living universe paints itself forth, but no fact is begotten by it; it cannot work, for it is not. It cannot work any good; it cannot work any harm. It is harm inasmuch as it is worse not to be than to be." [12]

If nature was an emanation from God, it followed that God could

[9] *Journals,* II, 274; IX, 491.
[10] *Journals,* V, 184.
[11] *Journals,* III, 283; II, 8; I, 103.
[12] *Essays,* I, 116.

be found in nature. This had been a game often played by Christian mystics, who had found everywhere analogies for the Trinity and the Atonement. With Emerson, influenced chiefly by Swedenborg, it assumed a different form; he found in nature manifestations of God's moral laws. "Every natural fact," he said, "is a symbol of some spiritual fact." "The laws of moral nature answer to those of matter as face to face in a glass." Heat was identical with love, and the laws of gravitation with purity of heart. "The axioms of physics translate the laws of ethics." The purpose of science was, therefore, not so much to discover the structure of the material universe as to shed light on God's moral laws. Nature was only a vast metaphor for morality; "what we ask of her is only words to clothe our thoughts." The attraction of science was in "the sublime delight with which the intellect contemplates each new analogy appearing between the laws of Nature and its own law of life." Correctly interpreted, all natural phenomena "hint or thunder to man the laws of right and wrong, and echo the Ten Commandments." "Wherever you enunciate a physical law," said Emerson, "I hear in it a moral rule." [13]

This conception of science as a branch of ethics is scarcely nearer to the world of the modern physicist than primitive animism or the medieval search for theological symbols. Even those persons who believe that, because Eddington's matter is less solid than Clerk-Maxwell's, idealism is once more admissible, will hardly identify the law of gravitation with purity of heart.

If it were merely a poetic fancy, we might dismiss it as, in reading Augustine, we dismiss his mysticism of numbers. But, by an extraordinary confusion of the planes of being, Emerson proceeded to deduce important consequences. If the laws of nature were identical with those of morality, then to understand them and obey them was a form of virtue; success in other words was a result of moral goodness. "Success," said Emerson, "consists in close appliance to the laws of the world and since those laws are intellectual and moral, an intellectual and moral obedience." "Money . . . is, in its effects and laws, as beautiful as roses. Property keeps the accounts of the world, and is always moral. The property will be found where the labor, the wisdom and the virtue have been in nations, in classes, and (the whole life-time considered, with the compensations) in the individual also." This was the basis of Emerson's optimism. "The league between virtue and nature," he said, "engages all things to assume a hostile front to its vice. The beautiful laws and substances of the world persecute and whip the traitor. He finds that things are arranged for truth and benefit." "An eternal, beneficent necessity is always bringing things right." Here was a transcendentalist reinterpretation of the Old-Testament Puritan belief that providence punished the wicked and rewarded the virtuous with riches. Among the Yankee farmers of Concord

[13] *Works,* I, 26, 40, 43; *Journals,* VIII, 536; X, 205; Miss Perry, *op. cit.,* 83.

it had a little plausibility. But its effect was to justify new forces, which were soon to destroy the rural society in which Emerson lived.[14]

That man had divinity within himself was a doctrine of mysticism; Emerson found it in Plotinus and the Indians. He arrived at it by way of the distinction between the reason and the understanding which he took from Coleridge. "Our compound nature," he said, "differences us from God, but our reason is not to be distinguished from the divine Essence." Emerson considered this to be the most important feature of his philosophy. "In all my lectures," he said, "I have taught one doctrine, namely, the infinitude of the private man." Emerson's use of it strongly recalls his ancestral Puritanism. Puritanism had declared that elect persons, after their conversion, had the grace of God within them, which the individual must obey. "Philosophy," said Emerson, "shakes hands at last with the simplest Methodist and teaches one fact with him, namely, that it is the grace of God—all grace—no inch of space left for the impertinence of human will." Calvin's rigid distinction between the elect and the damned reappeared in Emerson. Emerson the democrat could use words of the greatest contempt for the masses, who did not obey the Oversoul within themselves; they were "animals," he said, "in state of pupilage, and nearer the chimpanzee." But whereas for Calvin salvation was dependent on God's election and was reserved for a few, Emerson looked forward to a day when all men would surrender to the Oversoul.[15]

By "self-reliance" Emerson meant obedience to the Oversoul; as his son remarked, it should more accurately have been called "God-reliance." Man, he said, must surrender his individual will and intellect, and act only in obedience to the instincts of his soul; these instincts were the Oversoul expressing itself in him, and were identical with the forces which governed the material universe; they were, therefore, moral, and he who obeyed them could do no wrong. Man was great in so far as he made himself a vehicle for the divine spirit. This abandonment Emerson preached in the most uncompromising terms. "As the traveller who has lost his way throws his reins on his horse's neck and trusts to the instinct of the animal to find his road, so must we do with the divine animal who carries us through this world," he said.[16]

All religion is a self-surrender of the individual to something larger than himself. In traditional Christianity the individual surrendered to the City of God, whose earthly representative was the Church; the Church gave him moral standards which he used to evaluate his own experiences. Emerson recommended that the individual should surrender to his own unconscious. "The unconscious," he said, "is ever the act of God Himself." This doctrine had two causes. By combining mysticism

[14] *Works,* VI, 100; *Essays,* II, 221; I, 111; *Works,* X, 189.

[15] *Journals,* III, 235; V, 380; VI, 336; VIII, 456.

[16] *Essays,* II, 31.

with Puritanism Emerson had decided that the moral sentiment, the instincts of the individual, and the Oversoul were all identical. And he never found cause to alter his opinion because the strength of the moral censorship which his Puritan education had given him prevented immoral instincts from entering his consciousness—or at least from disguising themselves as angels of light. He did not shrink from deductions even more remarkable; instinct was still divine when it expressed itself in children and in crowds; children were naturally good; and as for crowds, a common danger or desire would "knit a multitude into one man," and rouse that "giant overcome with sleep," "the generic soul," whose eyes would "straight pierce through all appearances" and his tongue tell "what should be in the latest time." [17]

Surrender to an impulse is good or bad according to the nature of the impulse. Spontaneous goodness is usually the result of previous discipline. Emerson had been disciplined, and the impulses to which he surrendered were good. He did not find this surrender easy: "I have my own stern claims and perfect circle," he said; "if any one imagines that this law is lax, let him keep its commandment one day." Yet he never admitted a need for discipline, and he forbade any attempt to judge an impulse; rational or external moral standards would be an interference with the Oversoul. "Long before the opinion comes the instinct that a particular act is . . . wrong," he declared. "First thoughts are from God." And even more definitely:

> Our moral nature is vitiated by any interference of our will. People represent virtue as a struggle, and take to themselves great airs upon their attainments, and the question is everywhere vexed when a noble nature is commended, whether the man is not better who strives with the temptation. But there is no merit in the matter. Either God is there or He is not there. We love characters in proportion as they are impulsive and spontaneous.

Abandonment alone was good, no matter to what instincts or passions the individual abandoned himself. "What is love, and why is it the chief good, but because it is an overpowering enthusiasm? Never self-possessed or prudent, it is all abandonment." [18]

Emerson's "self-reliance" was a logical result of Protestant doctrine. Luther had taught that God communicated His grace directly to the souls of the elect; the result was to substitute, for the guidance of an external and rational system of values, the supremacy of Feeling. As long as Christianity survived in some form, Feeling was admitted as divine only when its impulses had biblical justification, and in the orthodox

[17] *Journals,* III, 325; IV, 52.

[18] *Essays,* I, 73, 74; *Journals,* X, 124; III, 323; *Essays,* I, 127; *Works,* I, 217.

churches of New England obedience to the Bible had almost wholly taken the place of Feeling; but the various antinomian sects had declared, like Emerson, that by obeying their wildest whims and impulses they were obeying God. Though, however, Emerson was predisposed to "self-reliance" by his ancestry, it was from Neo-Platonic mysticism that he actually deduced it. Not having had the true mystical experience, he imagined that the God in the soul was positive and gave positive commands. The heretical mystics of the middle ages had fallen into the same error and for the same reasons, though they did not have Emerson's justification of regarding the Oversoul as primarily moral. Amaury of Bene, for example, who had studied Erigena's translation of Dionysius, was burnt at the stake in 1204 for teaching Emersonian "self-reliance." The Beghards and the Brethren of the Free Spirit, later in the same century, declared that "more faith should be given to the things which come from the human heart than to the gospels; the soul's Inward Voice is safer than the truths preached by the Church." According to their enemies they claimed "to be divine by nature, and they make no distinction between God and themselves." "Whenever their nature urges them in any direction," said Tauler, "they follow the impulse, so that the freedom of the spirit may be unhindered." Similar doctrines were preached in the sixteenth century by the German Anabaptists and in the seventeenth by the English Ranters.[19]

Emerson's religion of the spirit was the consequence of "self-reliance." The man who obeyed the Oversoul within himself needed the aid of no institution. "The relations of the soul to the divine spirit are so pure that it is profane to seek to interpose helps." Poetic symbols might be useful, but the error of all established religions was in treating them as more than symbols; it was "the mistake of an accidental and individual symbol for an universal one." "The history of all hierarchies seems to show that all religious error consisted in making the symbol too stark and solid and was at last nothing but an excess of the organ of language." "Self-reliance" made all moral or religious authority unnecessary: "He, who has the lawgiver, may with safety not only neglect, but even contravene every written commandment." Such a man, being for all intents perfect, needed no secular authority either: "The appearance of character makes the state unnecessary." If there were "a reliance on the moral sentiment and a sufficient belief in the unity of things," then society could be "maintained without artificial restraints, as well as the solar system." This was the only reformation that was needed; teach men to obey the Oversoul, and not only wickedness and misery but "toothache and indigestion, cramp and croup, pain and poverty" would vanish.[20]

Emerson expected the reformation in the near future. "The distinc-

[19] R. M. Jones, *op. cit.*, 207, 208, 209.

[20] *Essays*, I, 66; II, 38; *Works*, I, 336; *Essays*, II, 210; *Journals*, V, 428.

tion of the new age" would be, he believed, "the refusal of authority." There was "a steady tendency of the thoughtful and virtuous to a deeper belief and reliance on spiritual facts." "This gradual casting off of material aids, and the growing trust in the private self-supplied powers of the individual" was "the affirmative principle of the recent philosophy." "The next age will behold God in the ethical laws—and will regard natural history, private fortunes, and politics . . . as illustrations of those laws." In other words, there was to be a new revelation and a new race of men. Emerson sometimes assumed the air of a John the Baptist prophesying a new Messiah. "The man who shall be born," he said, "whose advent men and events prepare and foresee, is one who shall enjoy his connection with a higher life." "I look for the new Teacher that . . . shall show that the Ought, that Duty, is one thing with Science, with Beauty, and with Joy." [21]

This mystical looking-forward to a miraculous future was strengthened by another mysticism—Emerson's faith in America. America has always inspired optimistic prophecies (Jonathan Edwards expected to see the rebirth of the Messiah); and the idea is by no means dead that in the new world there must inevitably be a new culture—a spontaneous generation from the soil, without parents or intelligible causes. In practice, since hatred of European institutions has been the chief cause for immigration, the American dream has usually been of a world where men can live without those institutions. For Emerson America meant freedom from all authority; every American would be guided by the Spirit. "A nation of men will for the first time exist," he declared, "because each believes himself inspired by the Divine Soul which also inspires all men." He believed that it would be the function of the United States to realize the spiritual religion of the future, and to embody the moral sentiment "in the laws, in the jurisprudence, in international law, in political economy." [22]

As a matter of fact, though Emerson did not realize it, this delusion first appeared at least a thousand years before the discovery of America. Almost since the foundation of Christianity heretical mystics dreamed of a coming Age of the Holy Ghost, when by some more or less miraculous revolution discipline and authority would be superseded and man would enjoy direct communication with God. The Montanists in the third century after Christ expected "the Church of the Spirit by means of the spiritual man, not the Church which consists of a number of bishops." Erigena prophesied an Age of the Spirit, and the prophecy was repeated by the Abbot Joachim and by Amaury of Bene; the Spiritual Franciscans and other medieval heretics preached the coming of the Paraclete, influencing even orthodox Catholics like Dante. After the

[21] *Journals*, IV, 495; *Essays*, II, 242, 247; *Works*, X, 222; *Essays*, II, 268; *Works*, I, 151.
[22] *Works*, I, 115; *Journals*, X, 144.

Reformation the Anabaptists, the Ranters, and some other Protestant sects declared that because man would be guided directly by the Spirit, Church and State were no longer needed.

This delusion has led always to the same consequences. For example: The marital tie is conspicuously an institution which man needs because he is imperfect. All the more extreme heretical mystics abolished marriage, declaring that the affections must be free and man should not restrict his love to a single person. The Vermont perfectionists in Emerson's lifetime made every male in their colony the husband of every female. From the same starting point Emerson arrived in due course at the same conclusion, though he expressed it much more cautiously. "The great and crescive self," he said, "rooted in absolute nature, supplants all relative existence and ruins the kingdom of mortal friendship and love. Marriage (in what is called the spiritual world) is impossible. . . . The universe is the bride of the soul. All private sympathy is partial." [23]

It is instructive to see how the old dream of the heretics, transplanted to a fresh soil, acquired an appearance of reality from union with the new dream of America.

## V

Historically, Emerson is important because he helped to destroy the New England theocracy. After him it was impossible for educated Puritans to accept the Christian myth or to think in theological terms; religion meant a vague respect for the moral sentiment, whether embodied in Christ or Socrates or Emerson himself. Emerson was so typically a product of New England, and his philosophy was so obviously a counter-irritant to Unitarianism, that it is not surprising that in his own section he should have had a large following. But, since he thought in terms which the modern world has almost forgotten, and since his position can easily be plotted on the map of the Christian heresies, it is strange that he should have had, and still have, so much influence in the world at large.

Something was due, no doubt, to his championship of America and his declarations of cultural independence; but a more important reason was that the main tendencies of his religious philosophy agreed with the secular beliefs of his, and our, time.

The modern faith is liberalism. According to liberalism men need no authoritative code of values, embodied in institutions, to guide or discipline them; they are happiest when left most completely free for self-expression. This attitude is not confined to any part of the world; but it has encountered least opposition in America. Its driving force has been its adoption by the new industrialism warring against agrarian conservatism. The weakness of liberalism has been that many of its advocates, in

[23] *Essays,* II, 78.

attacking outworn and obstructive forms of authority, have denied the need for objective moral standards of any kind; declaring that each man has a right to free self-development, they have forgotten that when values are no longer imposed by external authority, they must instead be adopted voluntarily by the individual. Much liberal thinking, therefore, particularly in the nineteenth century, when it was reinforced by materialistic conceptions of human nature, tended to encourage moral anarchy. Emerson's thought was medieval, contrasted with that of most other nineteenth-century thinkers; but it has contributed to the same result—the destruction of all moral standards. Men forget that he identified the law of gravitation with purity of heart and that by "self-reliance" he meant God-reliance; they remember him as the prophet of self-reliance.

The will, however, needs a code of values, and the individual, when deprived of authoritative guidance, cannot always discover his own system. Much modern thinking tends to solve this problem by denying the existence of the will. In practice the result is that one submits oneself to the tides of emotion, in the hope that they will overwhelm any rational doubt or control. Here again liberalism is reinforced by Emerson. He also counseled abandonment and spontaneity, declaring that our nature was "vitiated by any interference of our will," though he reached this conclusion by a wholly different route. "The one thing which we seek with insatiable desire," he said, "is to forget ourselves, to be surprised out of our propriety, to lose our sempiternal memory and to do something without knowing how or why; in short to draw a new circle. Nothing great was ever achieved without enthusiasm." [24]

Emerson himself, moreover, inspires the utmost confidence. This apostle of Dionysus was a water-drinker, a good husband and father, a citizen of the utmost integrity. He rose at six, studied assiduously, and for recreation walked in the woods. He had a gift for phrase-making rarely equalled in English literature; and though he may not have been a great writer, everything that he wrote had the texture of authentic literary personality. Emerson's virtues were the result of those institutions which his philosophy helped to destroy; but their effect was to justify that philosophy, to make it seem safe and respectable.

Nobody will deny that Emerson's philosophy gave too much encouragement to the worst tendencies of the time, to anarchical individualism, unchecked pursuit of wealth, and contempt for public spirit. Emerson himself was not blind to the faults of his contemporaries. When he curbed his moralistic propensities and applied himself to observation, he was always admirable (his best book is probably "English Traits"). Such a statement, for example, as that Americans had no passions but

[24] *Essays*, I, 300.

only appetites is worth all the "Essays." [25] Unfortunately, he was unable to readjust his philosophy in order to counter the evils which he observed. In later life he lacked vitality for original thought; beyond the age of forty he merely organized his stock of ideas and repeated them. For the last thirty years of his life he uttered only more and more dogmatic statements of his belief; and every fresh realization of degeneracy round him called out only a more emphatic assertion that confidence in the moral sentiment was the panacea for all human ills.

"I see movements, I hear aspirations," he said in 1867, "but I see not how the great God prepares to satisfy the heart in the new order of things. No Church, no State emerges; and when we have extricated ourselves from all the embarrassments of the social problem, the oracle does not yet emit any light on the mode of individual life. A thousand negatives it utters, clear and strong, on all sides; but the sacred affirmative it hides in the deepest abyss." "The gracious motions of the soul—piety, adoration—I do not find." Now that the old religions were dead, "we are alarmed in our solitude; we would gladly recall the life that so offended us." "Frightful is the solitude of the soul which is without God." In these words there was a note of despair, and Emerson's remedies did little to dispel it. "Heroic resolutions," he said, were needed. "A new crop of geniuses" might be born who "with happy heat and a bias for theism" would "bring asceticism and duty and magnanimity into vogue again." God's communications with mankind were as yet intermittent, but later there might be "a broad and steady altar-flame." [26]

If only the birth of "a new crop of geniuses" could save society, then society was probably doomed. The younger generation in New England took the hint. Some of them were already flying to Europe or to the Roman Church—a tendency which Emerson noticed and deplored. The remainder took shelter from a world of appetites behind the Genteel Tradition. This new conservatism was founded on culture and good taste; but because it had no real faith in the values which it adopted, because it had lost all vital links with any tradition, it could not absorb new experiences or master its environment. Fear and not a religious affirmation was its root, and therefore it was desiccated and without vitality.

[25] *Journals,* VIII, 321.
[26] *Works,* X, 218; *Journals,* X, 8; VIII, 500.

# Toward Melville: Some Versions of Emerson

*by Charles Feidelson, Jr.*

*Oh you man without a handle!*
H. JAMES, SR., to R. W. EMERSON

Emerson and Melville were the polar figures of the American symbolist movement. Whitman wrote poems in a form that Emerson might have adopted if he had been more consistent with his theory and less aware of its shortcomings. Hawthorne and Poe circle around Melville—not only because, like him, they are given to parading their hostility to all "transcendentalisms, myths & oracular gibberish," but also because in each case ostentatious hostility was only one aspect of a real mixture of attraction and repulsion. If we look for characteristic products of the complex tradition outlined in the preceding chapter, Whitman seems too pure a type; and Hawthorne and Poe, though more deeply involved than they knew, are too far off-center. Emerson and Melville are the poles.

Between them these two ran the gamut of possibilities created by the symbolistic point of view. Emerson represented the upsurge of a new capacity, Melville the relapse into doubt. Emerson was the theorist and advocate, Melville the practicing poet. Emerson embodied the monistic phase of symbolism, the sweeping sense of poetic fusion; Melville lived in a universe of paradox and knew the struggle to implement the claims of symbolic imagination. Yet neither was really an independent agent: their methods were reciprocal, and each entailed the other. Though Melville speaks to us today as Emerson does not, they stand on common ground, which is also common ground with our own sensibility. Melville assumed the ambient idea that Emerson made explicit, and if we feel Melville as one of ours, we must take Emerson into the bargain, whether we like it or not.

When Emerson says that the "perception of symbols" enables man to see both "the poetic construction of things" and "the primary relation of mind to matter," and that this same perception normally creates "the whole apparatus of poetic expression," he is identifying poetry with symbolism, symbolism with a mode of perception, and symbolic perception with the vision, first, of a symbolic structure in the real world and, second, of a symbolic relationship between nature and mind. The religious philosopher and the prophet of self-reliance with whom we are all acquainted was also a literary theorist greatly influenced by the problem of knowledge and a creative artist with a consciously adopted point of view. For him, both in theory and in practice, "the Imagination is Vision," poetic vision "is the perception of the symbolic character of things," and poetic structure, the form of this vision, is attained when the poet "no longer sees snow as snow, or horses as horses, but only sees or names them representatively for those interior facts which they signify."

Given due weight, this recurrent theme goes far to explain the substance and method of Emerson's work, the ultimate aim of which was to force a revision in philosophy that would justify and encourage literature, while at the same time it proposed the poetic outlook as a corrective to traditional metaphysics and epistemology. The crucial turn of his thought can be seen in a passage from *Nature* in which Kant's language is echoed but thrown into new perspective. "The sensual man," says Emerson—and he means the Lockian man—"conforms thoughts to things." But in Emerson's redaction of the Kantian tag it is the *poet* who "conforms things to his thoughts." The poet "impresses his being" upon material nature through symbolic vision, for "he uses matter as symbols" of his own feelings. What Emerson has at heart is not the old opposition of idealism and empiricism but a more general distinction between the canons of symbolism and of logic. The rationalist tradition, of whatever stripe, must make room for and profit by poetic method, which, as he said of the Platonic dialogues, "does not stand on a syllogism, or on any masterpieces of the Socratic reasoning, or on any thesis," but consists in "carrying up every fact to successive platforms and . . . disclosing in every fact a germ of expansion," so that "every word becomes an exponent of nature," and everything we look upon bears "a second sense, and ulterior senses." This world of multiple significance is thoroughly realistic. "The expansions are organic. The mind does not create what it perceives, any more than the eye creates the rose." For if "the poetic construction of things" is evinced in the ambiguity of every object, the "primary relation of mind to matter" appears in the organic experience of which both mind and object are functions.

As philosophy, these Emersonian dicta are often more naïve and create more problems than the "difficulties of a naïve dualism" against which his whole effort was directed. His theory has weight chiefly as a literary program, and his writings survive as literature. Yet his literary theory and practice were limited by the philosophic issues that led him to symbolism. While he gave a new prestige to aesthetic apprehension, he dwelt not on "the arts" but on Art itself; his subject was not the practicing poet but the human being, and Art was "nothing less than the creation of man and nature." While he urged an experimental attitude toward literary form, the "spheral" structure of his own poems and essays remained rudimentary—an immediate confirmation of his abstract monistic dream. Thus our sense of alienation from the Emersonian brand of symbolism is justified to the extent that he himself was remote from the specific possibilities of the *literary* symbol. Although the net effect of his philosophy was to give a new direction to literature by recapturing the sense of an autonomous language of poetry, he himself was more concerned with the other phase of his endeavor, the reorientation of philosophy in the light of poetic method. For him the awareness of "double . . . or . . . quadruple or . . . centuple or much more manifold meaning" did not primarily pose a literary question but suggested an answer to the rationalistic dilemma of his time.

As a result, it did not occur to him, as it did to Melville, to exploit the most exciting quality of modern symbolism—the tension between opposite meanings in paradox and the tension between logical paradox and its literary resolution—even though this very quality was implicit in his own approach. He was interested in reconciliation; and his great, though amiable, failing was too simple a confidence in the power of poetic harmony. Of course, conscious as he was of multiple meaning, Emerson necessarily lived in a universe of inconsistencies:

> I affirm melioration. . . . I affirm also the self-equality of nature . . . but I cannot reconcile these two statements. I affirm the sacredness of the individual. . . . I see also the benefits of cities. . . . But I cannot reconcile these oppositions.

Instead of going on, however, to make the most of paradox, Emerson usually beat a hasty retreat into transcendent unity. In his speculations the Oversoul was always available in emergencies; in his poems he was seemingly undisturbed by any resistance to metaphoric fusion, being comfortable in the belief that through all diversity

> A subtle chain of countless rings
> The next unto the farthest brings.

A poem like "Brahma" illustrates the limitation of Emerson's symbolism both in substance and in method. Just as the theme asserts a facile harmony of far and near, shadow and sunlight—a world where the slayer, the slaying, and the slain lose all individuality—the technique of the poem rests on the easy assumption that any image will do, that a literary unity can exist without a fully articulated symbolic order.

When this much has been granted, what remains is impressive enough.

Modern criticism has turned to Coleridge with the feeling that he aimed in our direction, that he was after something beyond the bounds of romanticism. Emerson, who did not possess Coleridge's knowledge and power of definition, throws another kind of light on the origins of modern taste. His works are like a continuous monologue in which the genesis of symbolism is enacted over and over. Though he never goes far beyond the breaking of the shell, he exemplifies in the most circumstantial way the new sensibility in the act of emergence. Emerson's failing was a lack of literary purposefulness, but his virtue was honesty. For all his absorption in the ineffable One, he was a faithful reporter of multiplicity. "A believer in Unity, a seer of Unity," he wrote, "I yet behold two." The essential drama of his work was the involuntary drama of his mind: the endless fusion and separation of the elements of his world, issuing in the "fragmentary curve" which was the characteristic structure of his essays. This adumbration of symbolic method is parallel to the concept of symbolism, which comes into being on his pages out of the pressure of the past and the needs of the present. It arises in his frank account of "the perpetual tilt and balance" of matter and mind, which urge their claims upon him like "two boys pushing each other on the curbstone of the pavement." Emerson's vision of symbolic reality was achieved out of the heart of a basic conflict of ideas. To follow the involution of his thought is one way of exploring what symbolism is.

The "inconsistency" for which Emerson is often censured was really the source of his power. The case against him has been drawn up by a recent writer as follows:

> The sum of Emerson's inconsistency from the beginning . . . is this: that sometimes the world seemed to him to have independent material existence, colored and interpreted by mind, and sometimes it seemed to him wholly dependent and ideal. He never could entirely make up his mind.

But to put the matter in this way is to miss both his problem and his way of solving it. The whimsical veerings that led him at one time to plump for absolute spirit and at another to acknowledge the independence of nature were actually, as he said, "somewhat better than whim at last," for each extreme was tacitly conditioned by a third view in which both became partial. Behind his fence-straddling was the feeling that the fence was his problem. His attitude was not so much indecisive as experimental, being founded on an acceptance of the intellectual world of his time and a willingness to immerse himself in the destructive element. Emerson was clear enough on the point that modern philosophy had been destructive, whether it led to subjective idealism or the scientific conception of matter.

The abstraction of the thinking ego—"the discovery we have made that we exist"—had necessarily drifted into "study of the eyes instead of that which the eyes see," and this interest in the *how* more than the *what* of knowing would eventually be "punished by loss of faculty." To the Greek the world simply "signified . . . Beauty," but the modern, bound up in his theories of knowledge, was increasingly incapable of such direct perception, and "skepticism, alas! signifies sight." On the other hand, the projection of a purely physical nature had made even the study of the eyes irrelevant. Poetry had faltered in minds that made a sharp distinction between the "real" world of objects and the world of value:

> The ancients probably saw the moral significance of nature in the objects, without afterthought or effort to separate the object and the expression. . . . But when science had gained and given the impression of the permanence, even eternity, of nature, . . . the mountain became a pile of stones acted on by bare blind laws of chemistry, and the poetic sense of things was driven to the vulgar, and an effort was made to recal [*sic*] the sense by the educated, and so it was faintly uttered by the poet and heard with a smile.

Emerson did not suppose that the steps of intellectual history could be retraced; given the results of dualism, he tried to think through to the other side. He realized that "the problems to be solved" were "precisely those which the physiologist and the naturalist omit to state." The solution, therefore, must not be by external fiat but by trial and redefinition of the established scheme.

*Nature,* for instance, sets out from and constantly returns to a formula that seems almost childish in its avoidance of any novel implications:

> Philosophically considered, the universe is composed of Nature and Soul. Strictly speaking, therefore, all that is separate from us, all which Philosophy distinguishes as the *not me,* that is, both nature and art, all other men and my own body, must be ranked under this name, *nature.*

But the simplistic dualism of this account really acts as a kind of reference point for a repeated shift of stance in which Emerson alters the whole meaning of the terms. Playing behind the commonplace disjunction is another concept, which comes to the surface in a journal entry of 1839:

> If, as Hedge thinks, I overlook great facts in stating the absolute laws of the soul; if, as he seems to represent it, the world is not a dualism, is not *a bipolar unity,* but is *two,* is Me and It, then is there the alien, the unknown, and all we have believed and chanted out of our deep instinctive hope is a pretty dream.

Put to the test, the opposition of Nature and Soul pointed toward the unsolved problem that the naturalist failed to state—"the relation between things and thoughts"—and suggested an answer that was actually a reinterpretation of the problem. The theory of "bipolar unity" transformed the conventional scheme by boring from within, "dualism" itself undergoing a change of meaning. There emerged a new basis for literature out of the wreckage of a system in which, as Emerson declared elsewhere, "poetry had been famished and false." Emerson's favorite term for the undifferentiated reality that persistently arose out of difference was borrowed from Coleridge and Wordsworth: "the marriage of thought and things." In the moment of genuine vision, "the act of seeing and the thing seen, the seer and the spectacle, the subject and the object, are one." The difficulty of maintaining the focus of this conception is obvious, since any statement of "bipolar unity" seems to postulate the very distinction that it denies. Emerson worked the sum over and over, starting from scratch every time. For, as he was perfectly aware, he was running counter to the mental habits of over two centuries, and each reprise of the "double consciousness" ended in the disintegration of two worlds that showed "no . . . disposition to reconcile themselves."

This was the case not only because of his ingenuous nature but also because of the very nature of his enterprise. Although Emerson's compelling desire to reduce multiplicity to unity is evident on every page that he wrote, his arguments for identity could not escape the implication of diversity. He was trying to define organic apprehension in rational terms; more particularly, he was trying to describe an ancient way of seeing by means of a modern vocabulary which had been designed to repress it. Inevitably, therefore, he spoke more truly than he himself perhaps intended. He could rehabilitate the monistic power of the symbol only in language that was heavily conditioned by the rational universe from which he departed; he could proceed at all only by a paradoxical method of self-contradiction. Thus by force of circumstance he both stated and illustrated the demands of "concrete fact" in the strictest sense of Whitehead's phrase. The paradoxical "union of opposites" which Whitehead would substitute for the "vicious dualism" of undisciplined abstraction is evident in the interplay of "oneness and otherness" in Emerson's mind. And the theory which is gradually thrown up out of Emerson's "hide-and-seek, blindman's play of Thoughts" reads like a free paraphrase of Whitehead's doctrine. What emerson calls "intellectual perception," which "severs once for all the man from the things with which he converses," is cognate to the abstractive strain in modern philosophy that Whitehead specifically repudiates. What Emerson calls "affection" —a mode of being in which the mental and the physical are identified without ceasing to be rationally distinguishable—is the counterpart of Whitehead's "occasion of actuality," wherein every dualism of the past is redeemed and finds its place. The focus of Emerson's speculation, and the rationale of his method, is the conception of a present reality from which subject and object are mere abstractions but which, paradoxically, can be defined only by reference to those abstract terms. What he wanted to depict as sheer unity emerged as unity in diversity: "Every fact is related on one side to sensation and on the other to morals." Fact was the keystone of the arch, the hypothetical point at which "the soul passed into nature" and nature into the soul. Through it ran the plane of reality, an "unsolved, unsolvable wonder," but a challenge to definition and an absolute presence in which the old categories became relative.

Using "fact" in another sense, Emerson said that the kind of perception he would advocate was "a continual reaction of the thought classifying the facts, and of facts suggesting the thought." His originality consisted in trying to take his stand precisely at the gateway through which these opposite movements pass. Again, his position is reminiscent of a very modern maneuver, one which would undercut the priorities assumed by idealism and materialism by maintaining that "the knowing relation is an entrance of the mind into external objects, or an entrance of external objects into the mind—whichever way one chooses to put it." By this means "concrete fact" is translated into the activity of knowing; the whole scheme of opposite substances is left behind in a shift of emphasis from substance to event; and the theory of knowledge, the need for which was symptomatic of all that was awkward in Cartesian metaphysics, is reoriented so as to destroy its own *raison d'être*. If Emerson ruefully accepted "the study of the eyes instead of that which the eyes see," he did so only to move the focus of study from the seer to the act of seeing; and from the act of seeing he worked back to the thing seen, which he reinstated as one aspect of the perceptual event. To become "a transparent eyeball" was to *be* nothing and to see all; at the same time "this manner of looking at things transfers every object in nature from an independent and anomalous position without there, into the consciousness." That may be idealism, as Emerson called it, but surely with a significant difference. What was important to him was not so much mind itself as "the habitual posture of the mind—beholding." Though Emerson often wavered, harassed by "a pernicious ambiguity in . . . the term *subjective*," his overall accomplishment was to speak of ideas and objects in a way that did no violence to the process of vision which presupposed and anticipated both. In his own words,

> he does not deny the sensuous fact: by no means; but he will not see that alone. He does not deny the presence of this table, this chair, and the walls of this room, but he looks at these things as the reverse side of the tapestry, as the *other end*, each being a sequel or completion of a spiritual fact which nearly concerns him.

With the proviso that the figures are in constant motion as the mind enters objects and objects enter the mind, it might be said that the tapestry, the field of vision, is Emerson's world. It is a realm in which "*subjectiveness* itself is the question, and Nature is the answer," where the precepts "Know thyself" and "Study nature" become a single maxim.

This is only to add that the *how* of knowledge—the process, the method, the form—is identical with the stuff of knowledge, the bipolar unity of idea and thing. The paradoxical fusion of "concrete fact" is also a unity of structure and content; equally paradoxical, since we always make the distinction, but even more fundamentally unified because mind and matter alike are instinct with form:

> There is in nature a parallel unity which corresponds to the unity in the mind and makes it available. This methodizing mind meets no resistance in its attempts. The scattered blocks, with which it strives to form a symmetrical structure, fit. This design following after finds with joy that like design went before. Not only man puts things in a row, but things belong in a row.

Here the primary question is not the locus of form with relation to subject and object but rather the locus of subject and object with relation to a formative process evident in both. Since "Nature works after the same method as the human Imagination," method takes on a kind of autonomy as a becoming in which nature and the imagination participate. Emerson found in this manner of speaking the surest way to point back at the oneness of idea, expression, and object which "the ancients" enjoyed without effort and the lack of which had left the mind in an "alien, . . . unknown" world. For, as he asked as though in reply to his friend Hedge, "what is classification but the perceiving that these objects are not chaotic, and are not foreign, but have a law which is also a law of the human mind?" To look at either pole of perception was to discover "the analogy that marries Matter and Mind"—the common structure that made everything in nature "an expression of some property inherent in man the observer" and that gave every "passage in the human soul," every "shade of thought," its predestined "emblem in nature." Reality was neither mental nor material substance but emerging form, and its locus, if one must give it a place, was the act of perception and the act of speech:

> The constructive intellect produces thoughts, sentences, poems, plans, designs, systems. It is the generation of the mind, the marriage of thought with nature. . . . It is the advent of truth into the world, a form of thought now for the first time bursting into the universe. . . .

While this passage may seem to cling to the "idealistic minimum" that Urban finds in any adequate theory of symbolism, what Emerson is trying to emphasize is the symbolic construct per se, quite apart from the premises of idealism. He is concerned, in Cassirer's phrase, with man as "animal symbolicum," not as "animal rationale"; the advent of truth is the growth of a language in which man realizes himself by discovering nature:

> So must we admire in man the form of the formless, the concentrations of the vast. . . . The history of the genesis or the old mythology repeats itself in the experience of every child. He too is a demon or god thrown into a particular chaos, where he strives ever to lead things from disorder into order. Each individual soul is such in virtue of its being a power to translate the world into some particular language of its own; if not into a picture, a statue, or a dance,—why, then, into a trade, an art, a science, a mode of living, a conversation, a character, an influence.

Though human speech was obviously the prototype of this vision of reality as radical symbolism, it was only one mode of the symbolic universe and in a way the least characteristic. Taken in isolation, verbal language withstood the realistic bias of Emerson, his "endeavor to make the exchange evermore, of a reality for a name." It had an arbitrary aspect that lent a certain credibility to eighteenth-century nominalism and that often left Emerson himself with a despairing sense of the "remoteness from the line of things in the line of words." But Emerson's purpose in generalizing his conception of "language" was precisely to compensate for the pull of rationalism on words and things alike. To describe all human activities as "intertranslateable language" was to redefine both reality and speech by putting both in terms of creative activity. "Words," Emerson said, "are also actions," just as "actions are a kind of words." Meaning, in whatever mode, was like "the figure, movement, and gesture of animated bodies," where the union of the spiritual with the physical and the submergence of both in sheer activity constitute a "silent and subtile language." Meaning was "not *what,* but *how,*" or rather the substance via the manner, like the recapture of being in becoming which Yeats imaged as the chestnut tree, the dancer, and the dance.

Though he dealt in theory, Emerson's whole enterprise had its origin in a state of mind. He had experienced a linguistic fact that made nonsense of rationalism:

> There lie the impressions on the retentive organ, though you knew it not. So lies the whole series of natural images with which your life has made you acquainted, in your memory, though you know it not; and a thrill of passion flashes light on their dark chamber, and the active power seizes instantly the fit image, as the word of its momentary thought.

Speech so experienced, as at once sensation and idea, could not be reduced to the status of the arbitrary sign. Language, the "quite wonderful city which we all help to build," was greater than the builder, claiming a kind of wisdom of its own:

> Each word is like a work of Nature, determined a thousand years ago, and not alterable. We confer and dispute, and settle the meaning so and so, but it remains what it was in spite of us. The word beats all the speakers and definers of it, and stands to their children what it stood to their fathers.

Meaning was the unchangeable potentiality of a word; what we call change of meaning was an alteration of the perceiving mind and the objective world:

> The great word Comparative Anatomy has now leaped out of the womb of the Unconscious. I feel a cabinet in my mind unlocked in each of these new interests. Wherever I go, the related objects crowd on my Sense and I explore backward, and wonder how the same things looked to me before my attention had been aroused.

Such passages of linguistic psychology are the trail left by a new mode of thought, which really demanded poetic utterance and could be fully conveyed only as a new poetic manner. What Emerson tried to render as metaphysical doctrine, and expressed more adequately by his very ambiguity of statement, was the resurgent capacity for symbolic experience, based on a peculiar sense of the inherent power of language.

Given this perspective, he moves back and forth from self-expression to impression, from language as the power of mind to language as the potentiality of nature. For him, "the seer is a sayer" and "that which cannot externize itself is not thought"; the word conveys "what I am and what I think . . . in spite of my efforts to hold it back." On the other hand, "nature is a language, and every new fact that we learn is a new word"; nature is a network of significant relations, so that the writer is also a reader. Although once again Emerson finds it necessary to invoke "Mind" and "Nature" in order to state a view that dissolves them, each partial statement entails the whole truth: that language is both self-expression and impression, that speech fundamentally refers neither to a preconception nor to an external thing but "to that which is to be said." Thus the old landmarks are relocated in the Emersonian landscape. The section in *Nature* on "Language," which sets forth the "threefold degree" in which "nature is the vehicle of thought," assumes a point of view from which each term—"nature," "vehicle," and "thought"—gives the others a new implication. Emerson begins with words as "signs of natural facts"; but when he goes on to say that "particular natural facts are symbols of particular spiritual facts" and that "nature is the symbol of spirit," natural fact in the sense of his first proposition no longer exists, the instrumental sign becomes an autonomous symbol, and spirit is simply the meaning of fact as symbol.

This position is oddly circular, for it both entails and assumes a theory of poetry. Emerson rightly supposed that his new sense of language was a rediscovery of poetic method: the "Namer or Language-maker" was distinctively the poet. What he said of language in general could be said even more precisely of poetic speech, which expressed the poet's thought, "but *alter idem,* in a manner totally new," while at the same time the expression was "the new type which things themselves take when liberated." Just as the kind of perception in which Emerson was interested turned out to be a verbal intuition, inherently meaningful language was essentially the poetic word:

> The poet names the thing because he sees it, or comes one step nearer to it than any other. This expression or naming is not art, but a second nature, grown out of the first, as a leaf out of a tree.

On the other hand, Emerson was most at home on the plane where philosophy and literature, science and art, are equally symbolic, and he justified his feeling that poetry is the essence of speech by the generalization that all true speech is poetic creation. He turned the tables on his predecessors and laid the groundwork for a conscious literary symbolism by assuming that all men, even Locke, are potential poets. The "progress of metaphysical philosophy," he suggested, was really "the progressive introduction of opposite metaphors":

> Thus the Platonists congratulated themselves for ages upon their knowledge that Mind was a dark chamber whereon ideas like shadows were painted. Men derided this as infantile when they afterwards learned that the Mind was a sheet of white paper whereon any and all characters might be written.

This generalization was bolstered by the apparent fact that "poetry preceded prose, as the form of sustained thought." All language was patently "fossil poetry . . . made up of images or tropes, which now, in their secondary use, have long ceased to remind us of their poetic origin." It followed that the objectivity of rational speech was an aberration, a distortion of the universal poetry. The basic division of mankind lay between those who speak "*from without,* as spectators merely," and those who "speak *from within* . . . as parties and possessors of the fact"—between those, as Emerson liked to say, who "speak about things" and those who "speak the things themselves." Here was the necessary counterweight to the rational orthodoxy of the modern tradition, as well as the sanction for a thoroughgoing symbolistic method in literature. Emerson found a new philosophic standpoint in the language of poetry, one that left the rationalist out on a limb, and at the same time he gave the language of poetry a new standing by reasserting the basic poetry of language. To feel the world as "two, . . . Me and It," had reduced poetry to "a pretty dream"; to turn about and feel the world as poetry gave dreams themselves "a poetic truth and integrity" as symbolic constructs: "My dreams are not me; they are not Nature, or the Not-me: they are both. They have a double consciousness, at once sub- and ob-jective."

It was just this resort to a generic symbolism that drew Emerson away from the specific problems of poetic art. In proportion as he dwelt on the heights where "all becomes poetry," thus establishing the symbolistic point of view, he lost touch with the practical conditions of poetic creation, which demand that the symbol be not only *found* but also *made*. For him, the poet's "expression or naming" was "not art, but a second nature." Instead of reflecting that the "first" nature, the material world, might well force a degree of art upon the poet, Emerson held that the "second" grows out of the "first" involuntarily, "as a leaf out of a tree." And he went on to maintain, as well as he could, that the order should be reversed—that the poet's unitary act of naming is really prior to the divisive language of common sense—although in the end he was still left with a "double consciousness, at once sub- and ob-jective." Emerson achieved his own aim only to the extent that he managed to represent the double consciousness as unified, not as a duality which must be forged into unity. While he was prepared to admit that poetic creation involves "a mixture of will, a certain control over the spontaneous states . . . a strenuous exercise of choice," his theory really left the poet no room for decision. The poet was a maker only in the sense that "perception makes"; the given "word" was literature itself rather than the raw material of literature; there was no need to build any tighter symbolic structure than such words impose upon themselves.

What is extraordinary about Emerson's writings is the way in which the problems he tried to ignore rose up again to dog him, lending a richer texture and content to his work. His flagrant inconsistency of method and the paradoxicality that he could never exclude from his theory were the product of his own encounter with the making of literature and with the claims of diversity upon every concrete fact. What is even more important is the seminal effect of his point of view, or the kind of thinking illustrated by it: the way his facile generalizations, which were intended as philosophic answers, communicated a new set of questions to the literary mind. While he spoke of the world as two only in order to suggest how it might be one, he thereby acknowledged a duality which is no less real because it is conquered in each instant of poetic speech. Emerson made way for a mode of writing which would dwell on the bipolarity of unity; in which "every act, every thought, every cause, is bipolar, and in the act is contained the counteraction. If I strike, I am struck; if I chase, I am pursued." He laid the groundwork for Melville, who freely accepted the ambiguity of the process by which "the artist informs himself in efforming matter." Emerson implied Melville, not as premise and conclusion, but as intuition is pregnant with the possibilities of new experience.

* * *

> See how cunningly constructed are all things in such a manner as to make each being the centre of the Creation. You seem to be a point or focus upon which all objects, all ages concentrate their influence. Nothing past but affects *you*. Nothing remote but through some means reaches *you*. Every superficial grain of sand may be considered as the fixed point round which all things revolve, so intimately is it allied to all and so truly do all turn as if for it alone.

Emerson describes a kind of existential poem, which, while in a sense it makes all lesser poems irrelevant, provides at the same time a rationale for the practicing artist. It provides him not only with a structural pattern but also with a status and function; for the man who can see the world of symbolic foci is himself an element in the universal poem—"a point or focus upon which all objects, all ages, concentrate their influence." Poetic man, the seer, is an instance of the structural principle which pervades his vision. It is by virtue of his power of vision that he occupies a unique place in the universal organism. The exercise of vision is a mode of being: *"so to be* is the sole inlet of *so to know."* But human being is distinctive in that it is really the becoming of the entire structure of which mankind, from another standpoint, is a part. While all things are potential centers of the world, man is the center of centers. "He is placed in the centre of beings, and a ray of relation passes from every other being to him. And neither can man be understood without these objects, nor these objects without man." Man, who from one point of view is a function of the cosmic structure, is unique because through him issues the whole relational world. He is "a bundle of relations, a knot of roots, whose flower and fruitage is the world." If the organic universe is the soil in which he grows, it is also, simultaneously, the product of his growth. It is both presupposed and created by the poetic activity of man.

The argument is frankly circular. It is no less paradoxical, in the final analysis, than Emerson's other attempts to formulate a world without absolute distinctions between man and nature, subject and object, the knower and the known. It serves, nevertheless, to remove the whole problem to another realm of discourse, where old preconceptions are less of a drag. Man, on this theory, is not essentially a mind dealing with alien matter; on the contrary, the human being begins where this disjunction ends, for he is defined as "the point wherein matter and spirit meet and marry." The organic principle hinges on the conception of a total man, without whose central presence as the vehicle of all becoming the world would collapse into the opposite poles of rationalism: "A man should know himself for a necessary actor. A link was wanting between two craving parts of nature, and he was hurled into being as the bridge over that yawning need, the mediator betwixt two else unmarriageable facts." So considered, man and the universe transcend the rational categories. Though Emerson continues to speak of "mind" and "matter," his basic scheme is really independent of those antonyms, being concerned with the mutual dependence of an organic creature and its environment.

These merge into each other; the figure of man is blurred and fluctuating. What seems at first an external relation between thought and the objects of thought turns out to be a single activity, more on the order of "sex, nutriment, gestation, birth, growth." The concept of mind gives way to the concept of organic function:

> The intelligent mind is forever coming into relation with all the objects of nature and time, until from a vital point it becomes a great heart from which the blood rolls to the distant channels of things, and to which, from those distant channels, it returns.

Even when Emerson falls back on a more conventional vocabulary, the old terminology is wrenched and modified by his new assumptions. The "mind" he invokes is not mental substance but a kind of behavior: "to think is to act." Mind is not divisible into areas like perception, knowledge. and will, but appears as a process where "each becomes other." And even this functional definition is ultimately inadequate, for "it is by no means action which is the essential point, but some middle quality indifferent both to poet and to actor, and which we call Reality. . . . Not action, not speculation imports, but a middle essence common to both." What is common to poetry and action, though indifferent to poet and actor, is the advent of meaning. Man, whether in thought or deed, is no more than the "faculty of reporting"; the universe is "the possibility of being reported." In the report itself, in poems and arts and systems, the human faculty and the universal possibility both become actual.

Thus Emerson gave the poet a role by transforming man and the universe out of all recognition. In his effort to shake off any links with the rational world view, he projected a world in which only symbols exist. We ourselves, from his standpoint, "are symbols," and we "inhabit symbols." The poetic image is identical not only with the universe it generates but also with the human being through whom it is actualized: "The value of a trope is that the hearer is one: and indeed Nature itself is a vast trope, and all particular natures are tropes." Emerson asserts, in effect, the identity of "I mean" and "it means"; he maintains that there is no distinction between the poet's act of "meaning," the poet himself, and the "meaning" of things. According to him, "a man is a method, a progressive arrangement, a selecting principle." To symbolize is man's function, but to symbolize is to *become* a symbol, into which, as a momentary mold, "the world is poured like melted wax." In this light the radically symbolic status of a poem is merely another way of viewing the symbolic structure it exhibits. Whatever one may think of Emerson's free and easy way with logic, his theory enables him to speak with equal assurance, and simultaneously, of the *why* and the *what* of literature, for it treats both of these questions as a single question of method. Emerson's reply to *why?* and *what?* is always *how*. He always returns to the realm of form, where "this refers to that, and that to the next, and the next to the third, and everything refers"—where the end and the essence of humanity are its formation and its formative power, so that "the delight that man finds in classification is the first index of his Destiny." Prior to the individual "thought" and "object" is the formal principle, which is the same whether we move from idea to thing or from one thing to another:

> I notice that I value nothing so much as the threads that spin from a thought to a fact, and from one fact to another fact, making both experiences valuable and presentable, which were insignificant before, and weaving together into rich webs all solitary observations.

The real implication of the organic theory, and, by the same token, the only scheme that would fully undercut the assumptions of rationalism, was a world of form, for this radical formalism did away with all static individuals. Here there was no substance upon which a form might be *imposed;* no thinking subject or isolated object of thought. Instead, one dealt in a web of meaning where the symbol—thought, word, or thing; the knower or the known—was a momentary point round which a whole took shape and which, in turn, received the delegated efficacy of the whole:

> The metamorphosis of Nature shows itself in nothing more than this, that there is no word in our language that cannot become typical of us of Nature by giving it emphasis. The world is a Dancer; it is a Rosary; it is a Torrent; it is a Boat; a Mist; a Spider's Snare; it is what you will; and the metaphor will hold, and it will give the imagination keen pleasure. Swifter than light the world converts itself into that thing you name, and all things find their right place under this new and capricious classification.

The sphere of meaning, perpetually redefined by its evanescent center, was simultaneously the milieu and the content of the work of art. In one dimension the artifact was itself a symbol, source and product of universal form: "A work of art is an abstract or epitome of the world." In another dimension it was the plenum of all symbols, since its meaning was unrestricted short of the entire universe.

This is the heart of Emerson's theory, the basic formula from which stem both its defects and its possibilities. By leveling the distinction between the "internal" structure and the "external" relations of the poem, so as to picture a spontaneous dance of self-determining and autonomous symbols, he left no means of control, evaluation, or limitation. On the other hand, his primary motive was certainly not the encouragement of artistic irresponsibility. He wanted to account for the psychological facts of creation, which otherwise he could only point at by alleging "the identity of the observer with the observed." It is a matter of experience that the poet *entertains* his vision of reality; he "suffers the intellect to see"; he undergoes "not instruction, but provocation." This is the differentia of the poetic attitude, and it seems to presuppose a distinctive kind of world. What that world might be is suggested by the further fact that such entertainment occurs as a formative process. Indeed, it could be defined as a state to which the two elements predicated by reason, the subject and the object, are inapplicable because they are always in process of formation; the growth of the vision is precisely the growth of the seer and the seen. "A man never sees the same object twice: with his own enlargement the object acquires new aspects." Emerson's theory is the metaphysical statement of this poetic psychology—the projection of a world of form to explain the formative essence of poetry.

It follows that there is little point in asking whether his doctrine is ontologically true. The useful question to ask is where the doctrine leads. Emerson is the appointed apologist of the symbolistic writer. His theory, partial as it is, establishes certain assumptions which any writer makes to a greater or lesser degree; it corresponds, by virtue of its very partiality, to the symbolist's obsession with the differentia of literature. The metaphysical structure which Emerson projects, circling round the figure of a man who "cannot help seeing everything under its relations to all other things and to himself," is readily translated into stylistic terms. When he declares that "there is no fact in nature which does not carry the whole sense of nature," that "the entire system of things gets represented in every particle," he is defining synecdoche. When he says that "experience identifies," that nature is "*one thing and the other thing,* in the same moment," he is describing metaphor. In practice, the self-realization of the symbolic universe is "Rhetoric, or the Building of Discourse."

The house of Rhetoric is built without logical mortar. Emerson postulates another binding force, which works through the collocation of words and thereby "gives . . . value to all the stones." He calls for a poem that

> shall thrill the world by the mere juxtaposition and interaction of lines and sentences that singly would have been of little worth and short date. Rightly is this art named Composition, and the composition has manifold the effect of the component parts. . . . The collated thoughts beget more, and the artificially combined individuals have in addition to their own a quite new collective power. The main is made up of many islands, the state of many men, the poem of many thoughts, each of which, in its turn, filled the whole sky of the poet, was day and Being to him.

As the last sentence suggests, the rhetorical unity of one part with another presupposes and makes possible the inherent reference of each part to the whole. Juxtaposition is a way of indicating a basic continuity, whereby every element is subject to a complete redefinition in the light of each of the others, so that (and because) each is a means of stating the whole. Or, to put the matter in another way, rhetorical structure has no finite elements. What is given in rhetoric is not a logical term, a "bounded fact," but a symbol which is really an expanding sphere presented at a "point where its rays converge to a focus." So regarded, each "noun of the intellect" or "fact of nature"—however one chooses to describe it—possesses "a double, treble, or centuple use and meaning." (This need not be consciously recognized in order to exist: "A man may find his words mean more than he thought when he uttered them, and be glad to employ them again in a new sense.") Art is habitual concentration on symbols, each of which is "the absolute *Ens* seen from one side":

> It is the habit of certain minds to give an all-excluding fulness to the object, the thought, the word they alight upon, and to make that for the time the deputy of the world. These are the artists, the orators, the leaders of society. The power to detach and to magnify by detaching is the essence of rhetoric in the hands of the orator and the poet. This rhetoric, or power to fix the momentary eminency of an object . . . depends on the depth of the artist's insight of that object. . . . For every object has its roots in central nature, and may of course be so exhibited to us as to represent the world.

Thus there is, as it were, no real question as to how the "parts" of a literary work become coherent. The literary term, by nature, includes and is included by its context, so that it is not a "part" in the same sense as a logical entity. Synecdoche is the principle by which the whole is vested in one of its aspects, and the term exists; metaphor is the principle by which "the world converts itself into that thing you name," and the whole exists. As Emerson notes, "poetry seems to begin in the slightest change of name," for this is the beginning of the combined detachment and magnification, derivation and imposition of meaning, which simultaneously establish the rhetorical unit and the rhetorical whole. The completed poem is a kind of movement, a progressive metamorphosis, of the total work and of each constituent term.

"Why should we write dramas, and epics, and sonnets, and novels in two volumes? Why not write as variously as we dress and think?" In setting forth the symbolistic ideal of a language where "every word . . . is million-faced," Emerson was proposing not an escape from form but an exploitation of the distinctive formal resources of literary speech. Yet Emerson had a theory of poetry which eliminated the particular poem, since it provided no means of halting the proliferation of metaphor and synecdoche. The poem he described, constructed wholly on the principles of multiple meaning, was chimerical. He himself could believe in its existence only because he was always able, given his premises, to slip from the "world" of the poem to the world at large. In any individual case, for the very reason that it *was* individual, an attempt to live up to his doctrine necessarily would lead to the difficulty he seems to have experienced—where, "if we go to affirm anything, we are checked in our speech by the need of recognizing all other things, until speech presently becomes rambling, general, indefinite, and merely tautology." In practice the most radically formalistic of literary doctrines was conducive to literary anarchy. Emerson would have liked to contend that, although "our tuition is through emblems and indirections, . . . there is method in it, a fixed scale and rank above rank in the phantasms." But nothing in his doctrine gave him a right to say this. He had destroyed the concept of fixity and with it the concept of hierarchy: his poet "derives as grand a joy from symbolizing the Godhead or his universe under the form of a moth or a gnat as of a Lord of Hosts." As an attack on the idea of intrinsically "poetic" material, this notion has its measure of validity. It implies a fundamental theme of modern aesthetics—that the work of art establishes a scale of value through formal means and does not depend on any external standard. Emerson, however, tries to do without the very concept of externality. He goes further and maintains that "the truth-speaker may dismiss all solicitude as to the proportion and congruency of the aggregate of his thoughts, so long as he is a faithful reporter of particular impressions." On this showing, the poem can establish no scale of value because it is wholly fluid, changing its shape as it moves from point to point. The symbolistic work is saved from such complete indeterminacy by the struggle to melt and reorder accepted distinctions; this intrinsic bond with the rational world gives the poem a focus. When Emerson projects a totally poetic universe, he deprives himself of any brake on the transmutation of form.

In general, then, while Emerson defines the presuppositions of a symbolistic literature, he does so in such a way as to make any literature impracticable. Thoreau's ultimate preference for the art of life over the life of art is only one symptom of the basic inadequacy of a purely symbolistic doctrine, which aims at creating a literature faithful to the status and form of sheer experience, but must finally settle for experience, not literature. Matthew Arnold's commendation of Emerson might be modified to read that "he is the friend and aider of those who would live in the symbol." But he is a friend whose aid must be suspect, as Melville perceived. What he gives with one hand he takes away with the other.

* * *

But Emerson came off very well under the circumstances. His rationale, which led him into many a theoretical mist, could also give shape and direction to the literary mind. For he himself was nothing if not literary.

Melville marked in his copy of the *Essays* a passage in which Emerson declared that the poet "disposes very easily of the most disagreeable facts"; and he noted in the margin, "So it would seem. In this sense, Mr. E. is a great poet." Here certainly was the bland inspirationalist, "cracked right across the brow," who was intent on drawing a veil before "the shark-maw of the Devil." Yet, as Melville conceded, Emerson was a "thought-diver." If he generally came to the surface with a premature conclusion that glossed over the battle in the depths, there was another and more important meaning in the very spectacle of his ever-renewed descent. What seemed a sermon was really a kind of object-lesson, a spiritual exercise. Though he was not a great poet, nor even a good poet, he was more a poet than a dogmatist. He was an artist in the medium of theory—in short, a dialectician—and his doctrines are better regarded as themes of his discourse than as elements of a system. He was ultimately faithful to no creed but only to the process of concrete thought which doctrine, as doctrine, always distorts.

"Dialectic" was his own term for his quasi-poetic method:

> As there is a science of stars, called astronomy; a science of quantities, called mathematics; a science of qualities, called chemistry; so there is a science of sciences,—I call it Dialectic—which is the Intellect discriminating the false and the true. It rests on the observation of identity and diversity; for to judge is to unite to an object the notion which belongs to it.

Dialectic claims the autonomous status of a poem, working in a realm constituted by the unification of objects and notions, and "discriminating the false and the true" on the basis of internal coherence rather than correspondence to an external reality. It is not a set of doctrines, but a process—"a long logic"—and "the moment it would appear as propositions and have a separate value, it is worthless." The characteristic form of dialectic is an approximation of symbolic structure:

> Each new step we take in thought reconciles twenty seemingly discordant facts, as expressions of one law. . . . By going one step farther back in thought, discordant opinions are reconciled by being seen to be two extremes of one principle, and we can never go so far back as to preclude a still higher vision.

In the dialectic hierarchy each general law is "only a particular fact of some more general law presently to disclose itself."

Emerson's fifty-year monologue was itself the best example of the genre he described. His ideas, as he pointed out, were like great circles on a sphere: they were "intertranslateable." Conversely, his main subject was the method he professed; he was never far removed from the act of expression as he himself knew it. In his usage a term like "World Spirit," whatever it means as a metaphysical entity, is also "our name for the last generalization to which we can arrive." God is the "algebraic *x*" in language, standing for a "residuum unknown, unanalyzable," which includes and is implied by the whole of recorded speech. If the writer is a "rhapsodist," and poetic creation is a "surrender of will to the Universal Power," this "attitude of reception" is cognate to the *entertainment* of meaning by which the symbolist and the dialectician extend the boundaries of present reality. In theory and in practice, Emerson cleaved to the concrete awareness which is the basis of literature: the sense of a whole which anticipates its parts; which is implicit in the parts and yet transcends them; which is known, therefore, by continual redefinition; and which is given as an immediate presence. He isolated these principles and thereby made them more available.

Of course, he oversimplified. The facile optimism that Melville censured was more than a matter of personality; it was inherent in the way Emerson put his basic question. "Cannot I conceive the Universe without a contradiction?" He was not fully alive to the complexity of the concrete fact in which he worked and to which his theory referred, for he took it as evidence that "the world of contradictions which the metaphysician finds" is not a real form of nature. Contradiction seemed only to prove that "the universality, being hindered in its primary form, comes in the secondary form of *all sides*. . . . Nature keeps herself whole and her representation complete in the experience of each mind." He resisted the idea that opposition might be more than a phenomenon, and he was always prepared with comforting reflections on the value of multiplicity:

> The surveyor goeth about taking positions to serve as the points of his angles, and thereby afterwards he finds the place of the mountain. The philosopher in like manner selects points whence he can look on his subject from different sides, and by means of many approximate results he at last obtains an accurate expression of the truth.

Emerson could never feel the potential disunity of thought, word, and object as a tragic dilemma; this was Melville's discovery. At his most skeptical, Emerson is lighthearted:

> It seemed to men that words come nearer to the thing; described the fact; were the fact. They learn later that they only suggest it. It is an operose, circuitous way of putting us in mind of the thing—of flagellating our attention. But this was slowly discovered. . . . Garrulity is our religion and philosophy.

He calmly foresees the disappearance of all language as "speech becomes less, and finally ceases in a noble silence." By agnosticism, if not by knowledge, the integrity of truth will be preserved.

He is more appealing in those moments of rueful confession when he *cannot* conceive the universe without a contradiction and therefore contradicts himself. As early as his sermon on the Lord's Supper, he was forced to modify his more categorical statements on the unity of thought, word, and object: "We are not accustomed to express our thoughts and emotions by symbolical actions. . . . To eat bread is one thing; to love the precepts of Christ and resolve to obey them is quite another." This disintegration of the symbol was one of the hard realities of a world where it was not always easy to transfigure the material fact. The symbolic ideal was perpetually unattained. "For language itself is young and unformed. In heaven it will be . . . 'one with things.' Now, there are many things that refuse to be recorded—perhaps the larger half. The unsaid part is the best of every discourse." Emerson was "not so foolish as to declaim against forms," but he was uncomfortably aware that his formalism walked a narrow path between the recalcitrance of the object and the vagaries of the imagination. He criticized Margaret Fuller for erecting a "dazzling mythology" without any "real meaning." Moreover, form itself was treacherous. The theme of the sermon on the Lord's Supper is the fossilization to which every form is subject when it degenerates from a creative force into a static sign. Even the creative symbol has its "intrinsic defect," for "language overstates" and exists as self-contradiction. Somehow "we cannot strongly state one fact without seeming to belie some other," so that "the only way in which we can be just, is by giving ourselves the lie." At the same time, language understates, with the same result: "The thought that I think excludes me from all other thoughts. . . . The symbols in which I had hoped to convey a universal sense are rejected as partial." We are sectarians in spite of ourselves:

> There would be no sect if there were no sect. . . . Something has been overstated or omitted by the antecedent sect, and the human mind feels itself wronged, and overstates on the other side. . . . Each of our sects is an extreme statement and therefore obnoxious to contradiction and reproof.

His concessions gave away his case: the world of contradictions, which he regarded as "secondary," became the primary fact of Melville's experience. Emerson's work has enduring value because his point of view, partial as it was, implied its opposite. When he tried to elevate his point of view into doctrine, he emerged with the jejune concepts for which he is famous. But in so far as he was faithful to his dialectic method, he himself was committed to "all sides," and his work pointed like an arrow at its antithesis. Melville's grudging praise—"Say what they will, he's a great man"—was the just reward of this "endless seeker," who transcended his own conclusions and who remained, as much for good as for ill, a "man without a handle."

# The Angle of Vision

## *by Sherman Paul*

*What is life but the angle of vision? A man is measured by the angle at which he looks at objects.*

EMERSON, "Natural History of Intellect."

*For the whole world converts itself into that man and through him as through a lens, the rays of the universe shall converge, withersoever he turns, on a point.*

EMERSON, *Journals.*

For the Emerson who defined the problem of insight in terms of the alignment of the axis of vision and the axis of things—"The ruin or the blank, that we see when we look at nature, is in our own eye. The axis of vision is not coincident with the axis of things, and so they appear not transparent, but opaque" (*C*, I, 73)[1]—the passage on the transparent eyeball is justly the representative anecdote of his experience of inspiration. "In the woods," he wrote, "we return to reason and faith. There I feel that nothing can befall me in life—no disgrace, no calamity (leaving me my eyes), which nature cannot repair. Standing on the bare ground—my head bathed by the blithe air, and uplifted into infinite space—all mean egotism vanishes. I become a transparent eyeball; I am nothing; I see all; the currents of the Universal Being circulate through me; I am part or particle of God." (*C*, I, 10) The original *Journal* record (*J*, III, 452-453)[2] is less compact, and except for an afterthought, less significant. The transparent eyeball is omitted, but its characteristic power is added: "There the mind integrates itself again. The attention, which had been distracted into parts, is reunited, reinsphered. The whole of nature addresses itself to the whole man. . . . It is more than a medicine. It is health." (*J*, III, 453) In terms of Emerson's visual experience, the trans-



[1] C—*The Complete Works of Ralph Waldo Emerson.* Centenary Edition.

[2] J—*The Journals of Ralph Waldo Emerson.*

parent eyeball was more than a lucky image. Twenty-five years later he noted that Plotinus had said of the heavens, "There . . . every body is pure (transparent), and each inhabitant is as it were an eye." (*J*, IX, 285) And throughout his many observations of the inspirational process, Emerson often converted thought into its visual counterpart, light: "Thought is nothing but the circulations made luminous." (*J*, VIII, 397) As a representative experience of inspiration, then, the famous passage in *Nature* indicates that for Emerson the primary agency of insight was seeing.

The eye was Emerson's most precious endowment. Everywhere in his writing it was a symbol of all the stages of inspiration, and still he could not resist the extended tribute he gave it in "Behavior." He confessed his own poor ear, knowing that he had compensation in his eye: "My lack of musical ear is made good to me through my eyes. That which others hear, I *see*." (*J*, V, 138) What his ear brought him, he often described visually; he compared the "thread of sound" in a singer's voice to "a ray of light," (*J*, V, 255-256) and the rippling pond struck his eye with a delight as great as that of an aeolian harp to the ear. (*J*, IX, 179-180) Light and music were analogous in their law, and he felt that in "the splendid function of seeing" he had the power of "recurring to the Sublime at pleasure." (*J*, IV, 173, 440)

The eye, then, was his prominent faculty. (Christopher Cranch, perhaps unwittingly, caricatured Emerson as an eye mounted on two spindly legs.) Seeing, for him, was constitutional: by bringing his total sensual response to nature, it was tantamount to spiritual health. He was aware of this in his youth because his eyesight wavered with his indecisions. The Emerson heritage (more dramatically revealed in the mental collapse of Edward) was transmitted, perhaps, in his weak eyes. (See *L*, I, 208)[3] When his eyesight failed him early in his striving for greatness, he wrote of his convalescence, "I rejoice in the prospect of better sight and better health. . . . Loss of eyes is not exactly one of Socrates's superfluities." (*J*, II, 99) How intimately his sight and health were connected, he was far from realizing here; but by the time of *Nature*, he could think of no greater calamity than the loss of his eyes.

For Emerson, the eye, in its own functions, focused the problem of his double consciousness of nature-as-sensation and nature-as-projection. Without the awakening stimulus of light, he was spiritually blind: "The light of the body is the eye." He would have agreed with Sampson Reed's attribution of the powers of Reason and Understanding to the eye, and especially with its unifying role in bringing the two awarenesses of nature into controlled equilibrium. "The eye," Reed wrote, "appears to be the point at which the united rays of the sun within and the sun without, converge to an expression of unity."

[3] L—*The Letters of Ralph Waldo Emerson,* edited by Ralph L. Rusk.

Emerson found this true of his own experience. The eye brought him two perceptions of nature—nature ensphered and nature atomized—which corresponded to the distant and proximate visual powers of the eye. These powers, in turn, he could have called the reasoning and understanding modes of the eye. And to each he could have assigned its appropriate field of performance: the country and the city. The sympathy with nature he hoped to attain by seeing, he found in cultivating the distant powers of vision of the eye; for in distant vision he discovered a state of perception in which he felt a heightened intimacy with the natural process itself. Dorothy Emmet has called this *feeling* of organic intimacy "the adverbial mode of perception." As a qualitative feeling of the total presence of nature, it might be compared to William James's pure experience or stream of consciousness. For from this undifferentiated total awareness, by focusing the attention, one selected or differentiated objects. Emerson, especially after he wrote "Experience," was aware of the selecting or accusative mode of perception. (*J,* VI, 242, 253) But before he saw nature as *flux,* he found one of the difficulties of attaining insight by seeing, in the almost inescapable accusative perception of the natural eye. As Dorothy Emmet has pointed out, of the senses sight is the most highly developed, seldom perceiving in the "primitive" adverbial mode. In seeing, one is usually aware of specific objects, unless one rises to the higher level of "aesthetic seeing" in which one again consciously attempts to enjoy the whole as well as to differentiate its parts.

As the agency of correspondence with nature and of inspiration, sight demanded a consciousness of its behavior that in itself might prohibit influx. It demanded, as well, scope of activity—the wide panorama—or the widening of Emerson's literal angle of vision, that is to say, the diffusion of his focus into a blur of relatedness. Before "strained vision" reconstructed his experience in nature, he had to achieve the "indolent vision" of reception. (*C,* VI, 178) In this way, Emerson's sensory equipment provided initial difficulties that Thoreau, for example, did not have. Thoreau was fortunate in his exceptional hearing—the sense that discriminates least—and held easier converse (sympathetic correspondence) with nature. But in other ways, Emerson found sight rewarding: chiefly, by converting his inspirational experiences with the stars and heavens into an astronomy of the imagination, he had the formal means for intellectualizing his experience that Thoreau never acquired.

The blur of relatedness of adverbial perception was achieved by Emerson in distant vision. When he began his essay, "Circles," he diagramed the need for this mode of vision: "The eye is the first circle," he wrote, "the horizon which it forms is the second." (*C,* II, 301) The distance between the eye and its horizon, however, could be progressively extended, and for Emerson, had to be extended. For one could view trifles as well as the stars: "Our little circles absorb us and occupy us as fully as the heavens; we can minimize as infinitely as maximize, and the only way out of it is (to use a country phrase) to kick the pail over, and accept the horizon instead of the pail, with celestial attractions and influences, instead of worms and mud pies." (*J*, X, 238) And what (or how much) one viewed made the difference between Reason and Understanding. With this in mind, he would have welcomed Ortega y Gasset's comment that " 'Near' and 'far' are relative, metrically . . . to the eye they have a kind of absolute value. Indeed, the *proximate vision* and the *distant vision* of which physiology speaks are not notions that depend chiefly on measurable factors, but are rather two distinct ways of seeing." Bearing out Emerson's own experience (*J*, V, 21), Ortega explains that in proximate vision the eye converges on a central object, thereby limiting its horizon of field of vision. The object closely *is taken possession* of by the eye: it takes on "corporeality and solidity." In this respect, proximate vision is atomic—dissociating, analyzing, distinguishing—and, for Ortega, a feudal mode of seeing. To the political implications of proximate vision, especially in the identification of a similar atomism in Lockean perception with the commercial but spiritually sterile England of the 1840's, Emerson might have assented. He knew that "there is nothing of the true democratic element in what is called Democracy." True democracy had to transcend a commercialism that possessed trifles. (*J*, IV, 95)

Democratic vision, for him as well as for Ortega (and Whitman should be recalled throughout), was the distant vision in which synthesis and relatedness were achieved. It was the wider look in which all things were alike or equalized. (*C*, II, 136) In distant vision, as in Emerson's angle of vision, "the point of view becomes the synopsis." In the "optical democracy" of distant vision, if "nothing possesses a sharp profile; [if] everything is background, confused, almost formless," still "the duality of proximate vision is succeeded by a perfect unity of the whole visual field." Democratic vision was a mode of sympathy, the result of the love that blends and fuses. (*L*, II, 377) Describing this change from proximate to distant vision, from feudal to democratic vistas, in respect to the almost tactile sense of objects or "trifles" that one has in the former, Ortega corroborates Emerson's own experience of the dislimning of objects:

> As the object is withdrawn, sight loses its tactile power and gradually becomes pure vision. In the same way, things, as they recede, cease to be filled volumes, hard and compact, and become mere chromatic entities, without resistance, mass or convexity. An age-old habit, founded in vital necessity, causes men to consider as 'things,' in the strict sense, only such objects solid enough to offer resistance to their hands. The rest is more or less illusion. So in passing from proximate to distant vision an object becomes illusory. When the distance is great, there on the confines of a remote horizon—a tree, a castle, a mountain range—all acquire the half-unreal aspect of ghostly apparitions.

Emerson made the same distinction in the reality of objects by distinguishing the masculine and feminine traits of the eye. "Women," he wrote, "see quite without any wish to act." And so with men of genius: "They have this feminine eye, a function so rich that it contents itself without asking any aid of the hand. Trifles may well be studied by him; for he sees nothing insulated." (*J*, V, 335-336) When he wrote that he was easily untuned by necessary domestic concerns and needed "solitude of habit" for inspiration, he confessed his "more womanly eyes." (*C*, VIII, 289) For the same reason he had to distance an object to see it: "If you go near to the White Mountains, you cannot see them; you must go off thirty or forty miles to get a good view." (*J*, VI, 156) Freed from the object, "the eye," he discovered, "possesses the faculty of rounding and integrating the most disagreeable parts into a pleasing whole." (*J*, III, 556)

This power to dislimn and integrate objects, an original endowment of the youthful eye, Emerson found hampered by culture or education: even the first shock of Reason, by destroying one's faith or instinctive belief in the indissoluble union of man and nature, interrupted its functioning. After this momentary skepticism, however, the eye of Reason helped the natural eye renew its distant powers.

> Until this higher agency intervened," he wrote, "the animal eye sees with wonderful accuracy, sharp outlines and colored surfaces. When the eye of Reason opens, to outline and surface are at once added grace and expression. These proceed from imagination and affection, and abate somewhat of the angular distinctness of objects. If the Reason be stimulated to more earnest vision, the outlines and surfaces become transparent, and are no longer seen; causes and spirits are seen through them. (*C*, I, 49-50)

And just as Emerson restores the distant powers with the eye of Reason, so Ortega connects the need for the integration of distant vision with the post-Renaissance trend toward subjectivism in epistemology. For when one tries to diffuse the focus of the eye and thereby "to embrace the whole field," objects lose their solid-convexity and the whole field becomes concave: the horizon literally becomes circular, as Emerson felt when he viewed "the bended horizon." (*J*, V, 46) The "limit," Ortega says, "is a surface that tends to take the form of a hemisphere viewed from within." And this concavity begins, as Emerson also noted, at the eye. The result was the exhilaration of feeling one's centrality and penetration of space, and Emerson felt this in viewing the landscape and the heavens. He noted Aristotle's notion of space as container (*J*, VI, 6) and pictured the world as "a hollow temple," the beauty and symmetry of which depended on the eye. (*J*, VIII, 52) Ortega confirms this sense of space in distant vision: "What we see at a distance is hollow space as such. The content of perception is not strictly the surface in which the hollow space terminates, but rather the whole hollow space itself, from the eyeball to the . . . horizon." In this way the eye can be said to form the first circle, because, paradoxically, in distant vision the object "begins at our cornea." "In pure distant vision," Ortega explains, "our attention, instead of being directed farther away, has drawn back to the absolutely proximate, and the eye-beam, instead of striking the convexity of a solid body and staying fixed on it, penetrates a concave object, glides into a hollow." Emerson recognized this *nearness:* "Really the soul is *near* things, because it is the centre of the universe, so that astronomy and Nature and theology date from where the observer stands." (*J,* VIII, 22) The eye (or soul), then, becomes the center of the angle of vision. Or, as Ortega says, "in fixing upon the object nearest the cornea, the point of view is as close as possible to the subject and as far as possible from things." The eye no longer revolves "ptolemaically" about each object, "following a servile orbit." In the Copernican change to distant-subjective vision—in the visual revolution of the epistemologies of Descartes, Hume, and Kant—"the eye . . . is established as the center of the plastic Cosmos, around which revolve the forms of objects." Emerson realized this change as early as 1831, when he wrote, "The point of view is of more importance than the sharpness of sight." (*J,* II, 399)

The requirements of distant vision compelled Emerson to arm the natural eye. Extremely "sensible . . . to circumstances"—he felt mean in the city streets (*J,* V, 146)—he needed as a condition of inspiration the wide, panoramic view. When only seventeen years old, he remarked on the scope of vision: "It is a singular fact that we cannot present to the imagination a longer space than just so much of the world as is bounded by the visible horizon." (*J,* I, 13) For the higher seeing he needed to go beyond this horizon (*C,* IV, 82); but, at least for the dislimning of objects by which inspiration was achieved, he needed to see *to* the horizon. The horizon, he would have admitted, was essential to his best working attitude: it was what the German Romanticists called the *Idealeferne.* He complained to his brother Edward, "I am trying to learn to find my own latitude but there is no horizon in C[hardon] St." (*L,* I, 330) And after he left the church, free to follow a literary life, he wrote to Lydia Jackson that in Concord he could possess his soul but that to go to Plymouth "would be to cripple me of some important resources." (*L,* I, 437-438) He felt that he must have "a scope like nature itself, a susceptibility to all impressions . . . the heart as well as . . . the logic of creation." (*C,* V, 253) For this, Concord was preferable.

One important resource was nature: in the rural landscape he found an attractive release from the visual confines of city life. "We need nature," he wrote, "and cities give the human senses not room enough. I go out daily and nightly to feed my eyes on the horizon and the sky, and come to feel the want of this scope as I do of water for my washing." (*J,* IV, 34) But even in the woods, unless he could fuse the detail by walking rapidly, he felt annoyed. (*J,* IV, 439) Of what use was his genius, he wrote, "if the organ . . . cannot find a focal distance?" (*J,* VI, 519)

His best focal distance was the unlimited extent: the heavens, the sea, the fields, and preferably the line of the horizon in which heavens and earth, sea and sky met. "The imaginative faculty of the soul," he wrote, "must be fed with objects immense and eternal." (*C,* I, 216) In the horizon he felt "the true outline of the world" (*J,* III, 264), and the "astonishment" of landscape was "the meeting of the sky and the earth." (*J,* VI, 76) Here was the mystic line, the visible symbol in nature itself of the dualism of the universe. And if the finite limit of the horizon suggested the illimitable, its hazy fading in the distance promised the bipolar unity of the moment of inspiration. For Emerson, the far was "holy," especially when the world itself began to dislimn (*J,* IV, 13); and haze, by doubling the distance (*J,* IV, 489), seemed to double the quantity of nature one grasped in his angle of vision. "From your centre," Emerson recorded, "Nature carries every integral part out to the horizon, and mirrors yourself to you in the universe." (*J,* VIII, 525) In this way the hazy distance tempted his eye and compensated for "the cramp and pettiness of human performances." (*C,* VII, 298) By providing intimations of spiritual release, a landscape—"a long vista in woods, trees on the shore of a lake coming quite down to the water, a long reach in a river, a double or triple row of uplands or mountains seen one over the other" (*J,* V, 470)—rewarded Emerson not only with first sight, but with second sight and insight. (*J,* V, 422) With only the horizon before him, he could launch himself into the sea of being, certain that he was able "to possess entire nature, to fill the horizon, to fill the infinite amplitude of being with great life, to be in sympathy and relation with all creatures, to lose all privateness by sharing all natural action, shining with the Day, undulating with the sea, growing with the tree, instinctive with the animals, entranced in beatific vision with the human reason." (*J,* V, 272)

This sympathetic correspondence with nature, the harmony of man and the vegetable, followed from breaking the artificial bonds of city life and expanding with the horizon of the "medicinal" fields. Coming into nature, Emerson wrote, "We come into our own and make friends with matter." (*C,* III, 171) This sympathy with matter, in a sense opening up the circulations of being, was the ground of the moment of ecstasy. Following the rapture of the transparent eyeball, Emerson immediately and significantly added:

> I am the lover of uncontained and immortal beauty. In the wilderness, I find something more dear and connate than in streets or villages. In the tranquil landscape, and especially in the distant line of the horizon, man beholds somewhat as beautiful as his own nature.
>
> "The greatest delight which the fields and woods minister, is the suggestion of an occult relation between man and the vegetable . . . [and] the

power to produce this delight does not reside in nature, but in man, or in a harmony of both. (*C.* I, 10).

Emerson's retreat to nature, then, having the precipitancy of constitutional need, was an advance on Reason. In the city he found more to be discontented with than the communion service. And, as we will see, he was much too gregarious (and ambitious) to seek forgetful solitudes for "romantic" reasons or for the picturesque alone. In an early sermon on "Trifles" (1829), he illustrated the wide range of the mind by comparing it with the distant and proximate powers of the eye: "It is like the range of vision of the eye that explores the atmosphere and catches the dim outline of a mountain a hundred miles distant and examines the anatomy of the smallest insect." (*Y,* 47)[4] But then he pointed out the dangers of close vision with which he himself was familiar. "If you bury the natural eye too exclusively on minute objects," he said, "it gradually loses its powers of distant vision." (*Y,* 48) And this tendency to magnify things, to lose the sense of relationship in an obsession with trifles, distinguished society. (*C,* VI, 153) In the perspectives of nature he tried to escape this tyranny of things.

For the city (and society) dissipated his energy and concentration, and waylaid his senses. He said the age was ocular (*J,* IV, 236), but he diagnosed its difficulties as ophthalmia. (*L,* III, 400) The city was shortsighted business. In America, he wrote Margaret Fuller, "We cannot see where we are going, preternaturally sharp as our eyes are at short distances . . . strange malady, is it not?" (*L,* III, 400) And the reason for the disease was that "the City delights the Understanding. It is made up of finites; short, sharp, mathematical lines, all calculable. It is full of varieties, of successions, of contrivances. The Country, on the contrary, offers an *unbroken horizon,* the monotony of an *endless* road, or *vast* uniform plains, of *distant* mountains, the melancholy of uniform and infinite vegetation; the objects on the road are few and worthless, the eye is invited ever to the horizon and the clouds. It is the school of Reason." (*J,* V, 310-311; italics supplied) One of the serious needs of America, he noted, was a "general education of the eye." (*J,* VIII, 550)

For the same reason, he would have put telescopes on every street corner! There they could remind the shortsighted—men with "microscopic optics" (*J,* III, 308-309)—that "they were born heirs of the dome of God" (*J,* IV, 281) and that the stars were the last outpost of God's providence. "God be thanked," Emerson wrote of his own need for the heavens, "who set stars in the sky! planted their bright watch along the infinite deep and ordained such fine intelligence betwixt us and them." (*J,* IV, 47) The stars seemed to him to take him beyond the horizon: "The blue zenith,"

[4] Y—*Young Emerson Speaks,* edited by A. G. McGiffert (Boston: Houghton Mifflin Co., 1938).

he wrote, "is the point in which romance and reality meet." (*C,* III, 172) And in astronomy he felt the visual promise of "everything"; the lawful heavens promised him successful moral navigation, and he took nightly walks under the stars to take his spiritual bearings. (*J,* VI, 187) Obsessed with astronomy throughout his life, he even symbolized the mind as a quadrant. By sighting the sun and stars, he hoped to find his latitude. (*J,* IV, 107) In the contemplation of the stars he participated in their animating law: "I please myself rather with contemplating the penumbra of the thing than the thing itself." And he found that this referred him "to a higher state than I now occupy." (*J,* III, 197-198)

When Emerson suggested that the American scholar—"the world's eye" —become an astronomer, he was speaking from this experience, and he was contrasting observation and vision. (*C,* I, 101) He wanted the scholar to feel "the grandeur of the impression the stars and heavenly bodies make on us." Then they would value their gleams more than an "exact perception of a tub or a table on the ground." (*J,* VII, 93) They would literally have a wide horizon for every fact (*J,* X, 331) and discover "the inextinguishableness of the imagination." (*J,* X, 330) In their penetration of space they would realize the "immense elasticity" of the mind (*J,* X, 330), and would be startled into wonder—and wonder reborn was the first affirmation of transcendental experience.

Even more than the distant vision it satisfied, astronomy gave Emerson a chance to speak for "the sovereignty of Ideas." (*J,* IV, 32) As a student of thirteen, he chose astronomy for the subject of a free theme (*L,* I, 29), and astronomy—imaginatively interpreted—excited him during the long remainder of his life. Herschel's great astronomy was his source book, and his "The General Nature and Advantages of the Study of the Physical Sciences," as much as Emerson's own delight in the Jardin des Plantes, directed him to the natural sciences. (*L,* I, 343; *J,* III, 197) In them, he was searching for the moral law, and astronomy—"thought and harmony in masses of matter" (*C,* I, 219)—seemed to Emerson its most grandiloquent expression. Calvinism and Ptolemaic astronomy lacked this moral grandeur for Emerson: they had yet to grasp the moral beauty of the Newtonian universe. They did not know "the extent or the harmony or the depth of their moral nature." Like the Unitarians, "they are clinging to little, positive, verbal versions of the moral law, and very imperfect versions too, while the infinite laws, the laws of the Law, the great circling truths whose only adequate symbol is the material laws, the astronomy, etc., are all unobserved." (*J,* III, 199) For to observe the stars was, for Emerson, to "come back to our real, initial state and see and own that we have yet beheld but the first ray of Being." (*J,* IV, 417) It was in the search for this experience that he began *Nature* (*C,* I, 7), and it was the end of all he said in *Nature* to bring men "to look at the world with new eyes." (*C,* I, 85) In viewing the stars he escaped into loneliness and health (*J,* III, 263, 390), because alone in an atmosphere "transparent with this design" he felt "a perpetual admonition of God and superior destiny." (*J,* III, 264) Again he undulated with the sea of being (*J,* IV, 417), rested his immortality in the immortal stars, and found in their great circles the laws that merger transformed into ideas. Properly *distant,* the natural unarmed eye achieved an angle of vision in which perception had a destiny. (*J,* VIII, 321) Properly distant, restored to its natural scope, the eye was no longer retrospective, but prospective. (*J,* VI, 190)

## II

Emerson's critics, understandably, seized the central and striking image of the eyeball. Cranch has left us nothing that will give him as much fame, perhaps, as his good-natured sketch of this passage. (*L,* II, 190) But the Very Rev. Henry A. Braun, reviewing *Nature* in *The Catholic World,* cited the passage as evidence of insanity: "We wonder, when he wrote that, whether he was not bilious and his 'eyeball' bloodshot as he looked at it in the glass?" He was using this "critical" bludgeon to prove that "Nature is not the correlative of the mind." *The Westminster Review* of London also singled it out as full of familiar truths, but here too much relied on and simplified: "They are propounded as if they lay on the surface of truth and within the grasp of all men, and contained not problems . . . in the solution of which the lives of thoughtful men have gone by, leaving the giant contradictions of our moral being just as they were, standing face to face, irreconcilable."

What these and other critics have often failed to see is that the transparent eyeball is only representative for Emerson of one aspect of the mind, and that the angle of vision as a metaphor of inspiration has its origins in Emerson's thought in the religious affirmation of compensation. For the problem of the mind, as it presented itself to Emerson, was that of a twofold process. Structurally, this process was represented by the two poles or termini of the mind: Intellect Receptive and Intellect Constructive. (*C,* II, 334) They recreated in man-the-microcosm the cosmological dualism of the universe. Functionally, they presented the problems of inspiration and its control, of passivity or "pious reception" and concentration or form. Between these poles the life of the mind played like a sputtering spark, and Emerson's creative task was to prohibit a surplus of energy to store itself at either pole and thus intermit the circuit. "Human life," he wrote, "is made up of two elements, power and form, and the proportions must be invariably kept, if we would have it sweet and sound." (*C,* III, 65) Seen in another way, this mental equilibrium required innocence and sophistication, that is, the openness of response and mature judgment that modern critics of the arts often remark on as impossible: "The lover of nature is he whose inward and outward senses are still truly adjusted to each other; who has retained the spirit of infancy even into the era of manhood." (*C,* I, 9) Although the receptive aspect of this process—certainly the more primary in Emerson's experience—was mystical merger, Emerson was not a mystic in the usual "visionary" sense of the word. He was not seeking in the angle of vision an escape from the world; as it formed, the angle of vision was to make *use* of the world. But mystical union, for him, was an epistemological necessity. Vision, he said of the inner seeing of the mind, "is not like the vision of the eye, but is union with the things known." (*C,* II, 325) The knowledge of merger, however, had its use only in the prudential world; if knowledge *began* in reception, it ended in action. Mysticism ended in rest. And "Man," he wrote, "was made for conflict, not for rest. In action is his power; not in his goals but in his transitions man is great." (*C,* XII, 60)

The transitions, or better, the transmutation of mystical power into form was his best description of the life of the mind. In this process the mind was a transmitter, a conduit through which the infinite was funneled from the spiritual reservoir to the prudential tap. Or again, to switch the metaphor, mind was the lens converging the rays of spirit on the daily affairs of man. Standing between the worlds of spiritual laws and prudential affairs, man's "health and erectness," Emerson wrote, "consist in the fidelity with which he transmits influences from the vast and universal to the point on which his genius can act." (*C,* I, 208-209) The point of action was found in everyday life, just as the only way of making the mystical power of insight available was by conveying it to men in the "language of facts." The ray of spiritual light, he pointed out in illustration, "passes invisible through space, and only when it falls on an object is it seen." Similarly, "when the spiritual energy is directed on something outward, than it is a thought." (*C,* II, 335) Speaking of his own experience of transition as ebb and flow, Emerson described the same process more "psychologically": "The daily history of the Intellect is this alternating of expansions and concentrations. The expansions are the invitations from heaven to try a larger sweep, a higher pitch than we have yet climbed, and to leave all our past for this enlarged scope. Present power, on the other hand, requires concentration on the moment and the thing to be done." (*C,* XII, 58)

In this twofold process of expansion and concentration, nature was instrumental both as the activator of insight and as the object of focus. Correspondence, therefore, as an inspirational means, was sympathy with nature, as well as the doctrine of its expression. And Emerson had in mind the natural history of its agency in inspiration when he gave his course in philosophy at Harvard in 1870-1871. He proposed early in "Natural History of Intellect" an aim that had absorbed the full span of his life. He explained,

My belief in the use of a course on philosophy is that the student shall learn to appreciate *the miracle of the mind;* shall learn its subtle but im-

> mense power, or shall begin to learn it; shall come to know that in *seeing* and in no tradition he must find what truth is; that he shall see in it the source of all traditions, and shall see each one of them as better or worse statement of its revelations; shall come to trust it entirely, as the only true; to cleave to God against the name of God. When he has once known the oracle he will need no priest. And if he finds at first with some alarm how impossible it is to accept many things which the hot or the mild sectarian may insist on his believing, he will be armed by his insight and brave to meet all inconvenience and all resistance it may cost him. He from whose hand it came will guide and direct it. (*C*, XII, 6-7; italics supplied)

How biographical this passage was, only those students knew whose fathers or grandfathers had witnessed and told them of the storm following *The Divinity School Address* (1838). To appreciate the miracle of the mind then had been to challenge the reigning miracle of tradition. Emerson had taken the word "miracle" in its traditional, linear sense and had reinterpreted it in terms of the vertical dimension of human consciousness. He said that "the word Miracle as pronounced by Christian churches gives a false impression. . . . It is not one with the blowing clover and the falling rain." (*C*, I, 129) By divorcing the miracle from an immediate sense of the presence of God in the process of nature, only known by man by sharing that process, the miracle that remained applied only to past events credited by historical testimony. "By withdrawing it [the preaching of the miracle] from the exploration of the moral nature of man, where the sublime is, where are the resources of astonishment and power . . ." the miracle as a support of faith became a dead word, not a living thing. (*C*, I, 141) In its sterility was the history of fifty years of America's waning spiritual life. And because of this, for Emerson, redemption was no longer to be sought in the Church but in the soul—in man's own experience of self-reflection. To his generation, long given to thinking of miracles as events of the past, his reaffirmation of their immediacy in consciousness was revolutionary. But as a result of this tremendous semantic shift, a generation later he could quietly say that truth was more likely to be revealed in psychology than in history.

In the early sermons one can trace Emerson's growing awareness of the fact that the revitalization of faith had to come not from "Miracles" (1831) but from "The Miracle of Our Being." (1834) Miracles were important to faith, because, as Emerson said, "a miracle is the only means by which God can make a communication to men, that shall be known to be from God." (*Y*, 120) For this reason Emerson retained it as historical fact (although he modified the usual interpretation by making the miracle accord with the moral expectations of man). To deny the miracle would have been to deny that God can communicate with man, and this was sufficient reason for him to keep it, in the face of a mechanistic universe that seemed to dull men's senses to the need for miracles. "There are thousands of men who, if there were no histories and if the order of natural events had never been broken, would," he explained the miracle as a departure from the order of nature, "never ask in the course of their lives for anything beyond a secondary cause and never ask for the first." (*Y*, 121) Never shocked into wonder, unless by a breach in nature itself, these "secondary" men (*Y*, 108) found sufficient the explanation afforded by secondary causes. But for Emerson, primary man himself must startle nature with "an instructed eye." He must discover the genuine miracle in his own life, that is, in his relation to the laws of nature—in the fact, for example, that he can will the raising of his arm, communicate his thoughts, and conduct his life, certain that the law of compensation will not fail him. Then he will realize that he can believe in miracles because he is "such a manifestation," because "all our life is a miracle. Ourselves are the greatest wonder of all." (*Y*, 122) Once he has recognized the informing law of his life and of nature, he will no longer find the miracle in departures from natural order, but in the moral bond uniting his constitution and that of the universe. Miracle at this stage in Emerson's sermon has been transformed into the awareness of a higher source of law operating in both nature and man: in the fact that man's sympathy with nature is the basic correspondence revealing God. What he omitted here, but emphasized in the later sermon, was the fact that only in self-reflection (as opposed to the observation of nature) man became aware of the need for a higher law as explanation of his sympathy with nature. For to reflect, he wrote, "is to receive truth immediately from God without any medium." (*J*, II, 409) And the noblest fact was that of "being addressed on moral grounds": "This fact is so close to the first fact of our *being*, that, like the circulation of the blood, or the gravity of bodies, it passes long unnoticed from the circumstance of its omnipresence." (*J*, II, 327)

When Emerson asked men to reflect on the miracle of their being he first pointed out the wonderful sympathy between nature and man, the way the universe was made to serve man and unfold his faculties. He distinguished, however, between superficial wonder in the external fitness of things and ecstatic wonder of man in the "bare fact" of his existence as a man. He significantly added, "This external fitness is wonderful, but I doubt if to those who saw this only, it would ever have occurred to remark upon the marvel . . . [because] it may be said of the things apprehended by the senses, that they are so nicely grooved into one another that the sight of one suggests the next preceding, and this the next before, so that the understanding in the study of the things themselves would run forever in the round of second causes, did not the soul at its own instance sometimes demand tidings of the First Cause." (*Y*, 203-204) The recognition of the *moral* fitness of the universe to man's needs, therefore, required one to get above the round of secondary causes, to get free from the enslavement to trifles, and to view the spectacle from the soul's vantage in the wonder of direct union with the First Cause. This was the supreme moment in the spiritual life of man, and it was toward this moment that Emerson had been groping in his need to destroy "the Chaos of Thought" of a morally unredeemed universe. "Rend away the darkness," he journalized when he was twenty, "and restore to man the knowledge of this principle [a moral universe], and you have lit the sun over the world and solved the riddle of life." (*J*, I, 257 ff.) And it was in "the exercise of reason, the act of reflection" that man lit the sun: "the chief distinctions of his condition begin with that act." Echoing Coleridge, he glorified man's release from "brutishness": "Awakened to truth and virtue —which is the twofold office of Reason, he passes out of the local and finite, he inspires and expires immortal breath." (*Y*, 206-207)

When the inspired primary man now *contemplates* the world about him, he discovers in himself "a point or focus upon which all objects, all ages concentrate their influence." He is now at "the heart of the world," at "the centre of the Creation." From this angle of vision the universe seems to exist only for his benefit. Life is no longer "an insupportable curse." Now "man lives for a purpose. Hitherto was no object upon which to concentrate his various powers. Now happiness is his being's end and aim." (*J*, I, 257) Now, like the "lowest natures"—a leaf, a grain of sand—he is intimately allied to the organic process. Emerson best described this intimacy—and he was a naturalist only to reveal it—when he wrote:

> Look at the summer blackberry lifting its polished surface a few inches from the ground. How did that little chemist extract from the sandbank the spices and sweetness it has concocted in its cells? By any cheap or accidental means? Not so; but the whole creation has been at the cost of its birth and nurture. A globe of fire near a hundred millions of miles distant in the great space, has been flooding it with light and heat as if it shone for no other. It is six or seven months that the sun has made the tour of the heavens every day over this tiny sprout, before it could bear its fruit. The sea has evaporated its countless tons of water that the rain of heaven might wet the roots of this little vine. The elastic air exhaled from all live creatures and all minerals, yielded this small pensioner the gaseous aliment it required. The earth by the attraction of its mass determined its form and size; and when we consider how the earth's attraction is fixed at this moment on equilibrium by innumerable attractions, on every side, of distant bodies,—we shall see that the berry's form and history is determined by causes and agents the most prodigious and remote. (*Y*, 207-208)

By recognizing in the humble blackberry one instance of the focusing of the beneficence of the universe, man himself could see that he, too, was a "center round which all things roll, and upon which all things scatter gifts." (*Y*, 208) Knowing the benefits of his implication in nature, he no longer felt caught in the web of circumstances; instead, in his new freedom, "he stands upon the top of the world; he is the centre of the horizon." (*Y*, 208) Emerson found this a favorite way of expressing the new release from events man discovered in viewing the activity of his mind as an angle of vision. When he looked at the rainbow, he believed himself "the center of its arch," and this feeling of centrality he found in viewing a landscape between his legs or in the rapid movement of a train. (*C,* I, 50-51) But he realized that these experiences were true of all men, that the angle of vision equalized, by making available to any man as much of the universe as his vision could contain. In this way, although dependent on nature, man was "absolutely, imperially free." (*J,* II, 272)

But the freedom of perception went beyond this awareness of the benefit of nature. Man, Emerson added, "is not designed to be an idle eye before which nature passes in review, but by his action is enabled to learn the irresistible properties of moral nature, perceived dimly by the mind as laws difficult to be grasped or defined, yet everywhere working out their inevitable results in human affairs." (*Y,* 209) Freedom was only to be found in the perception of the correspondence of the physical and moral laws. The whole message of compensation—the animating force in Emerson's vision—depended on perceiving this, that "the Creaton is so magically woven that nothing can do him [man] any mischief but himself." (*Y,* 209) The secondary man (the unregenerate), with his idle eye, will be ground to powder by the laws, will find in nature as much obstacle as benefit. But the primary man, armed by his perception of the moral necessity of law, will be defended from all harm he wills to resist; the whole creation cannot bend him whilst he stands upright." (*Y,* 209) The only freedom, like perception, was of this moral order.

The awakening of Reason was, for Emerson, this moral awakening: inspiration *was* moral regeneration. The moral sentiment (or Reason) was the "tie of faith" made alive by the human mind. The law it revealed as the basis of the human mind was the content of inspiration; when seen in nature it was "fatal strength." (*C,* VI, 221) And, as he repeated in his Harvard lectures, what was of greater worth than the dangerous knowledge of this power of the mind? "To open to ourselves—to open to others these laws—is it not worth living for? to make the soul, aforetime the servant of the senses, acquainted with the secret of its own power; to teach man that by self-renouncement a heaven of which he had no conception, begins at once in his heart;—by the high act of yielding his will, that little individual heart becomes dilated as with the presence and inhabitation of the Spirit of God." (*Y,* 210) Not only is this the religious burden of this sermon (as of the more secular essays on "Worship," "Inspiration," and "Spiritual Laws"), it is the religious context in which Emerson always thought of the experience of inspiration. When he enjoins men to see in the exaltation of Reason the transcendence of evil and the hidden spiritual good of their worldly failings, he is not mistaking the sense of power in inspiration for an irresponsible release of energies. "What is it," he says of the insight of inspiration, "but a perception of man's true position in the universe and his consequent obligations. This is the whole moral and end of such views as I present." (*Y,* 211) The power to overcome trifles resided in *this insight* and in no other, because, for Emerson, inspiration had no other "meaning" than that of compensation. If vision was to release him from the bondage of the senses, its message had to be a response to his most deeply felt need, had to answer his "metaphysical pathos." And in his moments of vision he found this assurance, "that the Father who thus vouchsafes to reveal himself . . . will not forsake the child for whom he provideth such costly instruction—whom every hour and every event of memory and hope educate. What does it intimate but presages of an infinite and perfect life? What but an assured trust through all evil and danger and death?" (*Y,* 212)

Inspiration experienced only as the ecstatic moment of heightened power was irresponsible, as one suspects from the passage on the transparent eyeball. But bringing with it the obligation (as well as the power) to communicate this insight to others, it made expression, either in act or word, its moral end. Men might feel at the receptive pole the spontaneous, instinctive flood of inspiration; they might balance it by reflecting on it, that is, by standing above it watch its operation and grasp its law. But at the constructive pole, this thought—"always a miracle"—demanded for its publication the control of the spontaneous flow. (*C,* II, 335) For in the very way he described the mind, for Emerson inspiration was always saddled with a moral rider; intuition was always coupled with duty. (*C,* VI, 224) "The poet," he instructed, "who shall use nature as his hieroglyph must have an adequate message to convey thereby." (*C,* VIII, 65) And because insight had to end in a message, the freedom of intuition demanded the necessity of precise form; and once Emerson became aware of this condition, he found, as all conscious artists have, that the reception of inspiration became even more difficult. (*L,* II, 342-343) He found that he needed *two* inspirations, one by which to see, the other by which to write (*J,* VII, 113); and by intellectualizing his vision of the laws, he saved himself from the decay of the first, and had more and more only to consider the ebb and flow of the second.

### III

Emerson intellectualized his vision by constructing an astronomy of the imagination. His constitutional need for *seeing* determined the spatial character of his thought; and his devotion to astronomy, especially the Newtonian revelation of gravitational attraction beyond the surface of the earth, provided him his symbols for expressing the fundamental correspondence of physical and moral laws. In the circle he not only found an equivalent for the Coleridgean Idea, but in its compensatory action he saw the moral law of compensation. (*C,* VI, 218-219) The daily life of the mind, its ebbing and flowing, he found he could express in the solar cycle of day and night; and this almost "primitive" dependence on the sun and stars, he made the visual metaphor of the process of inspiration. He believed that the most ordinary symbols were adequate to the fullest expression, and day and night were, indeed, the common pulse of the universe. (*C,* III, 17-18)

Men were literally born in darkness, he wrote: "Out of darkness and out of the awful Cause they come to be caught up in this vision of a seeing, partaking, acting, and suffering life." (*J,* V, 132) As in the womb, they rested in the "circumambient" unconsciousness of God (*J,* V, 385), becalmed on the ebbless sea of the Oversoul. (*J,* V, 292-490) And so when Emerson took his nightly walk, he felt that "nothing in nature has the softness of darkness . . . or the unutterable gentleness to the sense." (*J,* IV, 358) In darkness, as in sleep, he felt that he was falling back on God. "If I have weak . . . eyes," he wrote, "no looking at green curtains, no shutting them . . . are of certain virtue . . . but when at last I wake up from a sound sleep, then I know that he that made the eye has dealt with it for the time and the wisest physician is He." (*J,* IV, 143) In sleep and night were the restorative virtues of a return to the source of life; one ebbed or returned in the night only to flow with insight in the day. He copied from Sophocles

*Dost thou behold the vast and azure sky*
*How in its liquid arms the earth doth lie?*
(*J,* IV, 285)

and saw in the protective maternity of Lidian for little Waldo a similar image of God's providential care of man. (*J,* IV, 135) Darkness, then, far more than its usual associations with skepticism and atheism (*J,* III, 14), represented for Emerson a preparation—a night journey of sorts—for the day.

In Emerson's analogy, night was the creator of day (*J,* IV, 469), just as in Thoreau's, silence was the *background* of sound. For Emerson, day was the course of living the problems of life from their "uttermost darkness into light." (*J,* V, 74) Knowledge of God, he found in Scholastic philosophy, was *matutina cognitio,* morning knowledge (*J,* IV, 24-25 n.); and the self-recovery by which man regained insight and expanded beyond his previous limits he spoke of as *Easting.* (*J,* III, 477) Man's mind, he wrote, by "his efforts at self-knowledge . . . will revolve so far that the increasing twilight will give place to the Sun, and God will appear as he is to his soul." (*J,* II, 303) He likened conversion to "day after twilight" (*J,* II, 298), and the self-evidency of its truth was its sun-like light. (*J,* II, 516) In "Threnody" (lines 201-202) he called it the "super-solar blaze." If this ecstasy of inspiration was a "new morn risen on noon" (*J,* VI, 14; III, 239-240), immortality was the "Day" following the long life of morning. (*J,* X, 203)

But any change in the hodiernal cycle, suggesting the transitions of mind, represented the moment of inspiration. Sunset as well as the dawn expressed for Emerson the qualitative feeling of influx. (*J,* IV, 46) He believed "that no hour, no state of the atmosphere but corresponded to some state of the mind. (*J,* III, 386) But even in the bright day of inspiration he felt that the sun needed shadow. (*J,* VIII, 422) Realizing this polarity, he could accept the darkness and opacity of man and nature as the ground of light. (*J,* VII, 61) He could extend the analogy by saying that sin was opaque and innocence transparent (*J,* V, 309), that society mistook darkness for light (*J,* V, 108), and that the problem of inspiration in writing was to make daylight shine through the word. (*J,* V, 198) And in "Works and Days" he could contrast works and faith, "huckstering Trade" and the "deep to-day." His whole philosophy of the moment—of the time-transcending of the total response to nature—was expressed in this comparison: "Works and days were offered us, and we took works. . . . [But] he is only rich who owns the day." (*C,* VII, 168)

Emerson experienced the day in his adverbial perception of nature, in his feeling of intimate union with the law in and behind the natural process. His awareness of law, of natural order and harmony, was expressed in its mental correlative, the Idea. And the possibility of representing a total feeling in a thought derived from the basic correspondence of the mental and physical spheres. "The crystal sphere of thought," he wrote, "is as concentrical as the geological globe we inhabit." (*J,* V, 555) This correspondence made possible a method of expression that seemed to him to unfold thought according to the method of nature.

He liked Plato's expression "that God geometrizes." (*J,* VII, 92) Plato, too, he found, geometrized, and this made him both a poet and a man who "at the same time [is] acquainted with the geometrical foundations of things, and with their moral purposes, and sees the festal splendor of the day." (*J,* VIII, 43; VIII, 37) Plato was the "great-eyed," and his second sight explained his stress on geometry. (*C,* IV, 79, 84) His geometry of Ideas made possible the communication of inspiration and somehow preserved its splendor: "In his broad daylight things reappear as they stood in the sunlight, hardly shorn of a ray, yet now portable and reportable." (*J,* VIII, 45) A similar "geometric, astronomic morals" Emerson wanted for himself (*J,* VIII, 418), and demanded earlier of the teacher he would become: "The Teacher that I look for and await shall enunciate with more precision and universality, with piercing poetic insight those beautiful yet severe compensations that give to nature an aspect of mathematical science." (*J,* III, 434)

In Emerson's geometry of morals, the circle was the basic figure. He derived it, perhaps from his own sense of the bending horizon, from his own experience of the eye as the first circle and the horizon as the second; and like the horizon, it symbolized the Unattainable (*C,* II, 305) and the progressive ascent by which one advanced on the chaos and the dark. As the "primary figure," the "highest emblem in the cipher of the world," the circle represented as well the unifying Idea (as he adapted it from Coleridge), and its concentric expansion represented the process of ascending generalization, each step of which, in man's moral progress, was his highest knowledge of God. For God's creation of nature was also circular: "Nature can only be conceived of as existing to a universal and not to a particular end," he wrote, "to a universe of ends, and not to one,—a work of *ecstasy,* to be represented by a circular movement, as intention might be signified by a straight line of definite length." (*C,* I, 201) By similar ecstasies and self-recoveries man retraced in his own advancing circles of thought, the advancing circles of God in nature. And by taking up the angle of vision, every man could become the center of the circle, at one with God; for in Emerson's astronomy, as in St. Augustine's, God was "a circle whose center was everywhere, and its circumference nowhere." (*C,* II, 301) God was the "centripetal force" in "the depths of the soul" (*J,* IV, 215), saving man, in the unending antagonism of centripetal and centrifugal forces, from the circumferential ignorance. Man's life in God began from the moment of ecstasy, and from "there the Universe evolves itself as from a centre to its boundless irradiation." (*J,* III, 402) Again the circular growth of the self described this idea and god-seeking: "The life of man is a self-evolving circle, which, from a ring imperceptibly small, rushes on all sides outwards to new and larger circles, and that without End." (*C,* II, 304) And if God was the greatest circle, and the circle in its nature compensatory, Emerson could find in his notion of God as "the Great Compensation" a symbol of the Oversoul as container and resolution of all antagonism; and the Oversoul, as the circumambient atmosphere he felt overhanging him like the sky—a "heaven within heaven"— filled the intellectual circle with the content of his living experience. (*J,* VIII, 567)

Like the Ideas they represented, circles were compensatory. In the dialectic of inspiration (and thought) they represented the limit of each expanding ebb and flow. Each Idea, by compensating for a multitude of observations, was an ascent; each Idea became a higher platform from which to survey the prospect for a still higher generalization looming on a still more distant horizon. Ascending to thought in this way was the intellectual equivalent of distant visioning; the synthesis was in the focus of ever widening vistas—and one's visual reach was best achieved in ascent. (*J,* III, 373) Emerson described this intellectual visioning: "But now and then the lawless imagination flies out and asserts her habit. I revisit the verge of my intellectual domain. How the restless soul runs round the outmost orbit and builds her bold conclusion as a tower of observation from whence her eyes wander incessantly in the unfathomable abyss. I dimly scrutinize the vast constitution of being." (*J,* II, 223)

This intellectual restlessness was the true compensation. Emerson said that his cardinal faith was "that all secrets of the less [the prudential] are commanded by the larger generalization [the spiritual]." (*L,* II, 344)

And "ascent" was the proper word, because he always felt that the spiritual laws were *above* prudential concerns. The compensation of insight or self-recovery, then, lay in the power to press beyond the limits of a previous thought. When his center proved to be merely another circumference, he felt his powers decay. (*J*, VIII, 102) He felt the heart's refusal to be imprisoned in an Idea, and he expressed this by saying "that around every circle another can be drawn . . . there is no end in nature." Or to return to the analogy of night and day, "There is always another dawn risen on mid-noon" (*J*, VIII, 239), and " 'He who contemplates hath a days without night.' " (*J*, II, 478)

The possibility that with the returning life of influx he would regain a wider angle of vision seemed to him evidence in itself of God's presence in the universe. Unable to state the truth once and for all, unable to rest in an idea—these were signs to Emerson that in the harmony of man and the universe it was with man as it was with God: "There is no outside, no enclosing wall, no circumference to us." (*J*, VIII, 242) But the spasms of inspiration also showed him how humanly dependent he was, how fragmentary was the view from his angle of vision. He wrote that "a glimpse, a point of view that by its brightness excludes the purview, is granted, but no panorama. A fuller inspiration should cause the point to flow and become a line, should bend the line and complete the circle." (*C*, VIII, 273)

He could avoid the parallax of insight by a sympathetic correspondence with nature; in his own experience of distant vision and reflection he found that he could align himself with the axis of things. Whatever the magnetism of the universe was, for him, it directed his eye to the horizon and beyond to the "aboriginal self," to the "science-baffling star, without parallax." The deep force of "Spontaneity or Instinct" directed him, opened his eye in reflection to the source of being and light which he realized as Intuition. Beyond this his metaphysics of inspiration and self-reliance could not go. (*C*, II, 63 ff.) For he knew that he could not willfully make his inspiration consecutive; it was like the coming of day, dependent on the law, and therefore to be awaited with assurance. But its coming always predicted night. An idea might at the moment of its conception bind a fragmentary nature within its circle, but in the total demands of an angle of vision come full circle, it could only serve as an arc. Emerson learned this more and more from the infrequency of his inspirational experiences; and when his early static conception of nature gave way to one of illusion and flux, he found that the arc again provided the only way in which his angle of vision could accommodate the ceaseless flow.

By joining the static and mechanistic circle of Newtonian astronomy (his debt to eighteenth-century science) with the dynamic science of Ideas or dialectic of Coleridge, Emerson made his circle an organic symbol capable of representing both the unfolding mind and the ascending natural chain of being. His circle united his two desires: the desire for fixity or centrality in the universe of the spirit, and the desire for change and growth and freedom in the organic universe of prudence. He wanted it to show both the "evanescence and centrality of things." He wanted a symbol for what the ancient myths taught him was still true in human experience, that "things are in a flood and fixed as adamant: the *Bhagavad Gita* adduces the illustration of the sphered, mutable, yet centered air or ether." (*J*, VII, 29) The circle symbolized this sphered mutability, the growth that depended on a fixed center in being. As the center of the circle, God (through his sympathetic correspondence with Him) provided him the fixity and centrality he needed when nature became an ever-changing screen of "slippery sliding surfaces" (*C*, III, 48); the circumference of the circle, the human and natural limitations, receded in the ecstatic use of nature as the representative of law, whether that law was perceived directly in nature, or, later, through nature. That the perpetual *transformations* witnessed in the natural process expressed in their tendency the circular ascent of spirit were as much a miracle to Emerson as the mind's self-expansions. For both were affirmations of the infinite, of the compensation of ascent, of the power of new prospects. Limited by his human angle of vision and the fitful light of self-reflection or intuition, Emerson still had for his own the arc of nature, and the arc perceived in the fullness of his ecstatic insight promised a corresponding circle and represented for him its portable and reportable truth.

## *Chronology of Important Dates*

| | |
|---|---|
| 1803 | (May 25) Born at Boston, Massachusetts. |
| 1821 | (August) Graduated from Harvard College. |
| 1826 | (October 10) Approbated to preach as a Unitarian minister. |
| 1829 | (March 11) Ordination at Second Church, Boston.<br>(September 30) Married to Ellen Tucker. |
| 1831 | (February 8) Death of Ellen. |
| 1832 | (October 28) Resignation from Second Church accepted. |
| 1832-33 | (December-October) Travel in Europe. |
| 1834 | (November) Moved to Concord. |
| 1835 | (January-March) Lectures on *Biography*.<br>(September 14) Married to Lydia Jackson ("Lidian"). |
| 1835-36 | (November-January) Lectures on *English Literature*. |
| 1836 | (May 9) Death of brother Charles.<br>(September 9) *Nature* published.<br>(October 30) Birth of son Waldo. |
| 1836-37 | (December-March) Lectures on *The Philosophy of History*. |
| 1837 | (August 31) Oration on "The American Scholar." |
| 1837-38 | (December-February) Lectures on *Human Culture*. |
| 1838 | (July 15) Address at Divinity School, Cambridge. |
| 1838-39 | (December-February) Lectures on *Human Life*. |
| 1839 | (February 24) Birth of daughter Ellen. |
| 1839-40 | (December-February) Lectures on *The Present Age*. |
| 1841 | (January 25) Lecture on "Man the Reformer."<br>(March 20) *Essays, First Series* published.<br>(November 22) Birth of daughter Edith. |
| 1841-42 | (December-January) Lectures on *The Times* (published, in part, 1849). |
| 1842 | (January 27) Death of Waldo. |
| 1844 | (July 10) Birth of son Edward.<br>(October 19) *Essays, Second Series* published. |
| 1845-46 | (December-January) Lectures on *Representative Men* (published 1850). |
| 1846 | (December 25) *Poems* published. |
| 1847-48 | (October-July) Travel in England and France. |
| 1851 | (March-April) Lectures on *The Conduct of Life* (published 1860). |
| 1856 | (August 6) *English Traits* published. |

| | |
|---|---|
| 1862 | (May 9) Address on "Thoreau." |
| 1867 | (April 28) *May-Day and Other Pieces* published. |
| 1872 | (July 24) Burning of house. |
| 1872-73 | (October-May) Travel in Europe and the Near East. |
| 1882 | (April 27) Death at Concord, Massachusetts. |

# *Notes on the Editors and Contributors*

MILTON R. KONVITZ, Professor, School of Industrial and Labor Relations and School of Law, Cornell University. Author of *On the Nature of Value* (1946), and other works.

STEPHEN E. WHICHER (1915-1961), Professor of English, Cornell University. Author of *Freedom and Fate: An Inner Life of Ralph Waldo Emerson* (1953).

DANIEL AARON, Professor of English, Smith College. Author of *Men of Good Hope* (1951).

NEWTON ARVIN, formerly Professor of English Literature, Smith College. Author of *Hawthorne* (1929), *Whitman* (1938), and other works.

JOHN DEWEY (1859-1952), philosopher, psychologist, educator. Author of *Human Nature and Conduct* (1922), *The Quest for Certainty* (1929), and numerous other works.

CHARLES FEIDELSON, Jr., English Department, Yale University. Author of *Symbolism and American Literature* (1953).

NORMAN FOERSTER, formerly Professor of English, University of North Carolina and University of Iowa. Author of *Nature in American Literature* (1923), *American Criticism* (1928), and other works.

ROBERT FROST, outstanding American poet. His *Complete Poems* published in 1949.

WILLIAM JAMES (1842-1910), philosopher and psychologist, intimately associated with pragmatism. Author of many works, including *The Will to Believe* (1897) and *Varieties of Religious Experience* (1902).

FRANCIS O. MATTHIESSEN (1902-1950), Professor, Harvard University, 1942-1950. Author of *The Achievement of T. S. Eliot* (1935), *American Renaissance* (1941), editor of *Oxford Book of American Verse* (1950).

PERRY G. E. MILLER, Professor of American Literature, Harvard University. Author of *The New England Mind* (1939), *Jonathan Edwards* (1949), and other works.

HENRY BAMFORD PARKES, Professor of History, New York University. Author of *Jonathan Edwards* (1930), *The Pragmatic Test* (1941), and other works.

SHERMAN PAUL, Department of American Literature, University of Illinois. Author of *Emerson's Angle of Vision* (1952).

GEORGE SANTAYANA (1863-1952), noted American philosopher and poet. Among his many works: *The Life of Reason* (1905-06) and *Scepticism and Animal Faith* (1923).

HENRY NASH SMITH, Professor of English, University of California, Berkeley. Author of *Virgin Land* (1950) and other works.

# *Selected Bibliography*

## I. Bibliography

There is no complete bibliography of Emerson. The following bibliographical writings are, however, helpful:

Cameron, Kenneth W., ed. *Emerson Society Quarterly*. Since 1955.

Carpenter, Frederic I. *Emerson Handbook*. New York: Hendricks House, Inc., 1953. Bibliographies in four parts: (1) bibliographies, biographies, biographical articles. (2) text, textual criticism, aesthetic theory. (3) background of Emerson's ideas, critical studies. (4) Emerson's influence on world literature.

——— *Ralph Waldo Emerson, Representative Selections, with Introduction, Bibliography, and Notes*. New York: American Book Co., 1934. A volume in the American Writers Series. A critical and selective bibliography, with emphasis on material published between 1917-1934.

Spiller, R. E., W. Thorp, T. H. Johnson, and H. S. Canby, eds. *A Literary History of the United States*. New York: The Macmillan Co., 1948. Revised edition, 1953. Bibliographical Supplement, R. M. Ludwig, ed., 1959. Topical, selective listings.

Stovall, Floyd, ed. *Eight American Authors*. New York: Modern Language Association, 1956. "A review of research and criticism" of eight American authors, including a chapter on Emerson by the editor.

## II. Texts

Emerson, Edward Waldo, ed. *The Complete Works of Ralph Waldo Emerson*. Boston: Houghton Mifflin Co., 1903-4. Centenary Edition. 12 vols. The standard edition.

Gilman, W. H., A. R. Ferguson, M. R. Davis, M. M. Sealts, H. Hayford, and G. P. Clark, eds. *The Journals and Miscellaneous Notebooks of Ralph Waldo Emerson*. Cambridge, Mass.: Harvard University Press. Vol. 1. 1960, Vol. 2. 1961. This is a new edition of the journals and notebooks. Until completed, the former standard edition will remain useful: Emerson, Edward Waldo and Waldo Emerson Forbes, eds. *The Journals of Ralph Waldo Emerson*. Boston: Houghton Mifflin Co., 1909-14. 10 vols.

Rusk, Ralph L., ed. *The Letters of Ralph Waldo Emerson*. New York: Columbia University Press, 1939. 6 vols.

Whicher, Stephen E. and Robert E. Spiller, eds. *The Early Lectures of Ralph Waldo Emerson.* Cambridge, Mass.: Harvard University Press, 1959. The first volume of a three-volume work.

## III. Selections

There are many Emerson anthologies. Notable ones are the following:

Kazin, Alfred and Daniel Aaron, eds. *Emerson: A Modern Anthology.* Boston: Houghton Mifflin Co., 1959.

Linscott, Robert N., ed. *The Journals of Ralph Waldo Emerson.* New York: Modern Library, 1960. An abridgement.

Perry, Bliss, ed. *The Heart of Emerson's Journals.* Gloucester, Mass.: Peter Smith, 1960.

Van Doren, Mark, ed. *The Portable Emerson.* New York: The Viking Press, Inc., 1957.

Whicher, Stephen E., ed. *Selections from Ralph Waldo Emerson.* Boston: Houghton Mifflin Co., 1957.

## IV. Biography

Brooks, Van Wyck. *The Life of Emerson.* New York: E. P. Dutton & Co., Inc. 1932. A subjective life of Emerson; interesting as an interpretative study.

Rusk, Ralph L. *The Life of Ralph Waldo Emerson.* New York: Charles Scribner's Sons, 1949. The most complete and scholarly biography.

## V. Major Critical Studies

Berry, Edmund G. *Emerson's Plutarch.* Cambridge, Mass.: Harvard University Press, 1961. A study of Emerson's use of Plutarch as a source of his views of fate, becoming, and Stoicism.

Brooks, Van Wyck. *The Flowering of New England.* New York: E. P. Dutton & Co., Inc., 1937. Communicates a sense of Emerson's presence, stature, and character.

Cameron, Kenneth W. *Emerson the Essayist.* Raleigh, N.C.: Thistle Press, 1945. A detailed study of Emerson's development through 1836, especially important for an understanding of Emerson's use of the concept of Nature.

Firkins, Oscar W. *Ralph Waldo Emerson.* Boston: Houghton Mifflin Co., 1915. Biographical, but its main interest lies in the author's treatment of Emerson as a literary craftsman.

Hopkins, Vivian C. *Spires of Form. A Study of Emerson's Aesthetic Theory.* Cambridge, Mass.: Harvard University Press, 1951. Develops Emerson's concept of organic form as he applied it to literature and the fine arts.

Nicoloff, Philip L. *Emerson: Race and History*. New York: Columbia University Press, 1961. A study of *Emerson's English Traits* and its role in the development of Emerson's thought.

Paul, Sherman. *Emerson's Angle of Vision*. Cambridge, Mass.: Harvard University Press, 1952. A study of Emerson's idea of "correspondence" and its integral role in Emerson's thought.

Perry, Bliss. *Emerson Today*. Princeton: Princeton University Press, 1931. An excellent, sympathetic, critical discussion of Emerson's life and thought.

Pollock, Robert C. "Ralph Waldo Emerson: The Single Vision." From *American Classics Reconsidered*. New York: Charles Scribner's Sons, 1958. Edited by Harold C. Gardiner. A monographic study of Emerson that may be ranked, for breadth and interest, with "Emerson, Sixty Years After," by John J. Chapman, in *Emerson and Other Essays*. New York: Charles Scribner's Sons, 1898.

Whicher, Stephen E. *Freedom and Fate*. Philadelphia: University of Pennsylvania Press, 1953. Regarded by many as the most important study of Emerson's ideas in the twentieth century.

Woodberry, George Edward. *Ralph Waldo Emerson*. New York: The Macmillan Co., 1926. A volume in the English Men of Letters Series. Although ostensibly a biography, and written before Emerson's *Journals* were published, the book deals critically with Emerson's ideas.

Young, Charles Lowell. *Emerson's Montaigne*. New York: The Macmillan Co., 1941. The book discusses the affinity of Emerson for Montaigne as sceptic, moralist, man, and writer.